THIRTY-THREE
YEARS
THE UNFILTERED MEMOIR OF A COP

ROB G. ROTHWELL

Praise for *Thirty-Three Years: The Unfiltered Memoir of a Cop*

Rob Rothwell's new book: *Thirty-Three Years:The Unfiltered Memoir of a Cop* is engaging, revealing, at times raw.

Yet it is sensitive, and often funny, too.

Thirty-Three Years is a fascinating, 'inside' look at policing in a major city – Vancouver, BC – seen through the eyes of a police cadet, beat cop, drug squad detective, bike patrol Sgt., up to becoming a senior officer - a Superintendent - in charge of the homicide division, organized crime, terrorism, and more.

It reveals police procedures, tools and tactics – but, that's almost incidental. It's to help us understand the very human thinking underway as police and Rothwell, encounter a striking range of incidents, events, and challenges.

Dramatic, honest, revealing, compassionate - Rob Rothwell explains what it is like being a front-line cop, and eventually a high ranking officer, in very frank terms.

It begins with a stabbing & the death - right in front of Rob & his patrol partner, Randy - of 'Lonny' (no saint) - at a low-budget motel, and their arrest of his killer, a drug-crazy sex trade worker, Rose.

Highlights? Dozens, like rushing a transplant organ, a human heart, code 3 from the airport runway to straight to the hospital, like accidentally discovering a robbery and a sawed-off shotgun at a 7-11, to setting up the first anti-terrorism unit for a municipal police force in Canada.

After four decades of reporting crime and breaking big police stories for Global TV News in Vancouver, it is intriguing to read how many of the stories I was investigating and reporting were developing from 'the other side' of the Blue Line!

Example: The Stanley Park Six . . . a story I uncovered about patrol members dispensing 'paddy wagon street justice' to criminals - to protect merchants and citizens in the downtown core from this group of intimidating thugs . . .

Little did I know: Rob Rothwell was on the other side of that story as the Inspector heading the Vancouver Police Department's Internal Affairs (Professional Standards) dealing investigating the officers' questionable, violent, conduct.

Then there's the human tragedies: discovering what's left of a man when he's blown his head off with a shotgun, a horrific, macabre scene for which Rothwell is kind enough to give readers an early warning - in case they want to flip the page!

As I said, it is frank, and unvarnished. Like the tragedy Rothwell investigates when a 20 year old skipped Christmas Dinner with his family . . . only for them to return to discover him hanging dead by a necktie.

There are car chases, take-downs, face-offs with angry knife-wielding suspects, family interventions, mental illness, tragic stories of drug addiction.

And Rothwell is *not* the hero of the tale . . . he's a straightforward witness, admitting when he could have done better.

It's heavy stuff, but told in an honest, frank, informative, almost breezy fashion that had me flipping pages and reading well past bedtime.

There's the funny story of how he slipped esteemed defence counsel H.A.D Oliver, QC, into the secret undercover organized crime and intelligence building one night - and how Oliver held a 'Paper Chase' like court with the intrigued hardened investigators.

And how, at the door of a rough and tumble nightclub he had to let go of the angry suspect he was scrapping with - to retrieve his firearm, which had become unholstered in the struggle, and was skittering across the entrance tiles toward a crowd of stunned onlookers, all of whom may not have been 'police friendly'.

Rothwell confronts all the hot police topics now in the news - apparent police brutality, 'pile-on' take downs, controversial street checks (carding), cops in schools, buy & bust drug enforcement for street-level traffickers, rampant drug addiction, fentanyl, overdoses, deaths, demands for free drugs for addicts, 'wellness checks' that go sideways, mental health interventions, homelessness, suicides and PTSD for first responders.

Opinionated, yes. But it's not a polemic, not preachy, not political, just real.

Thirty-Three Years is a refreshing 'hands-on' insight to the troubling challenges facing police, society, and voters, everywhere.

It will hold special significance for those who live in Metro Vancouver, but *Thirty-Three Years* will resonate with anyone interested in public safety in major metropolitan centres.

Subtly sophisticated in that it deals with so much of human frailty, tragedy, and critical 'future of policing and public safety' questions - in a simple, easy-to-read 'buckle up' we're going for a ride' fashion - that will make you smile, maybe cry, and possibly raise your blood pressure . . . while you enjoy reading it like a rollicking detective novel . . .

Don't miss this new book.

John L. Daly
Global TV News Reporter (ret.)

 FriesenPress

One Printers Way
Altona, MB R0G 0B0,
Canada

www.friesenpress.com

ISBN
978-1-03-912343-4 (Hardcover)
978-1-03-912342-7 (Paperback)
978-1-03-912344-1 (eBook)

1. Biography & Autobiography, Law Enforcement

Distributed to the trade by The Ingram Book Company

This memoir is dedicated to my eldest brother, John. He was a force of nature and a fierce protector of all those in his life; a life that was ruthlessly taken following a brave battle with cancer.

Table of Contents

WELCOME TO THE SHITTY CENTRE

AS FAR AS KNIFE WOUNDS GO, IT LOOKED TRIVIAL. LONNY WAS laid out on the grim carpet of room 121 at Vancouver's notorious City Centre Motel, as it was regarded in the 1980s, but no longer. And which cops in the area referred to back then as the "Shitty Centre." Lonny was close to death as my partner, Constable Randy Mackoff, and I arrived, along with ambulance personnel with their large, plastic toolboxes of medical supplies.

Jumping around the room in a state of cocaine-induced panic was petite, pugnacious Rose Simpson. Well known in the hood as a low-track survival sex worker and addict, she had plunged a penknife into Lonny's chest exactly where his heart resided. They had been arguing, and it had escalated as these things always do.

The cut to Lonny's chest appeared no more than a half-inch long, and bled very little, yet he was in full cardiac arrest. We all knew what was coming. Despite emergency medical intervention, Lonny twitched and became ashen as his pulse and breath faded. Then we heard it: the death rattle that every cop eventually hears when someone's life departs their body. The final exhalation, which rattles the soft tissue of the esophagus as all the body's muscles and functions surrender to impending death.

We put handcuffs on Rose and arrested her for murder. Randy took custody of her and tried his best to calm her down. Despite all indications of Lonny's death, the paramedics didn't give up. They weren't doctors, and in a situation such as this, they couldn't formally pronounce death. With chest compressions underway, Lonny was raced to the hospital as I rode along in the ambulance, retaining continuity of the body, which would soon become evidence in a murder investigation.

At the hospital, Lonny was rushed into an operating room, where a surgeon drove a scalpel into the flesh covering his ribcage just below his left armpit. The ribs were forcefully separated, allowing room for the doctor to insert his gloved hand into Lonny's chest in order to manually stimulate his heart while also attempting to control the hemorrhage that was flooding his pericardial sac with blood and restricting his heart's ability to beat. Known colloquially as "chest cracking," resuscitative thoracotomy was a brutal, last-ditch attempt to save Lonny's life.

Sad as it is to see not one but *two* lives wasted in the dingy light of a rundown motel, as a cop, you've got to come out of the squalor and misery with a sense of personal survival. This need often manifests itself in black humour. In our case, we let a rumour quickly spread among our colleagues that, before Lonny's death, my partner Randy had left him with some good news and bad news. It went something like this: "The good news, Lonny, is that you're no longer on parole; the bad news is that you're being judged by a higher court."

Though Lonny had been on parole at the time of his encounter with knife-happy Rose, those words were never spoken by Randy. Nonetheless, it made an entertaining story that, in some perverse way, shielded us from the deep well of despair that all too often underscores police work. Over-worked cops repeatedly dealing with violence and death can be subject to unhealthy consequences, sometimes compounded by poor coping skills. The classic "holding it in" response is a syndrome far better understood in the realm of modern policing than it was even a decade ago.

Progressively minded police services have implemented robust psychological services combined with peer counseling and other support mechanisms designed to keep its officers mentally and emotionally healthy, in effect replacing the "bottle" with science-based programs, in which participation in many cases is mandatory following highly-charged incidents. Removing the "opt out" clause also removes the stigma of asking for help, and this has been a key factor in gaining buy-in and establishing trust in health services and programs that may have been previously perceived as pablum for the weak. While cops will often refer in jest to a visit with a police psychologist as "having my head read," or "having my head candled," the importance of these sessions is no longer in dispute. The rate of police divorces, suicides, and depression makes that clear to everyone who carries a badge and has sworn an oath to "protect and serve."

Interestingly, Randy pursued a PhD in clinical psychology and is now a psychologist supplying clinical services in the area of post-traumatic stress disorder to police agencies, as well as consultative services to police crisis negotiation teams.

MY ROAD TO THE SHITTY
CENTRE—THE EARLY YEARS

I WAS A COP FOR THIRTY-THREE YEARS IN THE CITY OF VAN-
couver, Canada. By accident more than intention, I found myself in the BC
Police Academy in 1979 at twenty-years of age. How'd I get there? It started
with a very unofficial ride-along with a young RCMP officer working patrol
in Surrey, BC. He was a few years older than me, growing up in the East Vancouver hood that I also called home. Late one night, Larry had me meet him at
the intersection of two backroads in a rural part of Surrey, where I dumped my
red '59 Austin A40, which I had bought for $475, and jumped into his Chevy
Impala cruiser. Surrey, a suburb of Vancouver, had a bad rap for crime and violence back then, and it didn't take long to prove itself.

With heroin being the era's drug of choice, codeine became the backup plan
when heroin availability ran low, making local pharmacies ideal supply-targets.
Cough syrup was boosted during break-ins and consumed in large quantities
for its codeine content. Now, I've never done heroin, but I'm told that codeine
is the poor man's heroin without the euphoric high. It stabilizes the hurting
addict, but nirvana it's not.

With officers few and far between in the mid-seventies, a cop in Surrey had
to be a one-man wrecking crew, a single force of nature, in order to take down
the lowlifes and criminal element that flourished in the drug-ridden areas of
an otherwise middle-class bedroom community. Our first call was a drugstore
break-in, and we were full-throttle, keeping the lights and siren off as we slid

into the lot of a non-descript strip mall. Without time to brief me on what to do, Larry bailed from the car, gun drawn. I remained back, a naïve, wide-eyed eighteen-year-old experiencing a rush of adrenalin like nothing before. "Wait here," Larry blurted as he ran through the smashed glass door. I stood by the car faking a brave face. Moments later, Larry emerged dragging a suspect by the scruff of the neck. Slamming him against the side of the car, Larry forcefully ordered me to "Hold him," as he went back in for crook number two.

That was it. That was the moment I knew I wanted to be a cop. Looking back, I was unwittingly similar to the addict, both of us seeking a high, except mine was legal and carried with it a sense of altruism—right conquering wrong.

Born in 1958, I grew up on the east side of Vancouver, in a tough, blue-collar neighbourhood where community pride—though occasionally misplaced—far outweighed pay-cheques. As one of five kids, money was tight, though we never went hungry. There was watered-down skim milk in the fridge and white bread on the counter. Praise for the Herculean efforts of our mom and dad to instill values in their sometimes-irascible brood cannot be over-stated. To Mom and Dad, my siblings and I owe an incalculable debt of gratitude.

I attended public school, where I recall never wanting to put forth more effort into passing each grade than necessary, though for reasons still obscure to me, I was awarded the most-improved scholar ribbon in grade four. I raced home to impress my mother without really knowing what I had done to merit the accolade. And frankly, I wasn't really interested in knowing. I just hoped for a little more leniency commensurate with the evidence of elevated scholastic skills. Funny enough, my laisse-faire attitude would be recognized decades later by one of my policing field trainers. I was taken aback when he noted in my performance appraisal: "Things you choose to do, you do exceptionally well, but in doing so, you choose to not do anything more than necessary." I was actually a bit rattled that he had detected this flaw in my industriousness. I certainly wasn't expecting it, though I've always given Rob credit for laying it out there. It was the reality check I needed at the time, and something I've been vigilant to address to this very day.

As elementary school gave way to high school, I was ecstatic to find that my high school was replete with shops. A metalwork shop, woodwork shop, and auto shop, all with heavy-duty machinery and open to students, especially those kids not identified for the academic stream of schooling that would typi-cally lead to university following grade twelve. I recall meetings with my grade nine counsellor, Mr. McDougall, in which he tapped me as a participant in the academic stream. I objected. All I wanted to do was unleash my creativity in various shop courses, in particular the automotive shop. Mr. McDougall found a way to accommodate. There was a hybrid blend that offered the best of both worlds, though with some compromise. I could take a limited number of shop courses but would also be required to complete a minimum grouping of academic courses that would keep the door to university open, or at least unlocked. I needed my parents' authorization to dumb-down my academic future, which was acquired with a signature on a form that I told my mother was simply to allow me to take a shop course, not undermine my academic future.

The sequel to this story is found in 1987. By this time, I was a school liaison officer at Templeton High School, the very high school I had graduated from. Only seven years separated my graduation from my return as the school's cop. One morning, I found myself in the records' vault following-up a case, when I inadvertently stumbled upon a card file that contained my name and a summary of standings from elementary school. There, typed in faded black ink, was my IQ. I actually recall writing what I now know were IQ tests in my primary years. The teachers never referred to them in that manner, but the instructions, such as, "Answer as many questions as possible, but don't worry about finishing," gave it away. I loved a test that you were told not to finish, but did my best to do so, nonetheless. It was surreal to be looking at a filing card bearing profile data that had followed me from elementary school to high school, and which had clearly influenced the proceedings with Mr. McDougall. Fortunately, the data didn't identify me as problematic or afflicted with anti-social tendencies. And the IQ? Meh.

So that's pretty much me. A decent kid from the East Side, who exhibited marginal ambition and would rather tinker with tools than calculators, but who also discovered a passion for writing thanks to the inspiration of Ms. Sharon Ross and her grade eleven Short-Fiction Writing class. I recall one assignment she placed upon the class, which connected with me. We were to select a favourite song and write about the meaning we found in the lyrics. My selection was "Candle in the Wind," from 1973. It was written by Bernie Taupin and performed by Elton John. I was a huge Elton fan back then, and I found immeasurable depth in the song inspired by the tragic life of Marilyn Monroe, whose real name was Norma Jean Mortenson. Despite my grade eleven lyrical introspection, my achievement malaise transcended not only high school but followed me into the BC Police Academy. More on that later.

3

IS THIS THE FELLOW THAT DAMAGED MY CAR?

SO HERE I AM, A ROOKIE COP IN VANCOUVER'S WEST END, ONE of North America's most densely populated neighbourhoods. Highrise apartment buildings shoot skyward from lots so small they barely accommodated the turn-of-century, Craftsman-style wood-frame homes that once defined Vancouver's West End. Standing side-by-side for blocks, today's tall buildings house many seniors, but are also home to much of Vancouver's gay population, emerging from the shadows to establish a diverse, vibrant West End community.

The caller reported that several male suspects were breaking into vehicles within the bowels of the underground parking garage of a Barclay Street highrise. My training officer and I were first on the scene. Running down the concrete ramps that accessed the lower levels, we heard the screech of tires and an engine screaming at full tilt. Whatever it was, it was headed our way—and fast. Careening around the corner came a red, 1970s Datsun pickup truck heading directly at us. We leapt from its path. As it went by, my partner threw his heavy cop-flashlight at the rear window of the small truck. The flashlight (sometimes known in cop parlance as a "bashlight") smashed through the rear window of the cab but missed the driver. My throw wasn't nearly as accurate, clanging off the metal of the truck's cab. We ran behind the truck as the driver madly raced up each ramp to the next level, striking the concrete wall with the right front corner of the car on each turn. Finally, on the last level, the driver carried far too much speed, lost control, and slammed into the rear of a pristine 1963 Cotswold blue Jaguar MKII. The resulting disfigurement was heartbreaking.

With the Datsun now jammed against the concrete wall, after body-slamming the Jag, the driver raced the engine but was unable to make progress. By this time, a K9 handler had arrived with a German Shepherd begging through its irrepressible bark to be admitted access to the Datsun's cab. Our suspect saw the K9 coming and tried to escape out the passenger door as the dog literally sailed into the cab through the driver's door. My quick-thinking partner shouldered the passenger door firmly closed from outside, preventing the suspect from hot-footing it. The dog effected a textbook arrest, shall we say. Once removed from the cab of the truck, the wiry suspect foolishly managed to wrangle himself free and sprint up the driveway leading to the street. Apparently, he had already forgotten about his canine friend. Just as I was about to give chase, I heard the K9 handler yell, "Dog out," and saw a furry-blur pass me en-route to our fleeing villain, who was nearing the street and potential freedom. Again, the dog made contact, bringing the suspect's thin taste of liberty to a biting end. Now here's where it gets interesting.

After a scrum to handcuff Mr. Tiggesmith, as he became known to me, I held him in place on the concrete driveway. Still in a state of drug-induced rage, Tiggesmith ranted, snorted, and squirmed in a manner not unlike one possessed by Satan himself. At about this point, a gentleman of senior years, dressed in what one might consider a smoking jacket of yore, ambled slowly over and looked down upon Mr. T. The refined chap then asked me, in a British accent that would have made the queen quiver with delight, if this was the fellow that had damaged his Jaguar.

"Yes sir," was my reply, expecting that to be the end of it—but it wasn't. Mr. de Landreau held his head high, clasped his hands behind his back, and walked several paces away before rotating on the balls of his feet and walking slowly back toward us. Without looking down, and with a rather exaggerated swing of his right leg, Mr. de Landreau booted our Tiggesmith square in the head.

"Oh, sorry about that old chap," said Mr. de Landreau as he carried forth. I've got to say, it was a bloody brilliant bit of theatrics that must have given the old chap a moment of satisfaction, though I'm not sure Tiggesmith felt anything in his elevated state, Mr. de Landreau's soft slipper doing no damage. For years afterward, I would encounter our man "Tiggy," as I came to name him.

Unfortunately, he continued with his drug-addled life of criminality. I'm not sure whatever happened to him. There's no doubt that he continued his pattern of victimization in order to sustain his addiction, which is a sad and pathetic existence for anyone, let alone a young man who otherwise may have had plenty of potential. He had no shortage of energy; that's for sure!

The event with Tiggesmith taught me two things: 1) drug-induced rage is real and presents a serious danger to anyone in its path; 2) don't mess with an Englishman's Jag.

4

THE ACADEMY

I ENTERED THE BC POLICE ACADEMY, SITUATED ON VANCOU-
ver's panoramic Jericho lands overlooking English Bay and the North Shore
Mountains, on May 7, 1979, as a recruit of the Vancouver Police Department.
I was among a class of sixteen recruits for the city, all of whom were men. Or
perhaps more accurately, some of whom were boys. I was twenty years of age,
while two of my classmates were just nineteen, the legal drinking age in British
Columbia. Though my high-school pals and I had bluffed our way into a few
bars while underage, I had a year or so of legal drinking status behind me when
I swore an oath to the queen to "serve and protect" her subjects.

The hiring philosophy back then went something like this: Hire them young,
then break them down and rebuild them as the officer you want. I wasn't one to
ascribe to such an outdated militaristic philosophy, but knew I had to tolerate
the boot-camp oppression of the academy to succeed. Though policing requires
firm discipline, and at times both emotional and physical toughness, we weren't
being trained to be Robo Cops. That's not what the community wanted of their
police officers. The concept of intelligence-led community policing was emerging as a progressive vision, and we were on the leading edge, contrary to the
boot-camp physical-training we endured.

Despite the renaissance taking place in modern policing, dealing with violence and conflict typical of large cities was no less real or dangerous for the
police. As a young cop, I recall being the only officer available to attend a family
dispute in which a son had been physically fighting with his father. The son was

older than I was. So, yes, being able to manage adversity at a young age was a paramount skill that had to be imparted by the academy, and in my case, at just twenty years old, it was more for my own survival than anyone else's. In that incident, I succeeded in separating and calming the two combatants, leaving them with some degree of dignity, and hopefully, a newfound tolerance for each other. I later reflected on the call and wondered if they knew how young and unworldly I was. Sometimes it just takes a fresh set of eyes, candid dialogue—and of course the threat of jail—to impart clarity in an embattled relationship that's too valuable to lose over bull-headedness. Having never fought with my father, or resented his parenting, this was as much an eye-opening lesson for me as it was for them.

If the success of my intervention was not underpinned by age-related wisdom, perhaps the "old school" ideology of the academy was more influential and effective than I had been prepared to give it credit for. Were the hours spent engaged in physical training and self-defence techniques, during the first fourteen-week block of our police training, the foundation that all young recruits needed before being thrust into society's dark side? If so, credit is owed to our academy supervisor, physical trainer, and self-defence instructor, the brutish Scotsman Pat McBride. Pat had been a Golden Gloves boxer in his day. Tough as nails, and not one to suffer timidity among his fledglings, he wielded an iron fist of leadership—a fist that met everyone's abdomen on the first day of months of self-defence training, which consisted largely of boxing.

Pat lined-up his brood of crew-cut newbies and walloped each of them in the abdomen with a right jab to ensure they could take slug to the gut and not go down. It was the first time that I had taken a punch to the gut with the ferocity of a runaway freight train. I managed to pass the test, barely. To further strengthen our resistance to abdominal incursions and fine-tune our abdominal reflexes, Pat's daily training regime had us prone on the gym floor while a partner dropped a walloping-big medicine ball repeatedly on the receiver's abdomen. The trick to survival was to tense the abs the moment of impact, otherwise the wind would be knocked from the lungs, and neither the breathless recruit nor Pat would be happy.

Pat made it clear during our sparring, wearing relatively light boxing gloves and head protection, that anyone not giving their "all" with punches would have to enter the ring with him. This was not a prospect any of us wished to avail ourselves of. The occasional bloody nose and black eye among us gave welcome credibility to the notion of "giving our all." On the lighter side of Pat's demeanour, he could be exceptionally funny and sarcastic. This was borne out when he badgered us with comments in his brogue Scottish accent as we struggled through round after round of sit-ups and push-ups: "Please, Mommy dearest, may I have another slice of pie?" he would mockingly utter.

Pat had a special name for me, which made me laugh whenever he said it. I wasn't the most coordinated of marchers on the parade square, which drove Pat absolutely mad. He took to calling me Rothman rather than Rothwell. Here's what he said to me in a pained voice during a fit of frustration when my foot-work was less than precise:

Pat: Do you know why I call you Rothman?

Me: No sir, I don't.

Pat: Because cigarettes kill people, and you're killing me! (Rothman's being a popular brand of cigarettes in the day.)

At this point, he ordered me to march everywhere on campus that I travelled. And believe me, he'd be hiding around the next corner to make certain I did. Fortunately, this rather humiliating technique of "practice makes perfect" only lasted a day. As much as Pat's teaching methods seemed barbaric and outdated, I have to give him credit. He took a ragged group of young men and turned them into a unit that operated with confidence and precision. I was never one to look for trouble as a teenager, but when I emerged from the police academy, I wasn't one to shy away from it either.

NO SWAT—NO TASER

DURING THE LATE SEVENTIES AND EARLY EIGHTIES, LARGER, more progressive police agencies throughout North America were establishing specialty units to increase the margin of safety when dealing with armed suspects engaged in violent acts. Hostage-takings, barricaded standoffs, and heavily guarded biker clubhouses, among other high-risk enterprises, required the policing community to rethink their response strategies in an effort to better manage risks that confronted first responders as well as potential victims and suspects. And so were born special, highly-trained units equipped with advanced weaponry, tactics, and skills.

The Vancouver Police Department was no different. It looked throughout North America to find leading-edge training for the creation of its Emergency Response Teams (ERT) and their Crisis Negotiator Program, both of which today are among the most advanced in Canada. Of course, neither resource was available the afternoon in the early 1980s when I donned heavy, metal ballistic armour before entering the basement of an east-end house in response to a "shots fired" call. The information was limited, as is so often the case when the police respond to a high-risk call. The upstairs tenant had heard yelling, then a series of loud bangs from the downstairs suite. Apparently, a lone male resided in the suite, which occupied only a portion of the basement. Roughly half of the basement remained unfinished, jammed with wood, tools, and an array of old boxes containing household items in storage.

As was the protocol of the day, the sergeant on-scene took command of the call and assigned roles. Mine was to use a battery-powered bullhorn to call commands to the subject believed to be residing in the suite. With the heavy, metal flack-jacket weighing me down, I took a position of concealment behind a parked car. The house was surrounded by the few officers free to attend the call. In a manner coordinated with the officers securing the perimeter, I attempted to make verbal contact with the subject. There was no script for me to follow, and no police psychologist to identify wedges to exploit with the suspect in an effort to gain compliance. I did my best to assure the suspect that we would not harm him, and that he must exit the house through the basement door with nothing in his hands or pockets. There was no movement from within and no response to my directions. This continued for twenty to thirty minutes before the sergeant made a decision: We were going to enter the unfinished portion of the basement and reattempt contact. Some of the factors leading to this tactic included the possibility that the subject was unable to hear us, or unable to respond due to injury or death, assuming he may have shot himself.

An even greater concern that could not be assessed from outside was whether the suspect had shot someone else in the suite or was holding a hostage. The police have a duty to protect life and render assistance. We could do neither from our exterior post.

Entering an enclosed area under the suspect's control is pretty much the last thing cops want to do. Today, ERT will use a number of techniques to gather intel on the activity taking place within the premises before committing to a blind entry. These include the use of video-equipped remote-controlled "throw" robots that can transmit live video back to the operator as they are driven throughout the premises. Throw phones and other electronic gear can also help establish a communication link with a suspect, or at least establish an audible communication path. More recently, drones are being used to look into windows without the need to have a human get anywhere near a residence. We, of course, had none of this modern technology.

Our entry was through the rear basement door. We viewed a roughly sketched floor plan provided by the upstairs tenant, so we had a vague idea of the layout. Across twenty feet or so of concrete floor was the hollow-core wood door leading into the suspect's suite. It was a typical inner household door that had never been painted. Scattered across the upper portion of the door was a series of holes, that given the circumstances, we took to be bullet holes. There were eight or so, each with splintered wood projecting away from the door. The conclusion was that the suspect had fired through the door from inside his suite.

I announced again our presence by bullhorn, convinced that he must be able to hear me given our proximity. Nothing. An arrest team with weapons drawn readied themselves. More commands to the suspect, and still nothing. Then suddenly movement was heard, along with an enraged voice yelling, "What the fuck do you want?"

Finally, communication.

"We just want to make sure that everyone is ok."

"Fuck off," came the hostile reply.

After more dialogue, the door suddenly opened. An agitated male emerged.

"Freeze!" I yelled.

"Fuck you," he yelled. He held in his right hand a kitchen knife, which he pointed toward us and waved side-to-side. Despite repeated commands to do so, he wouldn't drop it or follow commands.

Being in such close proximity to a knife-wielding suspect is to put your life on the line. A subject within twenty feet, with a knife, can race forward and deliver a fatal blow before a victim can perceive the advancing threat and take defensive action. "Step off the line of attack" is what they taught in the academy. An individual advancing at speed is unable to alter their course of attack if the target steps to the side at the last second. This tactic then allows enough time for the officer to point and fire before the attacker can pivot and take a second run. It's akin to a game of murder ball; however, the murder part is real.

There were three of us in uniform in the basement as the suspect pointed his knife. I was simply waiting for the crack of a pistol, taking the suspect down with deadly force. But just at that moment, while the suspect was focused on two of us, the third officer discreetly took hold of a piece of two-by-four wood, approximately four feet in length. In a flash, he came around from the side and swung the wood downward in a slashing motion, striking the suspect's out-reached forearm in a manner that would have impressed even the dirtiest NHL enforcer. The knife flew from the suspect's hand as we pounced and brought him into custody. What a sense of relief that was. Shooting and killing another person is the last thing a cop wants to do irrespective of how justified doing so may be.

We eventually learned that the bangs and resulting holes in the door were caused by a large fishing spear that the suspect had been angrily throwing at the door. He had then passed out after his cocktail of alcohol and drugs had taken affect, allowing him to sleep through our earlier attempts at communication. By yesterday's standards, our actions were fairly standard. No one was injured or killed, and the call wrapped up in an hour. By today's standards, we were impulsive, in fact bordering on reckless.

And the same could be said for this next call. Same era, similar life-threatening situation.

In this case, the suspect had a butcher knife. It was a wide, long-bladed implement such as a chef might wield in a commercial kitchen. We found ourselves on the street dancing around a couple of patrol cars as the suspect made numerous lunges toward the four cops in attendance. This, of course, preceded the use of tasers, in which two wired prongs shoot out of the conducted energy weapon (CEW) and lodge in the subject's skin. A high-voltage, low-amperage shock is immediately delivered, disrupting muscle function. The subject usually freezes and drops to the ground, but it's not assured. Thick clothing can prevent the prongs from connecting with the skin while some highly goal-oriented individuals can actually fight through the electric shock, especially when in a drug-induced psychosis.

Bean-bag shotguns had not yet taken hold as a less-lethal weapon to knock the fight out of an armed subject. While these assets can be invaluable in safely disarming violent subjects, they are not carried by all police officers. As a result, the likelihood of a taser or bean-bag operator being available in every critical instance is highly limited. If time can be bought, an operator can be hailed to the scene, but there's no guarantee of these less-lethal means of subduing a violent subject being effective.

Without either mechanism of less-lethal force, all we were left with was the use of our 38-calibre Smith & Wesson six-shot revolver, or a twenty-four-inch wooden baton that some, but not all, cops carried. Neither of these options was overly desirable from our perspective. This didn't deter Grant, one of the officers in attendance, from enacting option two in an effort to eliminate the need for an option-one response. While we strategically distracted the suspect by yelling commands at him, which he entirely disregarded, Grant quickly came from behind and did a two-handed Louisville Slugger swing, connecting his solid ash baton with the back of the suspect's head. Without doubt, I thought this would bring him down like a Jenga tower, but it didn't. The suspect stumbled forward, then regained his footing and stood erect, madder than ever. His rage had increased, for the moment that is. He soon started feeling the effects of the cranial blow and began slowing down. He was fatigued and hurting, but not willing to give up the fight. Fortunately, his laboured motor skills and waning vigilance gave an opportunity for a wrist whack with a baton, similar to that delivered to our spear-throwing basement dweller. The knife clanged to the roadway while the pile-on brought the suspect safely into custody.

The "pile-on" often looks dramatic on the evening news, yet for all involved it's one of the safest methods of immobilizing an unarmed combative subject, especially one with super-human strength underwritten by the veinal flow of a chemical cocktail. In a pile-on, each officer can restrain a limb while another manages the head, preventing jaws of fury from latching onto the flesh and bone of an arrest team. Handcuffing a resistive subject is far more difficult than armchair critics realize. Many physiological and psychological conditions can greatly heighten a person's ability to tolerate pain, which can render typical empty hand strikes and pain-compliance techniques ineffective. To illustrate my point, I once responded to a mentally ill male who was using a steak knife to castrate himself. Upon my arrival, he had partially severed his scrotum from his groin and was not deterred from his objective by pain. Imagine that— being so goal-oriented that you can take a steak knife, and without anesthesia, undertake a DIY castration. That level of determination may similarly apply to individuals equally intent on a mission to fight with the police and not be taken into custody.

Well, that was a bit of a divergence from dealing with an armed, barricaded suspect, but food for thought, nonetheless. Fortunately, police tactics in dealing with armed and barricaded individuals have evolved over the last couple of decades, bringing with them much safer outcomes for both the police and the offenders in high-risk encounters. While we got lucky on the two occasions I've described, a deadly outcome was a significant possibility for the officers responding to the threats and the suspects delivering them.

BEING A COP

THE VISCERAL NATURE OF POLICE WORK CAN'T BE COMPLETELY replicated on screen or in books. The attendant rush of adrenalin is unlikely to be triggered by words you read or screens you view. Yet find yourself in the front seat of a patrol car, and there develops a perilous need for adrenaline, which is so abundant among first responders. Why else would cops race to confront a madman armed with a weapon? Or why would firefighters enter a structure fully engulfed in flames? These ought to be acts that humans instinctively avoid, yet we seek them out. Altruism plays a major role for sure, but it alone is not the motivator. It's the adrenaline that flows from facing adversity, be it an armed suspect or a risky rescue, that feeds a penchant for action. Of course, my observations are anecdotal, but they are drawn from being immersed in cop culture for multiple decades. I'd venture to say that most cop spouses would back me up on my unscientific hypothesis around the uninhibited pursuit of adrenaline-fueled action.

In spite of the potential personal consequences and health risks that policing carries, it also delivers some of the most rewarding moments one can experience in a job. It could be something as humble as reuniting a lost child with frantic parents that keeps the motivational fires burning. Small victories count too, such as helping a family visiting Canada make it to their plane on time, despite being involved in a collision on the way to the airport in a rental car. In the latter case, a phone call to the airline managed to hold the plane as I whisked Mom, Dad, and the kids to the terminal in my police car. By turning a negative into a positive for a grateful family, I went home happy and certainly better emotionally adjusted than when the day ends with a fatality of some sort.

More often than not, it's these little things that restore a cop's faith in humanity, rather than the big calls. The most meaningful "thank yous" I've ever received were for the things that were, in my eyes, of least significance. Receiving a thank-you letter from the family that made their flight home to Europe following the collision was one of those moments. That said, a cop can never under-estimate the effect he or she may have on an individual, be it good or bad. Over the course of this book, I'll share with you many examples, but first, it would be helpful to zip you through a brief summary of my life with a badge:

> 1979–hired by the VPD at twenty-years of age (yes, I still wonder how sensible that was too)
>
> 1980–1983 worked uniform patrol in both the north and south sectors of Vancouver
>
> 1983–1987 successfully competed for a position as a school liaison officer, finding myself back in the halls of my high school.
>
> 1987–1989 uniform patrol work in downtown Vancouver
>
> 1989–1991 worked in a plainclothes crime task force, targeting residential and commercial break-in suspects
>
> 1991–1992 promoted to a corporal and assigned to the city jail
>
> 1992–1994 became a Drug Squad detective
>
> 1995–1996 assigned to the Vancouver Integrated Intelligence Unit (Russian Organized Crime and Gaming portfolios)

1996–2000 promoted to sergeant in-charge of bicycle patrol unit, downtown Vancouver

2000–2003 promoted to inspector in-charge of Internal Investigation Unit

2003–2006 inspector in-charge of Criminal Intelligence Section

2006–2008 inspector in-charge of Patrol Support Section, primarily a series of investigative units

2009–2012 promoted to superintendent commanding Criminal Investigation Division, Homicide, Robbery/ Assault, Arson, Financial Crime, Special Investigations

2012–Retired

2012–Hired back as the VPD's civilian manager of Fleet Operations, assessing fleet needs for the VPD, from patrol cars and trucks to motorcycles and boats, and working with city personnel to procure these assets.

Let's get back to police work!

MENTAL ILLNESS: LESSONS LEARNED

I WAS A BIKE COP RIDING A MOUNTAIN BIKE IN DOWNTOWN Vancouver. I was with a partner when we responded to an "out of control" male in the HMV music store on Robson Street, Vancouver's version of Rodeo Drive in Beverly Hills, California. The staff had vacated the store along with the customers for fear of this individual's aggression and his level of his unfiltered hostility. He was near the back of the store, and he was a human mountain. Maybe in his early twenties, the fellow was large, scary, and extremely belligerent. He had removed his underwear and had been throwing them at staff while hurling extremely hateful threats. He was demonic and possessed that night. It was clear to me that he was either mentally ill or under the influence of a drug, possibly crystal meth or crack, both of which are stimulants manufactured illegally and often cut with PCP or other psychosis-inducing chemicals.

We took our time approaching the subject and kept our cool. Nothing would escalate the violence more quickly than him reacting to threats levelled by us. We were firm though. We knew he had to either go to jail, if charged criminally, or to the hospital, if mentally ill. One way or the other, he needed to be restrained and assessed. We had an ambulance standing by, and after a slow cautious approach managed to calm the subject enough to handcuff him for the safety of us all. He was then forcibly restrained with leather straps on a stretcher and taken by ambulance to the hospital. Once he realized that we were not going to harm him, and in fact had his best interests at heart, he became much more manageable.

21

A few days later, I learned a powerful lesson about our interaction. I was in uniform, standing in front of our downtown Granville Street neighbourhood office when a group of four or so young people walked my way. A totally together male, whom I didn't recognize as the same madman from several nights before, spoke to me in the kindest voice possible. He apologized for his conduct, saying that he had been suffering a severe Tourette's episode and was greatly embarrassed by his actions. But most compelling of all, and the lesson that resonated so personally with me, is that he thanked me sincerely for treating him with dignity and respect. It almost brought tears to my eyes, and still in fact does. Here was a model young man that any of us would be proud to call a son or brother. It blew me away that he cared enough to open up to me. And it taught me that even amidst an episode of severe mental illness, people remember how they were treated by the police—good or bad. Once you learn that lesson, you never unlearn it.

I recall another case somewhat similar, which preceded this one by probably a decade, yet the parallels are uncanny. The parents of a young man in his early twenties called the police as the last resort in dealing with their mentally ill son who had become violent and was ripping apart the house. These were good people doing their best for a son they loved, and by all accounts, had done a marvelous job raising him. Yet his illness had become more than they could manage. I can't imagine the degree of pain the parents went through prior to making the call. They really had no idea how things would unfold after the cops arrived. What if their son grabbed a knife in the kitchen? Would the police react with deadly force? Would calling the police on their son further destroy the already fragmented relationship between them?

As we entered the house, I could hear the son swearing and raising a ruckus toward the back of the main floor. His mother implored us not to hurt him. His dad was in tears. All I could hope for was that this would go well—that he wouldn't rush into the kitchen for the aforementioned knife. Every cop knows how dangerous the kitchen is and how important it is to keep your suspect out of it. I can recall several brutal kitchen fights that I've battled through over the years, all the while thinking I've got to get control by any means possible before a knife or similar kitchen implement alters the dynamics for the worse. Fortunately, a brutal fight with the son was not part of this scenario, which ended with a calm approach followed by a quick grab by both my partner and me to gain control over the young man and handcuff him. Again, an ambulance with restraints attended and the subject was on his way to hospital. The parents thanked us profusely through their tears as they readied themselves to follow the ambulance to the psych ward.

One final example of mental illness illustrates that what is being espoused by a mentally ill subject may have meaning inconsistent with the words spoken.

A neighbour had called the police to report the sound of a major disturbance taking place in a nearby house. My partner and I arrived within moments and came upon a naked, middle-aged woman out in front of her house in a complete psychotic rage. We tried to calm her and take her back inside, but that was not going to happen given her irrationality and lack of cooperation. We obtained a housecoat from inside and did our best to have her drape it over herself. It was apparent that she had pretty much demolished the inside of her house. Almost everything had been smashed or upended.

We called an ambulance to transport the woman to hospital for a psyche evaluation. While being strapped to the gurney, she began to yell, "My baby! I need my baby!" I asked her if her baby was in the house. She said that it was. I ran back into the building in fear that I'd find a baby or toddler buried somewhere among the ruins, but I didn't. In fact, I didn't see a crib, a child's bedroom, or anything that would lend credence to "my baby." I ran back to the ambulance to ask her where exactly the baby was and how old. It was then that she said, "She's just a kitten." It took my breath away. Her baby was a cat. Perhaps I should've taken a little more time asking questions about her baby before running back into the house, but every cop's gut instinct kicks into high gear when a baby or child is involved; there is no greater driver of a full-scale police response.

Obviously, mental illness remains one of life's hidden truths, affecting people in all societies. I don't plan to get political in this book, but a recent study showed that thirty-five percent of the individuals the Vancouver police are required to deal with within the city suffer from some form or level of mental illness, which is a tragic state of affairs that contributes to crime, violence, and homelessness. (Lost in Transition—Vancouver Police 2008.)

8

VANCOUVER: DYSFUNCTION AMIDST BEAUTY

PICTURE PERFECT VANCOUVER IS CANADA'S GATEWAY TO THE Pacific. It lies on the West Coast, spitting distance from the Canada/US border. Vancouver enjoys a temperate rainforest climate, juxtaposed to the majority of this great nation, which endures colder winters and hotter summers intensified with greater humidity.

With a population nearing 700,000 residents spread over 114 square kilometres, Vancouver-proper is far from Canada's largest city. That distinction goes to Toronto, Ontario; however, Vancouver can boast mile after mile of sandy beaches in addition to being home to one of the largest urban parks in North America. Stanley Park is a 405-hectare public amenity surrounded by a seawall on which folks can walk or cycle the 8.8-kilometre pathway that circumnavigates the park, showcasing some of the most spectacular ocean sunsets on the globe.

Few cities are as tolerant, enchanting, and culturally diverse as Vancouver; few cities are also as expensive, drug-ridden, and politically dysfunctional as Vancouver. Yet, Vancouver is a five-star destination for tourists, international students, and immigrants seeking a better life for their families. The city is bordered by snow-capped mountains to the north and the Pacific Ocean to the west. In the spring, Vancouverites can ski the local hills, not more than thirty minutes from downtown, and sail the blue waters of English Bay on the same day. There's world-class hiking, biking, and fishing as well, all within a short drive or boat ride, but as delightful as it is, Vancouver has a dark underbelly.

Drug addiction, mental illness, and homelessness attach a much different definition to the Jewel of the Pacific. These appalling realities drive rates of property-related crime that are staggering and among the highest of any North American city. The cost of sustaining an addiction, be it crystal meth, cocaine, heroin, or MDMA, can easily run a user hundreds of dollars per day. An addict's return on stolen property is roughly ten cents on the dollar, which translates into several thousand dollars' worth of crime, per day, per addict. A walk-through of Vancouver's notorious Downtown Eastside, or one of its recurring tent cities, makes that strikingly obvious. All manner of stolen merchandise can be purchased in the bazaar-like atmosphere, in which the marginalized and the desperate scrape together a few bucks to see them through the day.

It's an endless cycle of crime, homelessness, and drug use for the addicts, many of whom are dual-diagnosis individuals, meaning they struggle with mental illness as well as addiction. But let's be clear, not all mentally ill individuals fall into the dual-diagnosis category; in fact, it's relatively few. The preponderance of mentally ill patients may otherwise be high-functioning individuals dealing with episodic bouts of mental illness, often triggered by a gap in medication, which we'll see as a recurring theme throughout this book.

The events presented here are all true, though some names, locations, and minor details have been altered to protect . . . well, everyone! The stories are not in any specific order. I thought about batching them together based on a timeline, or specific policing assignments, but chose to present them disordered, in the same way that the randomness of 911 calls and the unpredictability of crime ensure that no two days as a cop are alike. With the stage set, let's jump headlong into tales that can only accompany thirty-three years of policing a city as vibrant, diverse, and politically complicated as Vancouver, Canada.

9

SUICIDE: A LAST RESORT FOR MANY

I DON'T WANT THIS BOOK TO LEAVE ITS READERS TREADING water in a pool of emotion and misery, but I can't open the door on mental illness without addressing suicide. Police officers must investigate every case of suicide, largely to verify that the incident was, in fact, suicide and not homicide. Homicide is when a person's life is taken by someone else; however, homicide is not exclusively murder, despite murder always being homicide. Accidently killing a pedestrian with your vehicle is a case of homicide, which depending on the circumstances could be culpable (charge-worthy) or non-culpable. A justifiable killing, such as a police officer shooting in self-defence, is a non-culpable homicide, as is the accidental killing of a pedestrian with your car. Despite both events being non-culpable, they may be subject to non-criminal charges and various civil consequences, such as financial compensation.

The mechanisms for suicide are wide-ranging. Some suicides are structured to send a final, devastating message to those left behind, while some are structured to look accidental in nature, thereby garnering an insurance payout. Others are simply meant to end a life of suffering by the most efficient and painless means possible. Suicides I've investigated have included death by jumping, hanging, poisoning, overdosing, drowning, and firearm. I'll review three such cases and one case of successful intervention, the latter carrying with it a pall of absurdity.

She got smart and dumped a guy she saw no future with given his abusive nature and unproductive ways. In their mid-thirties, they were older than most dating couples, if their life with each other could be characterized as "dating." With some convictions for petty crimes and a love of the bottle that outweighed his love for her, he was sent packing. Unfortunately, he couldn't accept that she was successfully moving on. His final goodbye came to her late one afternoon. He knew she'd be home in her second-floor, east-side apartment. He also knew that she was unlikely to answer the intercom or phone if she suspected it was him calling.

The sound of objects tapping against her sliding patio door worked. He threw pebbles at the door knowing they would attract her attention but not break the glass, and he was right. She pulled back the curtain to have a look into the laneway. He was there, directly below and in front of her. As they made eye contact, he quickly placed the gun to his temple and pulled the trigger. She saw it all.

While this suicide by firearm was clearly intended to inflict one final, life-altering blow to a former lover, not all gun-related suicides carry such a graphic message of twisted love.

The callers to 911 were certain it was a shot they had heard emanating from the rented basement of the house they lived in. They ran downstairs to check. What they saw stopped them in their tracks. Scott lived alone in the basement suite. They knew he had firearms, and that he had been down on his luck of late, but suicide? No, wouldn't think so, but sadly, they were wrong.

I was nearby when the call came across the police radio in my cruiser. I arrived within moments with the intention of rendering aid if there was a glimmer of hope. There wasn't. The small, bachelor-style suite was comprised of a kitchenette combined with a living-room area where an old sofa was placed against the far wall, facing the TV. The ceiling was low, probably lower than code would permit, but that's how it was in many unauthorized suites on the east side of town.

The lights were switched off, but enough daylight flowed in through a single window that gloomy afternoon to present a clear view. Through the gunpowder smoke that still hung in the air, I saw him. He was seated on the couch. His butt was near the front edge of the seating area, and his torso was leaning against the rear cushion. Despite a somewhat slouched posture, he remained upright, facing forward. The scene was the most grotesque I had ever encountered. I will do my best to dispassionately describe what I was confronted with, but if gore makes you squeamish, time to flip the page, my friend.

The subject's head had literally been blown off. What remained atop the bloody stump of his neck was his lower jaw and tongue and a small section of skull, the occipital bone, with hair attached. Everything above had been obliterated by the blast of a shotgun, the base of which had likely been braced against the floor. It was quite evident that the barrel of the weapon had probably been inserted into the subject's mouth, pointing in an upward trajectory. The blast coated the ceiling and the upper portion of the wall behind the sofa with a dripping mixture of blood, brain matter, bone, and flesh, some of which had splashed back, coating the subject and the sofa with the same gruesome mixture of biological material.

Hollywood could not have created a more horrific, macabre scene. It's not something that can ever be "unseen." However, when perceived from a clinical perspective, in a manner consistent with that of a forensic pathologist, the ghastly scene becomes more of an exercise in science than horror. And I don't say that to diminish in any way the violent loss of a human life—clearly there were many people terribly affected by this tragedy—but for me to document the scene and complete my investigation, I had to extract my emotions from the analysis. I also had to go home without carrying the vicarious burden of a decision made by an individual that I didn't know, which I had no means of preventing. But I'm not without feeling. The Christmas suicide of a different young man proves that each December 25th.

It was Christmas. A young man with no more than twenty years on this planet was living temporarily with his grandparents in a condominium in an upscale part of town. Life at home with his parents was in turmoil. Like many teens, he couldn't live with them, and in some desperate way, couldn't live without them. He refused to participate in the family Christmas, despite urging from his grandparents before they left to join the rest of the family for dinner and gifts at the family home. Exactly what was going through the young man's mind that triggered his next decision we'll never know, but again, a gruesome message was delivered.

Returning home from the traditional dinner and festivities, the grandparents were hoping to find their grandson in a more congenial state. Sadly, that wasn't to be. After unlocking the door into the condo, they found it blocked by something from behind. The grandfather pushed harder and managed to see inside. What he saw will never leave him. His grandson was hanging by a tie, which had been affixed to a light fixture above the entry in the condo. Despite an urgent effort to cut him down and release the ligature, the grandson had passed.

The sadness upon my arrival was so intense that I could physically feel its weight surrounding me. The factors that led this young man to take his life on Christmas Day have gone to the grave with him. While the rest of his loving family celebrated Christmas, he chose to send a final "Merry Christmas" communique to them that was cruel beyond measure. I really don't know how families survive such tragedies; I just silently hope the best for them each Christmas.

Sometimes the absurdity experienced in police work leaves one shaking one's head in disbelief. A twenty-something woman shared a rental suite in downtown Vancouver with a similarly aged female roommate. The roommate had returned home and found a suicide note from her housemate. Her housemate had been having problems dealing with many personal issues, including depression, for which she had never been diagnosed or treated. The roommate called the police.

My partner and I visited the suite. The building they lived in sat within several blocks of the Granville Street Bridge, which spans False Creek, connecting the downtown peninsula with greater Vancouver. The bridge carries six lanes of traffic as it gently rises twenty-seven metres above the murky water of False Creek. It's a popular bridge for suicide as survival is highly unlikely.

My partner and I were bike cops. We figured the closest and most probable location for committing suicide in relation to the apartment was the Granville Street Bridge. We jumped on our bikes and rode like it was the Tour de France. As we were pedaling hard up the Granville Street Bridge from north to south along the west sidewalk, we saw her. She was nearing the apex of the bridge. Thanks to the silence of the bikes, she didn't hear us coming. Before she could react, we had her safely in our custody. She was indeed distraught, and it was clear what her intention had been had we not arrived when we did.

We had her transported by ambulance to Vancouver General Hospital under the authority of the Mental Health Act, which empowers the police to "take to a place of medical care" anyone who is a demonstrable danger to themselves or others. This legal hold then allows the subject to be admitted for an examination by a doctor, and possibly a full psych review. Now comes the absurdity.

On examination by a psychiatrist, our subject was deemed to suffer from a personality disorder, and accordingly, did not meet the criteria to be held pending a full psych assessment, despite what I believed to be reliable evidence to the contrary. From the medical staff's perspective, the finding required them to release her from the hospital if she so chose, which she did. But that's not the absurdity.

Despite knowing that her home was on the opposite side of the Granville Street Bridge from which she had intended to jump, they released her without an escort, effectively committing her to walking home over the same bridge. Upon learning of this outcome from the hospital, my partner and I shot back over to her place to check that she had made it home without a vertical detour. Fortunately, she had. It would've been difficult to accept any other ending after the steps we had taken to get her the help she clearly was crying out for.

Suicide ideation is not limited to any group or community within society. Depression and mental illness are probably more pervasive than any of us care to consider. Many environmental and emotional factors may negatively affect one's level of contentment with life, and the police know this all too well from within their own corridors. Cop suicides, while uncommon, most certainly exist, often occurring in small clusters within a law enforcement agency. I've seen it, and it's agonizing for the men and women who swear to protect the public but sometimes can't protect themselves or their colleagues from the very real consequences of their profession.

Day after day, cops are thrust into the misfortunes of others and the vulgarity of humanity. They also endure vicious harassment that segments of our population feel entitled to unjustly dispense whenever they see a cop. Through the routine of their duties, the police endlessly confront the dark side of humanity so that others don't have to. A constant diet of sorting out other people's shit can blind a cop to the joys of everyday life. How many child rapes and exploitations can a detective investigate without being beset with debilitating emotional trauma? How many homicide investigations is too many? And how many times can a cop confront the aggression and violence that we often see in protests today? Where's the breaking point for the humans sworn to protect others?

The day prior to my writing this passage, a young RCMP officer took her own life. Distraught and alone, she used her service pistol to end her life while her colleagues frantically searched for her. Words cannot convey the pain she must have been silently tortured by, nor the regret of the colleagues unable to find her before the demons took their toll.

While I was fortunate to make it through a thirty-three-year career relatively unscathed, not everyone is. Reflecting back, I'm not ashamed to say that I experienced mild symptoms of post-traumatic stress. They were nothing that had me question my purpose in life or its meaning, but more that they germinated a quick fuse combined with anger that simmered beneath the surface. Fortunately, the toxic mixture never boiled over in any violent or destructive ways, but it gnawed at me day in and day out for a period of years. I was a stoic idiot though and never sought help; I simply contained it. I know—wrong answer.

Only in recent years have the incendiary effects of policing come to the fore, replacing the historic "bottle in the desk" with prevention and treatment deliver by qualified professionals. Other safeguards apply now as well, including peer-to-peer counselling, wellness training, financial guidance, and an industry-wide recognition that cops are humans in uniform and subject to all of the inherent frailties therein. I'm so very pleased to see the progress—a renaissance of sorts—that is taking place in wellness for the modern-day cop. I just wish it was bulletproof.

COPS & DRIVING

I'VE ALWAYS LIKED DRIVING AND WAS ONE OF THOSE KIDS THAT couldn't wait to be a licenced motorist with a car of his own, both of which were achieved mere weeks after my sixteenth birthday. Funded entirely by my part-time job at Woodward's Department Store in downtown Vancouver, I went through a series of used cars in the next few years sufficient to fill a car dealership. I took advanced driving courses on my own and learned to drive an autocross course with reasonably good outcomes.

My driving background paid off in the police academy, where I had the second fastest time in our class through the highspeed course in dry weather and the fastest time in our class through the course in the rain.

Driving a police car is a bit of a dream for car buffs. Who wouldn't want to part the seas with the use of lights and a siren? Tactical driving is part of policing. Responding Code-3 (lights and siren) to life-threatening, in-progress events requires a level of concentration beyond anything I had formerly experienced. Motorists do unpredictable, illogical things behind the wheel when an emergency vehicle is approaching with its lights flashing and siren blaring. You literally have to be prepared for them to come to a screeching halt in front of you, blocking your only path through congestion. When not driving Code-3, simply being on the road for ten or more hours a shift can expose cops to unexpected driving hazards. Here are three examples, the second and third of which harmed nothing, other than my pride:

It was about three a.m. one chilly fall morning. I was driving our marked patrol car north on Main Street. My partner and I had just departed the local 7-Eleven store with treats to fuel us through the remainder of the nightshift. Chris was slouched in the passenger seat holding a bag of sunflower seeds (spits) in his right hand and a soda in his left. His window was half open. I was munching an O'Henry bar as we casually drove northbound in the number-one lane of the four-lane thoroughfare. (Police number lanes starting at the yellow centre line and moving toward the curb, so this put us next to traffic flowing in the opposite direction.)

The opposing traffic was passing normally when suddenly there was the massive grille of a 1979 Lincoln Continental taking up fifty percent of my lane, approaching with no more than a car length between us. With no time for braking, I swerved violently to the right. Despite the evasive manoeuvre, our two sedans sideswiped each other with a glancing blow sufficient to launch Chris's bag of spits out the window and his soda onto the floor of the car. I nailed the brakes and our Ford Crown Victoria Police Interceptor spun a 180, allowing us to see the taillights of the Lincoln disappearing down the road.

We were now fully awake, and with no further need for sugary treats, we gave chase. The Lincoln eventually pulled over. The lone male occupant, a prominent Japanese businessman of ill-repute, suspected Yakuza, was intoxicated. He was arrested and charges laid. The glancing nature of the impact with the Lincoln greatly reduced the intensity of the collision despite our combined closing speed of 100km/h or more. Had the impact been directly head-on, the consequences may have been far worse than a soda on the floor and a lost bag of spits. The sudden and unexpected nature of the collision delivered a strong message—even in the calmest moments, devastating accidents can occur instantaneously through no fault of one's own. After dealing with our impaired hit-and-run driver, Chris and I drove the route back to the scene of the collision. We were unable to find any evidence of the sunflower seeds or the bag they were ejected in.

Considered mid-size, the patrol cars in use when I started my career were mostly late 1970s Dodge Aspens with a 318 cubic-inch V-8 engine. These sedans were smaller than police cars typical of the era and were supposed to achieve superior fuel-economy. Dodge built them in response to the oil crisis, driven by an export embargo established in 1973 by the Organization of Arab Petroleum Exporting Nations, which sent fuel prices skyrocketing in North America.

The Aspens were a quick vehicle with decent handling characteristics for the era. They were, however, difficult to start on cold mornings, usually stalling a half-dozen times before hitting normal operating temperature. This was largely due to extremely lean fuel/air mixtures established by the manufacturer in order to improve fuel-economy. It was easy to hang the tail of an Aspen during aggressive cornering, so it posed some serious challenges in the wet. I learned this in a rather embarrassing manner that still makes me chuckle to this day.

It was a rainy afternoon when my partner and I received an emergency call requiring us to respond immediately, in the opposite direction to which we were driving. Switching on the emergency lights brought approaching traffic to a standstill. I spun the steering wheel to the left and fed in a healthy dose of throttle. The V-8's torque quickly reached the Posi-Track rear-end of the car, and before I could intervene, our sedan was spinning around like a top in the middle of the road.

Instead of performing the graceful 180 I had envisioned, we had spun 360-degrees, leaving us pointing in the same direction in which we had started—now looking straight ahead at the cars that had stopped to allow me to execute this slice of driving magic. To this day, I laugh to myself when I think of the drivers that watched my automotive pirouette and wondered, *What the hell was that?*

I'm sure another *What the hell was that?* moment occurred in a long, indoor carwash at a gas station. I was taking a marked police car through the wash, which was an automated affair that grabbed onto the front wheel of a vehicle and slowly pulled it through the various brushes, and detergent and rinse stations. The trick was to ensure that your vehicle's transmission was placed into neutral, a requirement I was aware of but had somehow missed on this sunny morning.

The first phase of the carwash covered the vehicle with foamy soap. As this took place, I directed my attention to my onboard computer, known more technically as a "mobile data terminal," or MDT for short. My mind was quickly absorbed into the salient notes of the next call I would be attending. A moment later, I felt a horrendous thump at the front of my patrol car. I switched on the wipers to clear the foam, and there pushed against my front bumper was a Yellow Cab taxi, which had been going through the wash well ahead of me.

How did this happen? I wondered. *Did he back into me?* A rapid check of controls suddenly revealed that I had not placed my patrol car's transmission into neutral. When I'd removed my foot from the brake, the car drove itself forward under its own steam rather than being pulled slowly through the wash by the facility's mechanism. I had clearly rear-ended the cab. I laughed at the absurdity of having a collision in an automated carwash as our two vehicles made their way to the end of the line. My car remained dirty at the front while the taxi was still dirty at the rear, given that no brushes could slide between our bumpers.

At the end of the wash cycle, the cab simply drove off. I guess the importance of grabbing a fare outweighed the need to check for damage. I examined the front of the Chev Caprice patrol car. Its bumpers were huge, designed to withstand a government-imposed collision of 8km/h, which in this case, it successfully had.

TO PURSUE—OR NOT TO PURSUE

AS ENTERTAINING AS DRIVING A POLICE CAR CAN BE, IT'S ALSO serious business, one in which car chases are not the thrilling, no-one-dies events portrayed by Hollywood. The cost of an innocent life is far too heavy a price to pay to apprehend a petty crook. It's for this very reason that most police agencies have adopted no-pursuit policies, including the Vancouver Police Department. To justify a pursuit, the risk to the public must be greater by not pursuing than by pursuing. Frankly, I can only think of a few scenarios that would be supported by such reasoning, the most obvious being the pursuit of an active killer.

Not pursuing doesn't mean not arresting. In place of pursuing, many police agencies, including the VPD, have adopted a "box and pin" strategy, which requires training and certification before an officer can apply the technique in the field. In short, the tactic is founded upon a strategy in which the police show little interest in the suspect vehicle while keeping it in sight from a safe yet accessible distance. Generally, the driver of the suspect vehicle also plays it cool, not wanting to appear suspicious. During this subdued "cat and mouse" phase, several police cars will work their way into the area with the goal of executing a tightly coordinated, perfectly-timed "box and pin" once the suspect vehicle comes to a natural stop, most likely at a red light or when traffic is backed up. The vertical push-bars on the front of patrol vehicles act like blades, creating points of high-pressure contact, effectively pinning the offending vehicle in place. The occupants are then removed from the vehicle before there's any opportunity for it to become mobile. If performed as intended, the occupants won't see the box and pin coming before it's too late to evade the blades of justice. This highly practiced immobilization technique is remarkably effective at preventing unsafe car chases while also foiling the escape by vehicle of those active in crime.

As much as I love competitive driving, engaging in a high-stakes pursuit was never a thrill I sought. The last pursuit I engaged in prior to the department's adoption of box and pin involved a mid-eighties white Buick sedan being driven erratically. The vehicle was speeding but not greatly. It had also run a red light. Equally concerning were the jerky, side-to-side movements of the car, which told me that there was something more unusual going on than was typical of a careless driver. When I activated my lights and siren—or as an old-timer once phrased it, "flicked on the jewelry"—the suspicious car increased its speed, showing no intention of stopping.

The vehicle had not been reported stolen and was, in fact, registered to a house within the area where I had encountered it. It was late at night with little to no traffic on the road as we careened around a few corners. I managed to get parallel to the fleeing vehicle and had a good look at the lone driver as he swerved, trying to run me off the road. At this point, I called off the pursuit. It was becoming too erratic for my comfort level. A short time later, I made my way to the address of the registered owner of the vehicle to follow up my investigation. I was confident that I would be able to physically identify the driver if I could locate him. What did I discover?

The driver was the mentally ill son of a very nice older couple. He had taken their car against their wishes and was now home in bed pretending to be asleep. Another officer and I pulled him out of bed. I physically identified him as the driver that I'd had a good look at while our vehicles were side-by-side down the main drag. He was in his early thirties. Described by his parents as an introvert, he had trouble making friends and was not comfortable in social settings. There's no doubt that he was truly frightened by the presence of a police car behind him and had panicked when I activated the lights.

By cancelling my chase and following up later, I had reduced the risk I was exposed to, as well as that experienced by the offending driver and other road users. I laid the appropriate charges and allowed the courts to take the condition of his mental health into consideration during the prosecution. The subject had no criminal history, and by all accounts, was a decent individual suffering from symptoms beyond his control. The case was justly diverted from the court system and dealt with through alternative means, which included help for him and his parents in dealing with his illness. It was a "win/win." His parents were very grateful that the events of that evening had concluded without tragedy.

Despite my penchant for competitive driving, early on in my policing career, I learned the human devastation that a car-chase gone bad can inflict. Though I was not engaged in the pursuit of an armed bank robber this busy afternoon, one of my colleagues was. I listened intently to his transmissions over the police radio, outlining the directions that the chase was headed, along with environmental factors, such as speed and road conditions. These are the variables, along with weather conditions and the number of people on the road, that must be monitored in determining whether to engage in a pursuit or to allow the offender to flee unencumbered by a police response. Unfortunately, on this particular day, the cancellation of the chase didn't come soon enough. The robbery suspect blew through a stop sign, broadsiding a mid-size wagon driven by a mother. Tragically, the collision took the life of her four-year-old boy riding in the rear passenger seat. The gut-wrenching pain surrounding this incident emotionally destroyed the pursuing officer. I can't imagine the crushing toll it took on the child's family. The dangers of a car chase crystalized for me at that point.

Policy changes within police organizations have greatly reduced (and in many jurisdictions entirely eliminated) car chases, which is the correct response. And while some folks involved in law enforcement and the criminal justice system viewed these restrictive policies as simply encouraging offenders to drive fast and dangerously to avoid arrest, that fear was never realized. Yes, some hard-ass criminals know to slam the throttle when their rear-view lights up red and blue, but for the most, part the abolition of car chases has not underwritten a pervasive MO for escape.

7-ELEVEN SHOWDOWN

WHILE SUSPICIOUS ACTIVITY INVOLVING A VEHICLE ISN'T always a case of criminality, it often is the catalyst for further investigation, as this next case highlights.

It's amazing how well attuned cops become to their environment. This enables officers to spot circumstances that are unusual or suspicious despite them not appearing as either to a typical passerby. It was with this mindset that I drove my police car into the parking lot of a 7-Eleven store in a mostly residential area in the southern quadrant of Vancouver. It was mid-afternoon and busy with lots of pedestrian activity and car traffic on the streets bordering the corner lot on which the 7-Eleven was situated.

I made quick observations that caused me concern. There was a large, older model Oldsmobile sedan backed into a stall just west of the 7-Eleven's front door. The car was a beater, and frankly, what person driving a beater cares enough to back it into a parking stall at a 7-Eleven? This was odd to me and made me think that the car was ideally positioned for a rapid get-away. A scruffy thirty-something male sat in the driver's seat. I looked past the car into the store through the large windows that lined the front. Inside, I saw two similarly scruffy ne'er-do-wells between the racks of food and other sundries of the twenty-four-hour convenience mart. Their eyes met mine. At such a moment, a trained cop can viscerally feel that things are far from ok. I radioed dispatch my location and advised that I would be checking a vehicle and several males associated.

Now at this point, a smarter cop would have stayed back and made observations while requesting back-up. I did neither. I first approached the driver seated in the car with his window open. Terrence Potter was cooperative enough, but only in the way that parolees cooperate in order not to have their freedom revoked. It was clear to me that he had done time, and his parole card was proof. I asked Potter to pop open the trunk, which he slowly complied with by pressing a button in the glovebox. Parolees know that any lack of cooperation with the police wouldn't be viewed favourably by their parole officer and could result in a revocation of freedom.

I walked to the rear of the car and began an inspection of the trunk. As I was focused on the contents of the trunk, an elderly lady on the sidewalk called out, wanting to ask me a question. "Officer," she politely hailed. I turned toward her and said that I would be over to see her in a moment or two. It was at this point in my trunk search that I found it. A sawed-off shotgun was tucked into the well of the trunk behind the driver's side rear fender. It was under a rag. I grabbed the weapon and threw it as far from the car as possible in the direction of shrubs lining the lot. Pulling my .38-calibre revolver, I quickly repositioned, pointing my weapon at Potter. After ordering him to put his hands out the window where they could be seen, the police radioed crackled with my call for immediate back-up.

The elderly woman awaiting my attention had a front-row seat to the action. She again called over to me in the sweetest voice, saying, "It's ok, Officer, I see you're busy." It was the strangest juxtapose. I was immersed in grave danger, trying to think tactically while holding a suspect at gunpoint, yet wanting to be polite and sensitive to the needs of a sweet old lady. Worlds were colliding; my respectful upbringing was in competition for attention with my police training. Thankfully, within moments, I could hear the approaching sirens of the cavalry. Every cop will tell ya that there's no sweeter sound when the chips are down. Somehow during the calamity, the two suspects in the store slipped out. Unfortunately, they were never located or identified.

Several more weapons were found in the car once the opportunity to properly search it was undertaken. These were a baseball bat and a two-foot length of extraordinarily heavy metal cable, each wrapped at one end with tape as a grip. Now came the legalities.

I spoke with the 7-Eleven attendant. He had felt extremely uncomfortable with the pair in the store and the positioning of the car by Mr. Potter. The two "shoppers" had arrived in the car with Potter, so my hunch that they were together was correct. But how to show that Potter had knowledge and control of the highly illegal sawed-off shotgun secreted in the trunk?

Interestingly, the 7-Eleven clerk had seen Potter in the trunk of the car moments before my arrival. The clerk could not see into the trunk enough to observe Potter's hands, but he described the arm motion of Potter as that of "cleaning a broom handle," one arm sliding back and forth toward the other. All of this was consistent with racking the shotgun and was inconsistent with anything else in the trunk, which was largely empty except for a spare tire and several shotgun shells.

Both the clerk and I attended Potter's trial. I gave evidence of the suspicious nature of what I had seen. I reiterated that I had asked Potter to open the trunk but did not compel him to do so. Back in the eighties, this was considered a voluntary action on the part of the accused, a parolee, and therefore admissible as evidence. The 7-Eleven clerk provided his evidence, which combined with mine, netted Mr. Potter two years less a day for possession of a prohibited weapon. I never sorted out the two loose ends to this case. The first was the identity of the two disappearing suspects; the second was the needs of the elderly woman sweetly asking for my assistance. Frankly, I care more about her than the two that got away.

If my encounter with Mr. Potter had not led to evidence of criminality, I would likely have completed a check-card on the event and moved on. Today, the issue of "carding" is a hot topic among liberals and advocates for the disadvantaged and those within the BIPOC and LGBTQ2+ communities. While I got lucky, in a sense, with my check of Mr. Potter, one could argue that it was entirely random and without cause. I had not been looking for a robbery suspect or parole violator when I chose to speak with Mr. Potter. Now what if the same circumstances had led to a parolee that had been convicted of sex offences against children? The check would've been random by definition; yet encountering a child sex offender at a 7-Eleven store midday when kids are buying Slurpees and treats could be of grave concern. Even if the subject's actions at the 7-Eleven were not suspicious, having a record of his presence in the area and the vehicle he was driving, by way of a check-card, could be the tip that a detective might need when investigating a sex assault against a child, or an adult for that matter.

Carding, as it is pejoratively referred to by opponents, is a highly useful investigative tool, and not a technique that, from my perspective, is inherently racist or bias. Yes, the improper application of street checks could be fueled by aberrant attitudes, but in my experience, that has not been the case. A person's actions or the environmental factors in which they are encountered are the variables that trigger a check by the police. A person walking down unlit laneways at three a.m., wearing dark clothes and carrying a knapsack and flashlight, is someone the police may want to have a word with irrespective of race, gender, or labels. I'd certainly hope such would be the case if it were my laneway.

Unfortunately, the outcome of the carding debate for the police is jeopardy. Stopping the individual in a laneway at three a.m., or parked suspiciously in front of the 7-Eleven, is today a practice that may generate a complaint against the officer for profiling an individual or for mistreatment of some kind. Even if the subject of the stop is completely ok with the encounter, in some areas of Vancouver, and most cities, there'll be a self-proclaimed delegation of anti-police advocates accusing officers of exercising bias or abusing their authority. As a result, the police may no longer be as pro-active in speaking with individuals whose presence or actions raise neck hairs as they once were.

This new reality is simply driving a greater wedge between the police and the citizens they serve. A fallout of the new-era contempt for the police is found in FIDO, which in cop parlance means "Fuck it, drive on." In essence, the hassle a cop is likely to endure by conducting a street check is no longer worth it. Unless there's a crime in progress, why expose oneself or one's professional career to accusations of racism, bias, or abuse by taking pro-active, self-directed steps to detect and detour crime before it happens? Does FIDO make neighbourhoods less safe? I'd argue that it does in areas of the city where crime rates are high and the moment an officer steps out of a patrol car he/she is besieged by a hostile, cell-phone-holding mob out to prove a cop is overstepping police authority or engaging in harassment of some sort. The sad reality is that the people most affected by an erosion of personal safety are the silent majority of citizens simply trying to eke out a life in what may be an extraordinarily perilous community.

Time to lighten the mood with a bit of humour.

WHEN CROSS EXAMINATION
GOES SIDEWAYS

THE ROLE OF THE POLICE IN A CRIMINAL INVESTIGATION IS TO gather evidence in compliance with all applicable legislation. That evidence is then presented in court where it can be tested by the defence and evaluated by a judge, or judge and jury. This is an adversarial system in which the Crown must prove its case beyond a reasonable doubt to secure a criminal conviction, while the defence need only establish a reasonable doubt in the minds of the judge or jury to acquire an acquittal. Some lawyers for the defence will engage all means of theatrics and double-speak to either intimidate witnesses or fluster them to the point of confusion. While these tactics can be an effective tool for identifying weaknesses in the Crown's case, they can also backfire. Here a few examples of the latter.

In the early nineties, I spent several years in the Drug Squad of the VPD where my partner Rob (not my former field trainer) and I specialized in the investigation of large-scale, illegal marihuana cultivations. A recent (at the time) court ruling had made it clear that the police were not entitled to gather evidence by entering upon a suspect's property without the authorization of a search warrant. The court ruling in question arose out of a case called *R. vs Kokesh*. In short, the Supreme Court of Canada held that a warrantless search of the property outside of a suspect's house was a breach of their constitutional rights. This meant that we could not walk into the suspect's yard, or step upon their property, to detect the odour of marihuana. This investigative limitation led to a testy exchange in court between me and an eager defender of the people.

During my evidence in-chief, I had taken great pains to describe in granular detail how I had made observations, which included seeking to detect the odour of marihuana at all four corners of the subject's property without entering upon the property. I further added observations made from neighbouring properties, all of which enabled me to localize the odour of marihuana to the house in question. From a neighbouring property, I used a monocle to determine the rate of electrical consumption by timing the revolutions of the disc visible through the glass dome of the electrical meter. By applying a mathematical formula, I was able to estimate the consumption level of electricity. An abnormally high reading might corroborate an informant's information that high-intensity grow lights are in use.

Upon cross examination of my evidence, a very wily defence lawyer walked me through every detail once again, while exhibiting a sense of disgust and disapproval. After having me reconfirm all of the steps I had taken in obtaining my observations, he asked—in the snarkiest of tones—one question, which he undoubtedly hoped would expose some illicit intent on my part.

Defence: So, I submit to you, Detective, that you engaged in this long litany of evidence-gathering steps in order to circumvent the spirit of Kokesh?

Me: (turning to address the judge directly) No, Your Honour, I did all of them in order to comply with the spirit of Kokesh.

Immediately after my response, the judge broke out in a smile, for he knew as I did, that the defender had simply reinforced the accuracy and precision of my evidence, which was beyond dispute.

"Any further questions?" the judge asked defence counsel.

"No, Your Honour," he sheepishly replied while taking his seat.

While a conviction was secured in the marihuana cultivation, with much thanks to the contribution of defence counsel, it wasn't the only time that defence had failed to serve its client well during my many appearances in court.

On this particular occasion, I was giving evidence against an impaired driver I had charged. During cross examination, defence counsel directed me to a point early in the investigation and asked, "Up to this point, Constable, was there anything about my client's conduct that caused bells to ring in your head?"

I'm sure that a rather incredulous look came over me while I considered an answer. The judge, having had enough of this lawyer's antics for the day, interjected, asking, "Counsel, are you seriously asking this officer whether bells rang in his head?"

Trying to redeem a last shred of dignity, the counsellor responded by explaining that he was using a figure of speech to try and elicit what I may have been thinking at the pertinent time.

"I see," responded the judge. "Well, for the record, I think we'll use the original question." He then turned to me and rather satirically asked whether any bells had rung in my head.

Though I wanted to partake in the judge's ridicule by responding with something cheeky, I played it safe and delivered a very factual, "No, Your Honour, no bells."

"Do you have any further questions?" the judge scornfully asked defence counsel.

"No further questions, Your Honour," stammered the lawyer as he retook his seat at the table. A guilty verdict was mere moments away.

Of course, not all trials have such a high entertainment factor; some may be a test in which a score is assigned. Such was the case when I found myself before the regal defender of peoples' rights, the late Honourable Herbert (Bert) Arnold Dimiti Oliver QC (1921–2011).

As a junior patrol cop in the early eighties, I investigated a case of sexual assault against a young woman by a similarly aged university student, whom she had met for a date. During the course of the investigation, I arrested and interviewed the suspect based on evidence detailed in a statement supplied by the victim. The suspect's interview and statement would become pivotal during the trial. As is often the case when a suspect makes incriminating admissions, defence counsel will do their utmost to impugn the statement and prevent it from being admitted into evidence. This is often accomplished by raising some doubt as to the voluntariness of the suspect's decision to speak with the investigator.

During my interview with the prosecutor in advance of the trial, I learned that the legendary H.A.D. Oliver QC would be defending the young man. Every cop worth his salt knew of Mr. Oliver's reputation and his tenacity during cross examination. "Relentless" and "brilliant" are adjectives that come to mind. While he wasn't a tall, imposing figure, H.A.D., as he was most often called, knew how to control a court room. His British accent and pompous demeanour added to his mythical persona. I had always likened H.A.D. to a blend of

John Houseman, who played Charles W. Kingsfield Jr. on the hit TV series *Paper Chase*, and former British Prime Minister Winston Churchill. Neither had suffered fools, and both could eviscerate with their choice of words, and frankly, so could H.A.D. Oliver.

There I was, not much older than the suspect I had charged, laying out the evidence before the court as H.A.D. furiously took notes during my evidence in-chief. I'm certain that his fastidious notetaking and subtle signs of alarm at my testimony were meant to intimidate me and cause me to question the validity of my own observations. And there's no doubt that such tactics have an effect on a young cop's confidence when giving evidence of a serious nature. Of course, over many years and many court cases, I grew intolerant of such tactics, which by then only served to fortify my confidence and resolve.

With H.A.D. now on his feet, pacing the floor between counsel table and the witness box, the inquisition was launched. His questions, couched in upper-crust British comportment, were designed to impeach the statement I had obtained from the accused. For he knew that, if the statement was denied standing, he would only need to raise a reasonable doubt about whether the victim gave her consent or not; the classic "he said, she said."

After a long series of questions seeking detail about my interaction with his client on the day he was arrested and interviewed, H.A.D. distilled it down to this: Was his client made fully aware of his right to counsel before the interview? And if so, was he granted the opportunity to contact counsel without delay at all points within the investigation? Yes, and yes, I asserted.

But H.A.D. retorted with: "Was there a phone in the interview room that he could avail himself of at any chosen moment?"

"No, there wasn't."

"Then how was my client to know that a phone was, in fact, available to him anywhere within the building?"

I took some time to explain to Mr. Oliver that when people need the police, they generally use a phone to make contact. And that the police will answer the phone call and respond accordingly. Therefore, the police station must be equipped with phones, which even his client ought to have known as general knowledge. Further to this, I had ensured the accused understood his rights by confirming, in colloquial terms, "the right to phone a lawyer."

With very little else at issue, H.A.D. completed his cross examination, and I stepped down from the witness box. As I made my way across the floor with armpits soaked in perspiration, H.A.D. stepped in my direction. Catching my attention, he leaned in and whispered words that made me smile, and that I'll never forget: "Eighty-three percent, lad." I loved it. I loved that like the character Charles W. Kingsfield Jr. of *Paper Chase,* H.A.D. had scored my cross examination and effectively given me a solid "B." Not only that, the statement in contention was admitted into trial, essentially sealing a conviction in the case before the court.

I came away from the proceedings emboldened in my testimonial abilities and with the greatest respect for the much feared and greatly revered Herbert Albert Dimitri Oliver Q.C. Yet I couldn't imagine how our paths would again merge many years later.

Within the Vancouver Police Department, the rank of inspector is a management position, while the higher ranks of superintendent, deputy chief, and chief are considered executive-level ranks. In keeping with tradition, inspectors and above are considered "officers," (think *An Officer and a Gentleman,* with Richard Gere) even though the term is applied broadly in society to represent any sworn member of a police agency irrespective of rank. The Vancouver Police Officers' Mess hosts an annual mess dinner. This is a formal occasion replete with plenty of tradition, pomp, and ceremony. The function will host many invitees of distinction, such as high-ranking representatives from law enforcement, the military, and politics.

I had been promoted to an inspector in 2002 and became a member of the Officers' Mess. This distinction required me to attend the annual mess dinner and ensure that our guests were well taken care of and enjoying the evening. From 1997 through to 2007, H.A.D. Oliver was the Conflict of Interest Commissioner for the Province of British Columbia. He was also engaged by Chief Constable Jamie Graham of the VPD to be the department's Conflict of Interest Commissioner. This role meant that Oliver would be an invited guest to the officers' Annual Mess Dinner.

In May of 2003, I was a new inspector attending my first Mess Dinner, which is traditionally held each spring at the Vancouver Club in downtown Vancouver. It's a formal affair, with tuxedos the expected attire, along with medals and ceremonial insignia. After quickly grabbing a refreshment, I began to mingle, greeting the many guests that I knew, both from within my agency and those that belonged to our partner agencies. I soon spotted Bert (H.A.D. Oliver). I hadn't had contact with H.A.D. Oliver since my cross examination by him nearly twenty years prior. He looked majestic in his black tuxedo with his striking Member of the Order of Canada medal around his neck. He was now in his early eighties but just as imposing a figure as he had been two decades earlier. I introduced myself, and we shook hands. It felt like shaking the hand of Sir Winston Churchill, Prime Minister of the United Kingdom 1940–1945 during WWII, and again 1951 through 1955.

After welcoming H.A.D. to the Mess Dinner, I couldn't help but raise the court case that had turned out to mean so much to me. Bert (as he asked to be called) said he remembered it well, and we shared a chuckle. I reminded him that he'd given me a score of eight-three percent. At that moment, I thought he was about to lecture me on how I could improve for next time, but he said that I had handled myself very well and should be proud of an eighty-three, because he's a tough marker. I mentioned to him that it was astonishing how such a small, informal—even comedic—gesture on his part had stuck with me for so long and strengthened my resolve on the stand. No other counsellor could intimidate me after surviving an H.A.D. encounter.

During the dinner, Chief Constable Jamie Graham asked me to make sure that H.A.D. got home safely. I let H.A.D. know that I would be his chauffeur when the evening was over. Turns out that he lived fairly close to me, so riding together made sense except for one minor point: H.A.D. drives a Rolls Royce. I was driving a two-door Honda Accord Coupe, which was a sleek, low-slung sports car with a roofline that required something akin to yoga's downward dog to enter. (It was not my regular ride, but a new car from Honda that I was reviewing in my role at the time as a part-time auto journalist.)

As the evening was winding down and cigars were butted out, I brought the Honda to the front door of the club. Bert was waiting by the front door, walking staff in hand and ready to go … that is until he saw a small import rather than an imposing Rolls-Royce behemoth awaiting him. But he was a good sport and embraced the challenge of dropping himself into the seat with some steadying from me. Once settled, he got a kick out of riding in the "quaint little car" rather than his massive blue Roller. Fortunately, he was in no rush to get home, so I suggested we cruise over to the VPD's covert building, from which we deploy our surveillance teams and undercover investigative units, so that I could change out of my mess kit (regimental tuxedo) and not have to go back the following day. This was the building I worked in as the inspector in-charge of the Criminal Intelligence Section. Bert was game to head over.

We arrived at the non-descript two-story building with a concrete exterior featuring small, highly positioned, security-enhanced windows. It was about eleven-thirty p.m. as I parked out front. The building operated 24/7 with shabbily dressed undercover detectives coming and going at all hours. Bert wanted to come in. He was intrigued by the clandestine operations and was keen to have a look inside the fortress. I used my proximity card to activate the front door and in we walked.

Now picture this. I've just walked into a near-secret police facility late at night with a person easily mistaken for Churchill. He's in a tux and is decorated with all manner of medals and insignia. He walks with a staff and exhibits a swagger belying his age. We immediately encountered detectives immersed in their work, and they looked up in a state of disbelief. Who is this chap that appears ready to command a Call to Arms?

I introduced Bert to everyone we met. He was truly enjoying the visit and all of the interest directed his way. As much as the detectives were captivated, so was Bert. A few of them adopted Bert and began showing him around while I hit the locker room and changed back to my jeans. I found Bert holding court with the detectives; it's *Paper Chase* all over. Soon after, Bert and I began the journey home chatting like old pals, no longer constrained by the formalities of the evening. This process pretty much repeated itself for the next half-dozen years or so. Always remarkably spry for his age, Bert remained as sharp the last time I drove him home as he had been decades earlier when he had me squirming in the witness box. Sadly, nature caught up to the Honourable Herbert Arnold Dimitri Oliver Q.C. in 2011. He was eighty-nine years young when he passed away, and I'm a better man (and evidence giver) for having known him.

While I managed a decent score on the stand being cross-examined by H.A.D. Oliver early in my career, it took years of giving evidence in court to become comfortable in my abilities and inoculated against the theatrics and strategies employed by defence counsel to unsettle witnesses or leave them in doubt of their own words and observations. Cops typically deliver testimony in a rote, almost mechanical fashion, in which emotion is usually absent or underdelivered.

Therefore, whenever I attended court, which was multiple times per week when assigned to the Drug Squad, I would take the opportunity to sit in various court-rooms and listen to the testimony of fellow officers and civilian witnesses. I would ask myself what I would make of that individual's evidence if I were the judge, Was it compelling and credible, or shallow and sketchy? This practice led me to realize that plain-speak rather than cop jargon is best understood and interpreted by a judge, and if present, a jury. I also came to the realization that a cop's clinical testi-mony generally failed to communicate the emotions that may have been flowing through the officer's veins during a calamitous event. Many of the incidents that cops testify about may have been traumatic for the officer or even terrifying. And these emotions should be clearly communicated, enabling the judge, and/or jury, to consider the evidence in a context that accurately reflects the full circumstances influencing an officer's decision-making.

To ensure that the quality of my testimony was the best I could offer, I devel-oped a number of tactics to defuse some of the hostility that often develops during an intense cross examination. Some defence lawyers like to ask rapid-fire questions to create a heightened sense of stress. I always counted to five before answering a question, which slowed the Q&A down to a pace that I controlled. When treated professionally by defence, I would look directly at the lawyer and listen intently to his/her question. My eye contact would then shift to the judge, during which I calmly answered the question. Witnesses in court need to remember that it's the judge a witness addresses, not the lawyers in the room. Lawyers hate when a witness knows and applies this technique; one's credibility is determined by the judge, not defence counsel. Eye-contact with the judge is commonly viewed as a strong indicator of truthfulness.

There were definitely times in court when a defence lawyer would agitate, throwing note pads onto the table, pacing angrily about, walking aggressively up to the witness box, waving documents, and basically over-acting his dismay in an attempt to intimidate me, or any such witness. I found it incredibly effec-tive (and frankly, highly satisfying) to look away, keeping my gaze on the judge as I awaited the next question. There's no rule that requires a witness to pay attention to such conduct. Depending on the judge in a particular case, I'd give His Honour a wry smile, which was usually met with a reciprocating smile—the unwritten communication acknowledging that the lawyer was acting like a jack-ass.

GO SLOW AND LISTEN

MY FIRST FULLTIME PARTNER FOLLOWING GRADUATION FROM the academy became a hero of mine. I recall arriving at the police station for my first patrol assignment. As was the practice back then, newbies were assigned to senior, well-seasoned officers as their first fulltime partners. This was a way of mentoring the young cops and acquainting them with the trouble spots within their patrol areas. Despite knowing of the practice, I was hoping to be partnered with a dynamic young cop with lots of gusto and drive. Heck, that's what I had, and it needed feeding. As patrol members arrived for the start of shift, I looked around at the selection and sized-up those I thought would be good and those, for no reason other than appearance, I thought would be less than optimal "first partners," shall we say. One less-than-optimal senior officer looked like Mr. Henry Mitchell, the father of the cartoon character, Dennis the Menace. *Please, not Mr. Mitchell*, my mind screamed, but to no avail. Dennis's father, with his tight-ass conservative appearance and black horn-rimmed glasses became my mentor, and as it turned out, I couldn't be more grateful.

Thomas was a quiet man who held strong opinions and wasn't easily ruffled or made a fool of. Highly intelligent and remarkably perceptive, he had a short fuse when it came to arrogant drunks. Yet he had all the patience and time in the world for helping those truly in need. He served the public with a deep well of compassion and kindness. Thomas wasn't reactionary; he was strategic. He didn't strike out at people who threatened him. Rather, he waited, and he planned, and usually he won. People would go to jail.

So away we drove for our first shift together. This could be a challenging time, and frankly more-so for him than me. I figured that he was a seasoned cop and obviously knew the streets. I could rely upon him, but really, how much could he rely upon me? I was a twenty-year-old kid with a uniform and gun. Sure, I did ok in the academy, including the many simulations we'd worked through. Plus, my field trainers had good things to say in my performance evaluations (excluding the revelation that I didn't do more than necessary!), but what reassurance would that be to Thomas at three a.m. when the chips were down and we walked into a bar fight, or worse?

As we chatted that first few hours together, I quickly realized that Thomas was highly insightful and sincerely upbeat about taking me under his wing. Not sure that all seasoned street cops would be as willing. With me behind the wheel, we were off and roaring from call-to-call, or at least from location to location. I thought that my "Richard Petty" persona behind the wheel would impress Thomas. He seemed to tolerate it for a while, but then (like a mindful father) he asked me to stop so we could talk. It was four a.m. or so during a nightshift when Thomas began his homily about why we should be driving slowly, with our windows down and our ears open.

Thomas patiently pointed out that, by driving quickly, I was missing so many tiny cues to suspicious activity and possible criminality. Not only should we prowl slowly, we should actually stop the car, kill the engine, and get out on foot. Most of all, "look and listen" he said. In the still of the night (my apologies to the Five Satins), sound travels.

"If we are quiet, we can hear glass break at the electronics shop; we can hear the screams of someone in crisis, or a car racing from a crime scene," explained Thomas. Furthermore, he said, when we make noise by driving aggressively, the bad guys hear us coming, and it gives us away.

Thomas's point was proven the next evening. For context, nightshifts can be extremely busy, with call-to-call demands leaving precious little time to skulk around in search of crime in-progress. I've always referred to the time between three a.m. and sun-up as the witching hours. That's when the call-load for the evening generally abates as drunks and other nocturnal miscreants either pass out or climb into bed. It's a surreal period of the waning night, with the roads dominated by police cars and delivery trucks. It's also the time favoured by the criminal element for break-ins to retail shops, warehouses, and all manner of buildings in which a profit may be turned.

One of our teammates, who also ascribed to the "nightshift crawl," had been slowly passing a car dealership with his window open when he heard the faint clang of something metallic. He rolled past and quietly exited his patrol car, then silently got an eye on the car lot where two suspects were removing the wheels off of a new car. Our colleague then called for backup, and that would be us.

Once we were in place, containing the lot, a dog-handler and his four-legged partner moved in for the arrest. Following a cacophony of canine rage, the next metallic sounds heard were the bracelets ratcheting closed. The crooks were smart enough not to run, unlike a crook from a previous call who thought he could elude a police dog by swimming into a small lake situated in an urban Vancouver park.

In that incident, it was dark. The dog was not on a long lead (leash), which is required these days. The German shepherd, hot on a perp's scent, didn't stop at the shoreline as the crook (and frankly, the police) expected. Shortly after, we could hear the furious battle between man and animal amidst a splash-a-thon. We couldn't see far enough into the darkness with our dim flashlights to make out their location, but we were soundly of the opinion that the animal was winning. A short time later, they both emerged onto the beach. You could say that the fishing was good for the dog. He was still latched onto the bad guy, who it appeared, he had dragged back to shore without the benefit of lifeguard training. I've often speculated on how scary it would be to have a police dog attack in the dark while treading cold water mid-point in a small lake. The lesson here: Don't try to outswim a police K9. Fortunately, the suspect's injuries were limited to a single arm, which the dog had clamped onto for the swim to shore.

Ah yes, back to our two crooks at the car lot. The benefit of "go slow and listen" was driven home to me that evening. Truth be told, there's no way I would've heard the faint clang that telegraphed crime to our colleague if I had driven past the lot like Mario Andretti. A good lesson learned.

As our weeks working together turned to months and even to a year, my respect for and admiration of Mr. Mitchell grew immense. It proved to me that, when it came to partners in policing, one shouldn't judge a cop by age or appearance, or gender for that matter. I worked with a number of policewomen and was always struck by how well they handled tense situations. Perhaps it was their maternal instincts that enabled them to gain the compliance of difficult subjects. Or maybe it's that most self-respecting guys won't act like an ass in front of a woman. In any case, having a woman on scene can be an effective means of defusing a hostile situation, especially one in which a male-to-male interaction is likely to escalate the potential for violence.

While my respect for the capabilities of policewomen is boundless, it was lessons from Thomas that I carried with me throughout my career and relied upon every day in uniform. These included treating all people with dignity and respect (well, maybe not arrogant drunks unless it's Frank Paul, the subject of my next story), along with being a strategic thinker and remaining unflappable in the face of adversity. If I'm honest with myself, though, I didn't always live up to those ideals. There were instances when I could have been more compassionate with victims and more understanding of the difficulties faced by those coping with poverty, mental illness, and marginalization in all its forms.

There are many instances in my career that I wish I could do over, but unfortunately "do overs" are limited to the imagination. Nonetheless, I am truly grateful for having been "Dennis the Menace" to Mr. Mitchell, and learning all I could from him, much of which guided me through the years of dealing with "one tough guy."

FRANK PAUL—ONE TOUGH GUY
(government failing, scapegoat cops)

IT WAS THE EARLY EIGHTIES. I WAS A PATROL COP IN THE PRE-Lululemon world of Vancouver's trendy, beachside neighbourhood of Kitsilano, known by locals as simply "Kits," or more disparagingly as "Skits." The latter designation was in reference to "schizophrenia," a pejorative attribution to the former hippie culture that Kitsilano was infamous for. At any rate, the operators of a corner store in the heart of Kits called the police to report that a drunk, abusive male was intimidating customers and causing a disturbance. Not an unusual call for the area due somewhat to the presence of a nearby government liquor store and the popularity of Kitsilano attracting a broad cross-section of society.

As I drove up, I saw the male leaning against the exterior wall of the store. He was a tall, strapping, Indigenous man around thirty years of age, and clearly drunk. I was reasonably familiar with the regular cadre of alcoholics that often made a nuisance of themselves in the area, and he wasn't one of them. Actually, I had dealt with four of them earlier that same day. They had convened in the parking lot of a 7-Eleven for a drinking party. Pouring out an alcoholic's booze is an unwelcome event that'll often trigger a fight, but with the public watching, I couldn't allow the open drinking to continue. I made a deal with the group: Pour out your drink, and I'll buy each of you a coffee and chocolate bar inside the 7-Eleven. Knowing that my offer was the best of a bad situation, it was reluctantly accepted. Out went a few beers and in went the crew. Massively large coffees and a bountiful selection of snacks were procured while I waited at the till with credit card in hand. I'm certain that my "quartet of guzzlers" had more booze stashed in the nearby bushes, but they all agreed to wander off with their javas and treats for the time-being.

But back to our friend outside of the corner grocery.

Despite being intoxicated, he was coherent and willing to talk. He had a large piece of white gauze covering a significant wound over his left eyebrow. From what I could see, the gash appeared fresh around the edges, but what really got my attention was the erratic, spider-web-like pattern of black thread that had been sewn over the gauze to hold it in place. I knew that no legit medical clinic had performed this treatment. The thread was stitched through the skin of the gentleman's forehead in six to eight places, in what appeared to be a random pattern. Where the thread passed through the skin, it was taut, causing the skin to stick up like miniature mountain peaks. I asked him who had sewn the bandage to his head. In a slow and deliberate manner, he answered, "I did."

"Wow," I said, "you're one tough guy. From this day forward, you and I are going to be friends."

He cracked a smile, gave me a chuckle and said, "Ok."

I told him my name and asked for his full name.

"Frank Paul," he said with a sense of certainty.

I jokingly called him "The man with two first names," referencing in my mind a John Prine song—the late John Prine being one of my all-time favourite musicians, his songs often clever, witty, and deeply poignant. I had the privilege of seeing John Prine in concert twice. Once with his former sidekick, the late Steve Goodman. It's funny how you remember the little things more-so than the main attractions. I recall a shy John Prine smoking on stage during his performance in the eighties. I can still see him with long hair and a moustache placing the unlit end of his cigarette between the E-string and the head of his folk guitar while he launched into another heartfelt tune. The lyrics of "Six O'clock News" describe the tragic life and death of James Lewis, "a kid with two first names." Sadly, it turns out that the tortured spirit of James Lewis fit Frank Paul in more ways than having two first names.

Frank told me that he was new in town, coming from the Island, which I took to mean Vancouver Island, just off the BC mainland. Despite several initial physical cues that I interpreted as precursors to violence, Frank remained calm and cooperative. Among others, such cues often include clenched fists, a fifty-yard stare (looking past the officer), a bladed body (standing at an angle), heavy breathing, and a tense facial expression. Frank was definitely not welcoming my approach; however, I think he was disarmed by my concern for his wound and my lame use of humour to lighten the situation. It was likely not what he was expecting from a cop in uniform.

Frank agreed to leave the store and find a place to lay low for a while. As he made his way toward the nearby train tracks, I had no idea that our paths would continue to cross over the next dozen or so years, or that his death would trigger a major shift in the practice of the police investigating themselves when conduct-related complaints were lodged.

Over the next few years, as I worked on and off in the Kitsilano area, I would continue to encounter Frank. He was usually drunk, and the subject of a call from a citizen regarding his combative behaviour.

Each time I dealt with him, I would remind Frank about our first meeting and our agreement to be friends. "Frank," I would say, "it's Rob." He always remembered and never gave me any serious trouble. I liked Frank, and on occasion, handed him a sandwich or other food items from my lunch. As my career moved on, I found myself promoted to a corporal in 1991 and assigned to the city jail as a supervisor.

Frank's physical health had deteriorated greatly before our next meeting, which was shortly after I embarked upon my role in the jail. Frank arrived under police escort. He had been arrested for being in a state of intoxication in a public place (SIPP), hostile, and unable to care for himself. Frank was often a fighter when confronted by cops, a behaviour he was displaying this particular day. I got in front of him and sternly said, "Frank, it's Rob. Take it easy." This calmed him somewhat. It had been several years, but he still recognized me. I made a deal with him. If he agreed not to fight, I would get him some food. He did, and I did. A lukewarm coffee, banana, and yogurt usually did the trick on his many arrivals at the jail while I was the supervising corporal. The last time that I encountered Frank before his sad demise would've been in 1996.

By then, I was a patrol sergeant working in uniform on the west side of Vancouver. The manager of a Dairy Queen phoned the police to report that a drunk male had taken residence in a toilet stall in the DQ's washroom and was refusing to come out. I had no idea who I'd find when I opened the door, but there was Frank. He had made a terrible mess in the stall and wasn't willing to cooperate. I said, "Frank, it's Rob. How ya doing?"

He grunted but that was about it. It was clear that his physical condition had deteriorated well beyond what it had been during our jail encounters. There was no way that I was going to enter the stall to physically remove Frank. Based on the mess he had made of the toilet and surrounding area, Frank was not well from an intestinal perspective. I told him that if he was willing to come out, I would get him a hamburger and a drink. I'm not sure that Frank recognized me any longer, but the offer of food still did the trick. I walked to the counter and told the manager that he would voluntarily leave if I could give him a burger and a drink. The manager had a plain burger and pop quickly bagged, and then charged me something like $4.29. I guess I had technically ordered a burger and a drink (a small price to pay to gain Frank's cooperation). I paid and went back to see Frank. He slowly got himself together and came out. Based on his physical state outside the washroom, I felt that Frank was strong enough to carry on under his own steam, which he did while declining any medical assistance. That was my final encounter with him. The deterioration in his health had been startling, and I felt bad for him. He lived a tough, unfulfilling life largely defined by alcoholism and mistreatment at all levels of government and society.

In December of 1998, Frank's life ended. He had been picked up, as he had hundreds of times before, for being drunk and unable to care for himself. Due to his combative nature, Frank had been barred from the province's Detox Centre, leaving little option but jail for him to sleep it off. The sergeant in charge of the jail that fateful evening refused to admit Frank, believing that his level of intoxication didn't meet the required standard despite his inability or unwillingness to be self-ambulatory. As a result, Frank was physically dragged from the jail and dropped off near the Detox Centre, from which he was barred. Sadly, he passed away that chilly evening.

The actions of the officers involved in dealing with Frank came under investigation by the Homicide Unit of the Vancouver Police Department. No criminal charges were recommended at the conclusion of the investigation. There was clearly no intent on anyone's part to end Frank's life. As was the practice in the era, a subsequent investigation was launched pursuant to the BC Police Act, which would examine whether any officer breached the act's code of conduct. This investigation landed in my lap. I was now the inspector in-charge of the

VPD's Internal Investigation Section. Frank had come full circle with me, and now no amount of food or joking about being a man with two first names would bring him back.

I assigned the investigation to two of the unit's top investigators. The investigation was subject to civilian oversight by the Office of the Police Complaints Commissioner. I met with the commissioner and his deputy a number of times during the course of the investigation. Disciplinary penalties for failing to provide an adequate "duty of care" were imposed upon the sergeant of the jail the evening in question and upon the young officer who had transported Frank in the prisoner wagon, ultimately releasing him in a manner that had contributed to his death. Public pressure around the treatment of Frank, an Indigenous man originally from the Mi'kmaq reserve in Big Cove, New Brunswick, resulted in the Davies Commission of Inquiry into the Death of Mr. Frank Paul. Many recommendations flowed from the inquiry, including the formation of an Independent Investigation Office (IIO) to relieve police agencies of having to investigate themselves when someone has sustained serious injury or has been killed by the actions of police. The IIO's mandate is to exert investigative jurisdiction over any matter in which a citizen's life was lost or a citizen sustained serious injury in relation to any action, or inaction, of the police. The IIO engages its own investigators to investigate such events while remaining free of any conflicting interests with the involved agency.

Though two officers were disciplined due to their inadequate "duty of care" for Frank, they were in some ways scapegoats for a government that had failed to establish services equipped to handle difficult patients such as Frank. The provincially-funded Detox Centre that most alcoholics were at the time transported to by the police for sobering is an excellent facility, but it was not suited to the admission of combative individuals. It was this shortcoming that, in many ways, left Frank out in the cold. Without a suitable sobering centre for uncooperative drunks, jail was the only alternative, yet it wasn't appropriate either. Such individuals had not committed a criminal offence, so why should they be jailed? They were in need of treatment not incarceration.

In retrospect, the jail sergeant that fateful evening should not have ordered the removal of Frank Paul, irrespective of his mistaken belief that Frank was not drunk. The young constable driving the prisoner van felt that by leaving Frank next to the shelter of a building very near the Detox Centre, he would be seen and checked on occasionally as officers drove past with additional clients for Detox. As well, Frank was accustomed to life outdoors and had been passed out on an exterior display bench in front of a local store when he'd been picked up that evening for drunkenness. There's no doubt that he deserved better from the police that evening, but he also deserved better from all levels of government that had passed the buck over and over around caring for the Frank Pauls of the world. Fortunately, there now exist better options for the care of combative drunks. Though Frank had lived a forsaken life, it wasn't without legacy, which includes enhanced sobering services in the city and the formation of the Independent Investigations Office of British Columbia.

Had the IIO existed when I was a drug detective, my partner may have had some difficult questions to answer as you'll see in the next story.

16

SORRY FOR SHOOTING YOU, HONEY

WHILE THIS STORY ISN'T ABOUT AN EVENT THAT I WAS DIRECTLY connected with, it's definitely entertaining and was delivered to me firsthand the morning after.

My partner in the Drug Squad was Rob. He was a few years older than me, but we got along well. He was an insightful partner who wasn't shy of sharing his opinion or engaging in esoteric debates ranging from politics to poetry. While we both answered to "Rob," it was clear that we'd need a way to distinguish between two Robs on the same team if we were to be permanent Drug Squad partners. This would be particularly important during radio transmissions on our private Drug Squad channel. The use of first names for such communications was the operating protocol, and with that, my partner became Rob-one while I answered to Rob-two.

This story told to me by Rob begins the preceding day, during which we had been at the gun range for our annual firearms qualification. As a point of clarity, all police officers in BC are required to meet an annual minimum standard of firearms proficiency in order to carry a firearm. The testing was composed of various shooting exercises and scenarios, all of which were timed, requiring the participant to unbuckle their holster, raise, aim, and fire a prescribed volley of shots into specified locations on the printed human silhouette. These challenges took place at varying distance intervals and required the shooter to adopt a range of firing positions, which included standing, kneeling, and prone. The use of concealment tactics meant that the shooters had to keep their bodies behind

61

wood posts, which simulated a wall or barricade of some kind. The courses of fire were designed, as much as possible, to reflect real-life scenarios, though they remained highly artificial.

A lot of magazine reloading (pistol magazines are often incorrectly referred to as clips) would take place during the course of the day, and it wasn't unusual to arrive home with a few spare rounds in your jacket pocket. This was the case with Rob. At the end of our shooting day, he threw a half-dozen leftover rounds into a plastic baggie and placed the baggie into the trunk of his $750 beater Buick, which he had bought for commuting. (His argument for the "beater" was that it could never depreciate more than $750, and if it needed expensive repairs, he'd simply replace it with a vehicle of similar value.) Rob was a wise "money man" whose stock portfolio was legendary. Pulling carefully into his garage, which was part of his sprawling suburban rancher, Rob carefully parked beside his prized Mercedes-Benz 380SL sports car, which he'd gingerly drive with the roof down when the weather cooperated.

Hearing him arrive home, Rob's lovely wife (we'll call her Mary) made her way into the garage to greet him as she often did. Rob was pulling gear out of the Buick's trunk as she walked toward him. Somehow the small baggie containing a cluster of bullets became snagged and fell to the concrete floor. There was a loud *bang,* and Rob knew immediately that one of the bullets had been fired, likely by another bullet in the bag striking the primer of the discharged bullet as they hit the floor. Now a bullet that fires without being in the barrel of a gun has vastly reduced velocity because the explosion is not constrained the way it is in the barrel of a firearm, which focuses all of the exploding energy into a singular direction. Nonetheless, like most guys, Rob's first instinct was to examine the polished fender of his 380 SL, fearing that he might find damage, or worse yet, a bullet hole. Contemporaneous with Rob's intensive fender examination, he heard Mary's distraught voice cry out, "You shot me!" Imagine the panic they both must have been feeling at this moment.

As it turns out, either the bullet or the casing had shot forward and grazed Mary's lower calf not far above her ankle. It left a reddened furrow in the flesh, which fortunately didn't require medical attention beyond basic home-based first aid. As Rob told me the story the next morning, still in a bit of shock over the event, I kept thinking about how things could've spiraled out of control had Mary's injury necessitated a trip to the hospital.

"What happened?" the emergency physician would ask.

"My husband shot me," would be the honest answer, though completely out of context. Even if Mary tried to explain that the incident was accidental, the attending physician would have a duty to report the shooting to the police. Many victims of domestic violence may be too frightened to report abuse at the hands of a partner for fear of reprisal, so a reporting-onus exists upon the physician. The impending call to the authorities would likely have the police responding to a report of a victim of domestic violence, shot by her husband.

Testing a suspected shooter's hand and clothing for gunpowder residue is a given in a shooting investigation of late. Rob would test positive on both counts due to our day at the range; plus, his pistol would also have evidence of fresh usage. Hmmm, this is not looking so good for old Rob-one. No doubt, a modest amount of investigation would uncover the accidental nature of the incident, but you never know how far sideways things could go until then.

I guess the lesson for Rob was this: Check the wellbeing of your wife before your SL 380.

CHASING CRIME

FOR A COP, CHASING CRIME CAN LITERALLY MEAN RUNNING after criminals. Here are two such cases that had me hotfooting it after suspects.

Running was always great way to break-up an eleven-hour nightshift. To non-shift-workers, the thought of heading out for a run at two a.m. on a chilly, rainy evening is less than tantalizing, but for a nightshift worker it can be highly energizing while also improving one's sleep when the lights finally go out. My partner and I had just completed a lengthy run. It had been wet, and cold enough to turn some of the drops into wet flakes. With the run behind us, we were back in our patrol car nursing our fatigued legs and enjoying the heat blowing out of the ventilation system. We were no more than a couple of kilometres from the station, stopped at a red light at the end of a bridge that carries traffic over Vancouver's False Creek and into the city's downtown core. *Screech ... wham.* A small Ford Ranger pickup truck slammed into a car stopped at the same intersection. I'm sure the occupants of the car were glad to see the police no more than a few metres away. The same can't be said for the driver of the truck.

As we walked to the crash scene, the driver's door of the truck flung open and a large-sized male jumped out and started running. Damn. My legs were like jelly from the extended run not more than thirty minutes earlier. I took off after the driver while my partner tended to any possible injuries among the car's occupants. For an overweight, big fella, this dude could run. He was fueled by adrenalin, me by sheer determination. One block, then two blocks, and more as he kept running west along a main downtown thoroughfare. He cut into a dark alley and kept booking it. With my tank running dry and my legs becoming wobbly, I made one last charge to close the distance. As I did, I drove the palm of my hand into his back between his shoulder blades. It was enough to cause him to pitch forward and lose his footing. I still remember the sound of his head hitting the pavement like a watermelon. The blow robbed him of his fight, and I managed to handcuff him without too much resistance on his part. Yup. As suspected, he was drunk, and of course, belligerent.

Due to his cranial wallop, I had an ambulance drop by to check him out. His vitals were stable and his head wound was a lump but not bleeding, nor was he exhibiting signs of something more serious. We managed to get him to the police station for a breathalyzer test, but it was evident that supplying a suitable sample of air from his lungs was not on his "to do" list. We charged him with impaired driving, hit and run, and refusing to supply a breath sample. His truck was impounded, and he was lodged in jail.

A court trial was scheduled approximately six months later, at which time his lawyer worked-out a plea agreement with Provincial Crown. He was fortunate that no serious injuries were sustained by the innocent occupants in the car he rammed. It was a fairly severe impact, and I have no doubt that their heads and necks were probably just as sore the next day as those of our impaired driver. And as for my legs that night, I could barely walk back to the police car. But knowing that the fleeing scoundrel would face justice for the crimes that he otherwise would've gotten away with was the best therapy ever. A good set of legs and lungs will take a cop far, as I learned one night in the Drug Squad.

I spent two years in the Drug Squad of the Vancouver Police Department, which turned out to be a fascinating assignment. I worked in a small team of drug cops, with Rob-one as my partner. One of our mission was to deal with street-level drug trafficking, which was burgeoning in scope and seriously affecting community safety in the Downtown Eastside of Vancouver. One of our standard enforcement strategies was to use an undercover detective to make drug buys, then arrest and charge the dealers. Given that I was the youngest among my cohorts in the Drug Squad, and the scrawniest, the role of buyer often fell to me. I used several personas to "fly under the radar," so to speak. The dealers were always wary of undercover cops, so acting cool, talking the talk, and not looking like a cop was essential to success.

One of my more effective personas was that of a university student needing a little help to get through exams. I was doing a lot of cycling in those days and had all the gear: spandex, Italian road bike, and knapsack. Riding slowly through the high trafficking areas, I was constantly offered crack cocaine, weed, and various other chemical concoctions. I'd snap out of my clipless pedals but sit on my bike to make a transaction, pulling money from one of three pouches on the back of my cycling jersey and replacing it with the drug du jour. I'd then provide my cover team with a pre-arranged signal and ride off while they moved in quickly to make the arrest. After completing a transaction, dealers are always hyper-vigilant, looking out for a possible arrest team. This was the case after a buy that was made by one of my teammates in a notorious part of the Downtown Eastside called Pigeon Square.

I was part of the arrest team on this occasion. As we moved in for the arrest, the astute dealer twigged and launched into a sprint. Three of us started after him. One drug cop dropped out after going no farther than across the street. The other made it half a block, leaving me as the only remaining runner giving chase. The dealer was lean, and probably coked up, based on his speed and demeanour.

One of my tactics in a foot chase was to try and unnerve the suspect with comments such as: "I know you're getting tired, but I can do this all night. You may as well give up; I'm not going away." It's surprising how effective these comments can be in altering the mindset of someone you're chasing. In reality though, I was nearing the end of my rope, and there was no way I could carry on the pace much longer.

We ran full-tilt three blocks to the east, one block south, then back westward again. It was a warm summer evening. I was overdressed for running, wearing a black fleece pullover and body armour, and was definitely overheating by then. I knew the rest of the cover team was out in vehicles looking for me and that they'd alerted the police dispatcher to the circumstances, yet no one had found us on the circuitous route.

I could see that the suspect was also running out of steam. He saw an opportunity. It was a cab stopped at a light with no passengers. The suspect swung open the rear door and jumped in. Before the cab could move or the suspect could figure out how to lock the door, I had it open. I yelled "Police" to the driver, who was yelling, "Get out! Get out of my taxi!" in a thick, South Asian accent. I grappled with the suspect and pulled him from the cab.

The two of us ended up rolling around in the filth of a Downtown Eastside sidewalk—me trying to apply a choke hold, him trying to break free. Just at this moment, and being only a block from the Main Street police station, an off-duty officer came around the corner by happenstance. With some helping hands, the suspect was finally handcuffed and taken into custody. Was it worth the physical risks and aggravation? Probably not, but there's something prehistoric about the chase that doesn't let you give up. He was the prey, and I was the predator.

Despite its potential perils balanced against the significance of the crime, or perhaps insignificance (as it would be viewed in today's liberalized drug scene), I was determined to make the arrest. Through today's lens of social tolerance, the efficacy of our "buy and bust" strategy may appear pointless, even pernicious. And while such an argument can be made, in my view we were making the streets safer for the citizens that lived in the affected areas. They too had the right to safety and security, the essence of which was taken from them by drug traffickers and the criminality they attracted. In addition, with each drug-related conviction, the courts were in a position to impose sanctions that relieved the neighbourhood in question of the disorder wrought by traffickers. They could even commit addicted offenders to recovery programs in the hope that they'd leave behind their lives of addiction and crime.

Rolling around on sidewalks, grappling with suspects, as I did with the drug trafficker, is not a highly unusual event for a cop, so I'll pop one more into the book before moving on to items less abrasive than bare skin on concrete.

"WE'RE GOING OUTSIDE TO FIGHT"

IT WAS THE LATE EIGHTIES WHEN THOSE WORDS WERE SPOKEN by an individual listed on the police database as an ex-member of the military, who was both anti-police and a martial-arts expert. He was also just plain nuts.

Our military man had discreetly been bothering patrons in one of Vancouver's most counter-culture vegetarian restaurants. He would pull up a chair and begin helping himself to whatever meatless morsels were on a table while trying to engage the patrons in small talk. The management had quietly asked him to leave, but that was not on our friend's menu. It was a busy night, not only for the restaurant's staff but for the cops as well. I attended the restaurant with the hope of quietly escorting the "help yourself" patron from the premises.

Now, a little about the restaurant, which was generally a place of tranquility. The Naam is an institution in Vancouver's Kitsilano neighbourhood. There are probably more scraggly beards and tie-dyed shirts in the Naam any given night than in all of San Francisco. I was in uniform. One can't wear a uniform and be discreet in the Naam; it would be easier for Denzel Washington, one of my favourite actors, to fit into a Klan rally.

The manager explained the problem and pointed out the culprit. He was seated quietly at a table near the back of the restaurant with a nervous young couple he didn't know, eating their food and trying to converse. I recognized him the moment I saw him in the glow of the candle-lit table. I knew of his background, which included military service and expertise in martial arts. He had a penchant for violence but was civil as I approached. I very calmly asked him if we could chat outside.

"No. Why?"

I could see that an easy resolution was not in the cards. "Look," I explained, "the management has the right to ask you to leave. You can't just sit with strangers and eat their food, so why don't you discreetly leave, and no one will be the wiser?"

Now becoming agitated, G.I. Joe (I'll reference him as GI for short) jumped up and slyly whispered those ominous words: "Ok, I'll go outside, but we're going outside to fight."

Now keep in mind that every eye in the place was on us. I imagine, from their perspective, the suspect was being cooperative and agreeing to quietly leave the restaurant. And fair enough; that's exactly how it would've appeared to anyone out of earshot, yet in reality, it was anything but. I sensed GI's demeanour change. His posture stiffened, his chest thrust out, and his walk became deliberate, almost as if marching into battle.

I walked behind GI as we passed a long line of tables and made our way to the front door. Now, the front of the restaurant is essentially all windows. Even the front door and vestibule are composed of glass, so there was no hiding from the laser-lock gaze of every patron in the place. I knew that going toe-to-toe with this maniac was not an option. And even if that were to develop, every cop knows that maintaining custody and control of their firearm is critical to survival. Many police officers have been murdered by creeps that have taken hold of an officer's firearm, so being knocked unconscious by GI was not going to happen. With these thoughts flashing through my mind, and some reticence about whether any of the counter-culture patrons would jump to my defence, I had to act strategically (remember Mr. Mitchell). As GI walked out the front door like a gladiator headed to the ring, I jumped him from behind, throwing him into a headlock and taking him to the sidewalk, where I hoped to control him until backup arrived.

The plan was executed as intended. I squeezed, hoping to keep GI from breaking free as we rolled on the sidewalk. How this apparent "unprovoked" turn of events appeared to the soy-eating clientele I can only speculate. And while I hadn't counted on help from any of them, a nicely dressed young man did leave the restaurant and come to my aid. Turned-out that he was a newly-hired Vancouver Police recruit. I guess serendipity does exist. With the recruit's assistance, GI was taken safely into custody without blows being exchanged, following which he was charged with mischief and resisting arrest for his epicurean lawlessness.

I have one last word about officers protecting their firearms. A few years earlier, my patrol partner and I were in plainclothes. We attended a call of a disturbance at the Biltmore Pub, which at the time was a hangout for a younger crowd into heavy metal and such. There was a lineup at the door this particular evening, and a couple of jack-asses were causing trouble by cutting in. My partner and I each took hold of one. Before anything could be said, the fight was on. We were both trying to gain control of our fighters. I got my arm around my guy's neck and swept him over my back from the right side to my left side, in order to bring him down hard on the pavement. In doing so, his body or outer clothing somehow snagged the butt of my revolver and pulled it from the substandard plainclothes holster that was issued back then.

The gun flung forward, hitting the slick clay tiles along which the patrons awaiting entry were lined up. It was completely surreal. I can still see my gun flying in slow motion and landing like a flipped pancake, and how its forward momentum caused it to skittle along the tiles and into the feet of patrons, all of whom were jumping to try and avoid the out-of-control weapon. I dropped the suspect I was grappling with and literally made a dive for the gun. My fear was that the suspect or someone sympathetic to him might beat me to the punch. The shock created enough distraction that both suspects quit struggling and were arrested without further resistance.

One last mention of the Naam Restaurant must be told before moving on to other topics. It pertains to my time in the Drug Squad, probably five years after the GI event. We generally worked an afternoon shift in the Drug Squad, which would start at four p.m. and fade out at two a.m. Though we worked primarily in partnerships, we came together as a team for large-scale events, such as search warrants, surveillance, and undercover activity. In addition, we always made an effort to meet for dinner at a cheap and cheerful restaurant, somewhere that served meat and plenty of it. Restaurants in Chinatown were favoured. Chicken with black bean sauce, sweet and sour pork . . . you get the idea—six or eight large scruffy males clustered around a circular table and a scattering of plastic chopsticks up for grabs.

Inevitably, one of us would complain about the chosen location, so we made a pact that whomever won a random numbers game, played with coins, at the start of each shift could pick the location, and no one was permitted to complain or suggest an alternate locale. Though my colleagues seized upon the fairness of the process, I saw an opportunity for fun. Whenever I won the game, I picked a restaurant that I knew would challenge the gastronomic horizons of the group with eclectic menus, artsy atmospheres, and so on. They began to catch on. I was warned. Then re-warned. My partner Rob-one advised me not to do it again, but I couldn't help myself. Hello Naam!

Now, I know that in my previous story I made Naam sound like nirvana for wool-wearing millennials, but it sincerely is a cool restaurant. It's one that I've eaten at many times, even in uniform, and the staff were always kind and welcoming. While basking in the glow of my "numbers" victory that evening, I reminded my colleagues of the game rules and went on to describe Naam as serving delicious Mexi-Cali fare.

"Does it have meat?"

"Of course," I reassured them.

Rob and I parked nearby at the allotted time and met the rest of the Drug Squad on the sidewalk in front. They became suspicious. Very suspicious. Suddenly, the sandwich-board out front verified their concerns: VEGETARIAN. I ran. They chased me. They were like raging bulls, and I was a scarlet-red matador in full retreat. Fortunately, my partner jumped into the car, raced ahead, and swung open the passenger door. I jumped in, and we squealed our way to safety.

From that day onward, I was prohibited from playing the numbers game. I pled my case, and they eventually allowed me to play again, but I had to pick from a short list of approved locations. To be honest, it was so much fun working with my fellow meat-eating narcs that I still chuckle to myself when I reflect back on some of the antics. And while some of our nutritional endeavours could be considered odd, I served two years as the president of a real Odd Squad.

ODD SQUAD

THE ODD SQUAD IS A CHARITABLE, NOT-FOR-PROFIT ORGANI-
zation, whose core is composed of a small group of Vancouver police officers
with longstanding experience policing Vancouver's infamous drug-ridden
Downtown Eastside (DTES). Established in 1997, the Odd Squad, including
its volunteers, staff, and board members, has been producing video content to
help educate youth about the importance of their decisions around drug use
and lifestyle. The first production, *Through a Blue Lens,* released in 1999, was
a ground-breaking, award-winning documentary that transported the viewer
into the world of despair that consumes drug-addicted individuals surviving in
the DTES. Since the release of *Through a Blue Lens,* the Odd Squad has delivered a most compelling library of videos and educational literature addressing
the risks of drug use, gang life, and criminality.

This content is used nationally by schools to educate students in a manner
that resonates and connects with young people. Odd Squad members and
their volunteers travel throughout Canada delivering presentations combined
with healthy-lifestyle coaching and positive choice-making exercises. The participants are empowered through the principles of judo and teambuilding. The
Odd Squad's latest video production is a three-part educational series on the
dangers of fentanyl, as seen through the eyes of users, their families, and surviving loved ones.

As a non-profit charitable organization, Odd Squad Productions is administered by a board of governance. I had the honour of serving as the president

of their board of directors for a two-year term from 2005-2007. It was truly a privilege to be a small cog in this globally-unique machine, and to see the immense difference it was making to lives at risk. I'll never forget participating in the Odd Squad's "On Track" program, in which a cohort of high school students, many of whom were started down a darkened path, spent the day building rapport with the participating police officers while seeing firsthand the outcome of addiction among individuals not much older than themselves.

The "On Track" day started with breakfast before moving onto an orientation session of judo, following which the group was divided into smaller segments. Some headed onto the water in the police boat while others engaged in a number of well-organized events with specialty units of the police department. After the groups had rotated through all of the activities and chowed down a catered lunch, they were partnered with Odd Squad officers for an immersive walk into Vancouver's menacing DTES to see up-close and personal the devastation of drug addiction and to meet some of the locals struggling with the consequences.

I was never assigned to the DTES as a beat cop, but I spent plenty of time working the area as a drug cop and also as a bike cop, so I was no stranger to the pall of hopelessness and despair that permeates the area. Nor the squalor of the single-occupancy rooms that provide little refuge for those trying to beat the odds and survive another day. That said, I was blown away by the willingness of many drug-addicted souls to speak earnestly with our youngsters, describing the personal circumstances and poor decision-making that consigned them to a life of misery and addiction. In true expressions of altruism, the addicts wanted to prevent the young adults in our groups from becoming one of them, or worse, an overdose statistic.

One story I vividly remember came from Tony. He was in his early twenties, though drugs and strife had marked him as older. We encountered Tony in a back lane where he was furtively looking to score. While he wasn't a vision of health, Tony was passionate about telling his story to the kids. And as he recounted the precursors to his life on the street, I recall thinking how smart and well-spoken he was. I figured that, without the devastation wrought by the chemicals he needed daily (more like hourly), Tony would have found success and made his family proud, but that was far from the case. Yet, it was clear that Tony was from a family that cared and had tried desperately to save him.

For Tony, it had started with pot when he was thirteen. He described pot as a gateway drug that primed him for chemical-induced highs. Crack cocaine was huge with Tony, crystal meth ranked high, and by the point of him being on the street, anything he could get his hands on would do. Like so many families confronting addiction, Tony's loved ones begged him to get help. They pleaded with him to participate in rehab, but he refused to acknowledge a problem despite stealing money from his dad's wallet and his sister's piggybank to score dope. Tony described the agony he put his family through and continued to do without end. He knew how much he had hurt them and cried about it in front of us as he described the last straw, which severed any remaining ties with his broken-hearted family.

Tony's father was a life-long collector of baseball cards. He cherished them, and many of them had substantial value. Tony knew which one was the most valuable, not just financially but emotionally to his father. It was a 1952 Mickey Mantle worth $30,000. Despite knowing its rarity and value, and what that card meant to his father, Tony stole the card from his dad's collection and sold it for thirty dollars at a pawn shop for a quick fix. The raw emotion and guilt Tony shed reciting this story brought tears to the eyes of a few of the students, and frankly had me tearing up as well. I'm not sure that I've ever heard a more heartfelt, sorrowful confession, and certainly not one told by a thieving drug addict, but there you have it. The reality of addiction.

Tony wasn't the only one that opened up. Margaret was a woman in her sixties. It would be fair to say that, under the ashen complexion of a heroin addict, she was an attractive woman bearing the telltale signs of class and dignity. She was a high-functioning heroin addict, with her addiction seemingly under control thanks to participation in a methadone program. She invited our group up to her room in a rundown, single-occupancy building. These facilities are often informally referred to as rooming houses. Despite the dilapidation and decay of the old building, her tiny room was an oasis of plants and artwork. Margaret had done a fabulous job of decorating her four walls with watercolour artwork that she had created. Also in her room was an upright piano, which she played for us with delicate beauty. The only other item that fit into the small rectangular space was a cot to sleep upon.

With the grace of a grandmother, Margaret told her story to the kids. She had been happily married long ago, raising two children to adulthood. She held a high-level managerial job in a major bank, but she was deeply stressed. She was offered a hit of heroin by a well-meaning associate, and that was it, she was hooked. Margaret kicked off her black pumps to show the kids the scars in the arches of her feet where she would stick the hypodermic needle loaded with heroin. This was the only location where no one, including her husband, would see her tracks. Her addiction eventually grew out of control, as they always do, and destroyed everything she had. Homeless and penniless, Margaret resorted to the sex trade to support her habit. Now, some thirty years later, Margaret has things under control for the most part. The methadone helps her tolerate going clean, which is a bottomless fall into hell for an addict. There's no magic wand that restores the addicted to their pre-addicted life. The best most can do is manage the day-to-day angst with the help of recovery programs and less-harmful drug alternatives. Margaret's story challenged our group's perception of a drug addict, shattering the convention that drug addicts are street people and criminals with no future or social contribution.

To this day, the Odd Squad continues its work, and have expanded their mandate, membership, and supporters along with their sphere of outreach. This wasn't always the case, though. During my volunteer term as the board president, I was the superintendent commanding the VPD's Investigation Division. This was an executive-level position within the department, and one in which I was a member of the chief's inner cabinet. Loyalty to the chief in such a key role goes without saying. In my case, my loyalty stretched back to the first days of the police academy when Jim Chu and I were classmates. Now as chief, Jim was my boss. Early on in my presidency, Chief Chu was for the most part a supporter of the Odd Squad, but that notion soon came into question.

The Vancouver Police Department and the community it serves benefit greatly from the Vancouver Police Foundation, which is a non-profit philanthropic society focused on a mandate to fund police-led programs intended to promote community well-being, increase public safety, and prevent crime. It's truly a wonderful organization comprised of caring, generous donors hoping to improve life for the vulnerable and those most at risk in our city. I have nothing but the greatest admiration for the foundation, its service to the community, and its members. Where things got a little ugly, though, and perhaps too political, was in the chief's desire to have the Odd Squad abandon its independence as a non-profit society and become an entity under the framework of his office.

This would mean that the Odd Squad Board of Directors would be dissolved and our status as a non-profit society decommissioned. In return, the Odd Squad and its programs would receive stable funding through the auspices of the Vancouver Police Foundation. The appeal of regular, reliable funding is compelling for any non-profit that must constantly fundraise for its survival.

While the proposal from the chief wasn't without merit, it would put me in a major conflict of interest with the Odd Squad Board if I were to arbitrarily pull the trigger on the chief's plan. Rather, I took the plan to the board of directors and to the members of the Odd Squad, seeking their position on the proposal. It became immediately clear that neither the board nor the Odd Squad members had any desire to dissolve the board and the society by adopting the proposal. They were, however, highly appreciative of the offer. I totally respected the collective decision and was committed to defend it regardless of the cost. Principles matter.

I met with the chief and updated him. He wasn't pleased. If the Odd Squad wasn't supportive of the proposal, Chief Chu wanted to sever its association with the VPD. The chief drew up orders that forbid the Odd Squad from wearing their uniforms at any Odd Squad event, training session, or function. The Odd Squad could no longer use VPD branding on any of its literature or materials and could not undertake any action in support of the Odd Squad while on-duty or in any VPD facility. Simply put, Odd Squad had become persona non grata with the chief and could not represent the Vancouver Police Department in any manner. Then to hammer home his displeasure, Chief Chu initiated the transfer of several Odd Squad members from Vancouver's Downtown Eastside, where they had worked closely with community members and those in the media and medical fields to create programs that educated youth around the dangers of drug use and gang affiliation.

The chief had effectively neutered the Odd Squad, and in doing so, had placed me in an untenable conflict of interest. I was president of the Odd Squad Board, and this was a board of highly talented and deeply committed professionals. I would not abandon them. At the same time though, my loyalty to the chief and the executive committee tore at me. I had always been supportive of the chief—in fact, *many* chiefs over thirty-plus years—but this action by Chief Chu felt to me to be excessive, lacking in both foundation and justification. It wouldn't be overstated for me to declare this phase in my thirty-three years of policing as possibly stressful and disappointing, yet it had nothing to do with actual police work.

There's no doubt that Chief Chu had his reasons for imposing the restrictions. There was, at the time, some concern expressed to him suggesting that Odd Squad officers were losing direction and not meeting objectives or completion expectations. I was addressing these issues in my role as president, none of which merited in my mind, throwing out the baby with the bath water. Bear in mind that the Odd Squad is comprised of volunteer officers who also maintain busy family lives and highly demanding police careers.

Though controversial, the decisions of Chief Chu no longer aggravate me or get my heart pumping as they once did. Why? Because the Odd Squad survived! And then some.

Kicked but not down, the Odd Squad and its board dug deep and found the resolve needed to overcome the politics of Chief Chu. They acquiesced to his demands, picked up the pieces, and put the organization back on its feet with even more determination to do the right thing. They found additional benefactors, and strong, influential supporters that believe in the mission. United and committed, all of those connected to the Odd Squad lifted the organization out of the Chu era with dignity while achieving astonishing results.

Following Chief Jim Chu's tenure, a new chief took over the Vancouver Police Department in 2015. Like Chief Jamie Graham, who'd preceded Chief Chu, Chief Adam Palmer immediately recognized the success of the Odd Squad and the unmatched value of its service to the community. Chief Palmer has re-established a productive relationship with the Odd Squad. More than ever, the Odd Squad is a dynamic organization producing outstanding video and educational documentaries, drug and gang educational presentations, peer-to-peer content, and physical literacy programs. They are now based in a new, two-story custom-finished facility encompassing classrooms, video-production labs, and a fully sprung gym floor. Their reach has never been greater and neither has their success in building resilience and self-esteem in youth-at-risk. I am so proud of them all.

Further information on the work of the Odd Squad can be found at www.oddsquad.com.

Further information on the work of the Vancouver Police Foundation can be found at www.vancouverpolicefoundation.org.

LOVE BITES

WHILE JIM CHU'S TREATMENT OF THE ODD SQUAD MAY BITE, the bite in my next story is far more literal.

Under the category of "you can't make this shit up," I have a couple of penis-related stories that may have those whose chromosomes include a Y squirming in their seats. It was roughly eleven p.m. on a relatively quiet evening when multiple calls to 911 were received from residents of a tri-level walk-up apartment on the west side of Vancouver. They were reporting a madman running naked through the halls, banging on doors, and screaming for help. My partner and I raced to the scene. Once inside the building, we quickly found our agitated streaker. He was buck naked, holding his manhood wrapped in toilet tissue. Blood was seeping out.

Despite being in the throes of pain more severe than I care to imagine, his injury wasn't his primary concern; his girlfriend was. He led us into the suite they shared. She had been suffering from a seizure but was coming out of it upon our arrival. We immediately called an ambulance for her, and as it turned out, for him too. At this point, you may have an inkling of what had occurred that led to the maniacal call for help. Our two consenting adults had been engaged in oral sex when she suddenly suffered a seizure and clamped her jaw forcefully closed, subjecting her boyfriend to a penile variant of a leghold trap. He couldn't extract himself until his erection subsided and his girlfriend's jaw muscles slackened enough for him to pull out. Once liberated from the jaws of agony, he ran for help, hoping someone would call an ambulance. Cell phones had not yet populated every butt pocket, and as new tenants, our young couple's landline had not yet been hooked up.

Though not completely severed, the penile laceration would require surgery to close. Prior to both of our subjects heading to hospital, we confirmed the boyfriend's story with his girlfriend. While she had no memory of the actual seizure, she confirmed the beforehand consensual activity. As my partner and I departed the building, we assured the residents that everything was fine, and they had nothing to fear. The naked madman pounding on doors was sincere in his need for immediate help for him and his girlfriend. Yes, I guess love bites at times.

HERE'S A TIP

THAT Y CHROMOSOME I REFERENCED IN THE PREVIOUS STORY can induce its carrier into engaging in stupid human tricks that should never be attempted, even by the dimmest of wits.

I was working at a Vancouver Canuck's hockey game one evening when I was alerted to an injured male in the men's washroom. How do men get injured in a public washroom? They're usually so drunk that they fall and split open their heads on porcelain. But not in this case, despite the elements of drunkenness and blood.

Four young men were operating on a cocktail of alcohol and testosterone, and that's a risky combination. Somehow, they had managed to smuggle firecrackers into the game. Now, these weren't bad lads, and they were likely the pride and joy of their parents. But like over-stimulated teens everywhere, their common sense was plainly in the toilet that evening. They got together in the large public washroom of the arena for some hijinks: teens, booze, firecrackers. You get the idea . . . but actually you don't. Tossing firecrackers around to create a little panic wasn't in their playbook. No, they had a more daring idea. Well, at least one of them did.

You see, it's mandatory for teens with firecrackers to show their—shall we say balls—and their misconceived sense of invincibility by holding bigger and bigger firecrackers while they detonate. The trick, as I recall from my days of limited common sense, was to hold the incendiary device by the edge of its base using the tips of the thumb and index finger. The arm was held outstretched in an upward trajectory to keep the ensuing explosion away from one's face. This technique was pretty much the norm, and it seemed the worst of potential consequence was a stinging sensation at the points of contact. Through a sporting sense of one-upmanship, the teen with nerves of steel, and perhaps the most alcohol-enriched blood, decided that holding the firecracker by inserting its non-fuse end into the tip of his penis would enlarge his reputation . . . and it did.

I arrived moments after the big bang, followed by the big scream. Despite the firecracker only being a "Lady Finger," a name that adds to the spirited nature of the act, the flaw in the plan pertained to an error in the depth of insertion. The resultant fleshy tear and expanding puddle of blood were evidence of the miscalculation. I could barely believe my eyes. Here was another bleeding penis in my career, and another male headed to the hospital for a surgical response. Yes, I can't help but think of this case every Halloween and wonder what other errors in judgement may befall such users—some of those errors carrying with them much greater consequences than the results of a misplaced Lady Finger.

22

"IT WAS US!"

WHILE WE ALL OCCASIONALLY MISPLACE AN ITEM, I MAY HOLD some kind of inglorious record for what's next to come.

The words "it was us" were spoken with a visceral sense of alarm by my partner Rob-one in the Drug Squad as he arrived back to the office after a trip to the washroom.

"What are you talking about?" I asked him.

"The car! The car! The missing car! It was us! Don't you remember? You and I had separate cars at the start of shift. We then met up in South Vancouver to work a file, and you jumped into my car. We left yours parked on the street."

I suddenly had a lightbulb moment, soon accompanied by pangs of guilt.

Our misadventure had started nearly three-weeks prior. The Drug Squad had just received four new undercover vehicles. Rob and I each took a car at the start of our shift on the day in question in order to perform follow-ups on our respective files during the first half of our day. As planned, we went late into the evening to work together for the remaining hours. I parked the new Chevy Corsica sedan I had been driving under a large maple tree on a side street lined by well-kept middle-class houses in South Vancouver. I hid the keys for the car behind one of the wheels so that any one of us could grab it if needed, and away we went in Rob's car. Not only did I leave the car behind, but my memory with it.

Our shift ended around three a.m. after a busy evening. For the next few days, the car wasn't missed. The assumption was that it had been borrowed at the last minute by one of the department's surveillance teams. This was not an unusual event. On occasion, a surveillance car may take a "burn," meaning that the targets had taken an unusual interest in it. In such a case, the surveillance team might grab a covert car from us, or any other undercover team, to replace the heated-up wheels. Usually, a note was left along with the keys to the burned car so that our team had its allotted number of vehicles. But like children with their toys, accountability doesn't always happen, which inevitably results in finger-pointing and a rush to judgement. And that was the case when our Chevy had not materialized the following week.

"I'm sure they've hidden it so that we can't get it back," I figured. My Drug Squad colleagues agreed. Yet, our surveillance colleagues denied any knowledge of the missing Chevy despite our assertions to the contrary. Such claims of innocence were expected. But as two weeks turned to three, our sergeant was losing his cool. If the car wasn't back by the end of the week, he vowed to report it stolen. This was getting serious, and we were actually wondering if someone had stolen the new Chevy. That was until Rob had his urinary epiphany. I'm sure all men will agree that standing before a urinal relieving oneself is where much critical thinking gets done. It certainly did for Rob that day of reckoning.

"How the hell are we going to get it back?" I asked him.

We quickly came up with a plan, grabbed the spare keys to the Corsica, and flew. Our incessant chatter on the Drug Squad radio made us sound busy, checking a file on the opposite side of town. Soon, our abandoned car was in sight, covered in tree sap with one of its tires appearing low on air. A huge sigh of relief left my body as the car's V-6 engine came to life.

Part two of the plan: I would follow Rob down to the police station but hold a few blocks away as he scoped-out the underground lot, in which the covert cars were kept, to ensure that the coast was clear. We didn't want to encounter any colleagues from surveillance or any other investigative unit while driving the missing car.

I got the pre-arranged signal from Rob over the portable Drug Squad radio and quickly swung the Chevy down the multiple ramps descending to the basement. While covert cars did not have assigned parking spaces, each team (be it surveillance, drugs, etc.) had a specific level of the parkade allocated to their fleet. As planned, I roared down to the level of the surveillance teams, bypassing the level assigned to the Drug Squad.

I parked the car at the far end, as if it might have been there all along. By now, Rob was on the elevator heading to the offices of the surveillance teams to verify that they were all out on the road. This was a late-evening operation, so no daytime personnel were around either. I zoomed up to the surveillance offices and met Rob. We gained access to the cupboard that held keys to all of the surveillance vehicles and hung the Chevy's keys on a non-descript hook. Then we jumped into the car Rob had been using and got on with the remainder of our shift, grinning ear-to-ear that we had pulled-off "Operation Recovery."

We knew it wouldn't be long before the Chevy was discovered by surveillance personnel, and that we'd be vindicated when they sheepishly came over to return the keys the following day. As planned, two surveillance guys showed up with the keys at the start of our shift the next afternoon. They smelled a rat. They knew that someone in the Drug Squad had set them up to take the fall for the missing vehicle, and they weren't about to roll over. Lots of indignant finger-pointing was accompanied by swirling accusations but none of it sufficient to implicate. With a reasonable doubt shared equally between "the usual suspects," our exasperated sergeant threw his hands up and simply demanded that it never happen again. Until this day, the story has remained untold.

And a funny note about those four new vehicles: Unbeknownst to Rob and me, these were the first vehicles in the police department to arrive with key fobs, which remotely locked and unlocked doors and opened the trunk. I personally had never owned a car with key fob access at this point in my automotive history, so the emerging technology was somewhat foreign to me. Essentially, this was the first year that remote entry hit the automotive landscape in any meaningful way.

Two quick-thinking members of my Drug Squad secretly removed the fobs for the new cars from the keyrings before anyone was the wiser. With the fob to our vehicle tucked in their pocket, they would ask to meet us in an empty lot somewhere. As we pulled our cars side-by-side, the door locks on our vehicle would inexplicably begin locking and unlocking. Then our trunk would pop open. It began to freak us out, and we named the car Christine after a 1983 slasher flick based on a book by Stephen King, in which a vehicle named Christine violently destroys anyone coming between it and the owner that restored her.

The next day, we grabbed a different new car for fear of the events of the preceding day. Again, our mischievous colleagues asked to meet, and again the car went berserk. At about this point, we began to figure it out. Christine was dead and the mystery solved, which was a little disappointing, I have to say. I loved the notion of a "possessed" car in our fleet. Of course, key fobs and remote locking are the norm today, but not so much in the early nineties when Christine struck fear in the hearts of the mechanically gullible.

WE'RE FUCKIN DETECTIVES

IN THE EVENT THAT OUR BAFFLEMENT IN RESPONSE TO THE fob hoax has you questioning whether we were actually detectives, the following circumstances should provide clarity.

Let's stay with the Drug Squad theme a little longer. In doing so, I want to tell you about the Russians. I have several stories pertaining to my interactions with this former die-hard gang of Eastern European criminals who had intended to take over the drug trade in Vancouver in the nineties. Their arch enemies were the Hells Angels.

The Russians introduced themselves to the Angels by shooting up the clubhouse of the East End chapter with automatic gunfire. That little "get ta know ya" definitely got the attention of the HA, and kicked off a gang war between the two notorious organizations. I'll have more to say about the interpersonal skills of the Russians later in the book, but for now, I want to cover the events of a day we spent surveilling the Russians, in particular, Alexander Alekseev and his younger brother Eugene Alekseev.

I was working with my partner, Rob-one. The other members of the Drug Squad were in partnerships as well. Each partnership drove a covert surveillance vehicle; ours happened to be a high-performance 1992 Camaro Z28. Yes, loud and obnoxious, and to be honest, not a good vehicle for blending in. Nonetheless, the day of surveillance had been going reasonably well. The Alekseev brothers had been driving to various locations during the day to support their criminal enterprise. Our surveillance team had been making

progress in identifying associates and addresses related to their marihuana cultivation and distribution business.

The Russians were difficult and challenging to surveil. They used counter-
surveillance tactics, in which two other members of the gang would follow a short
distance behind, conducting surveillance of their own in an attempt to identify
police vehicles engaged in surveillance. One of the favourite tricks employed by
the brothers was to drive partially up an on-ramp to a bridge, then pull to the side,
stop, and examine the passing cars. Obviously, any surveillance vehicle committed
to the on-ramp had to drive calmly past the targets and over the bridge, effectively
removing them from the surveillance. After watching the traffic, the Russians would
U-turn and drive the wrong direction down the ramp, returning to the main road
they had originally been travelling on. From their perspective, any vehicle that had
pulled over on the main road rather than committing to the on-ramp was clearly a
surveillance vehicle. They were often correct in their assumptions.

As morning turned to afternoon, we found ourselves tailing the lads in
Richmond, a quiet suburb separated from Vancouver by the Fraser River. It
could be that they saw two long-hair scraggly dudes in a Camaro Z28 once
too often during the day, and they pulled a U-turn on a busy four-lane road
and got behind us. They closed the distance and began following us. I hoped
to shake them by running a late light, forcing them to stop at the red, but they
went through as well. Next, I looked for the most obvious destination to bury
the car and disappear on foot into a store. It was a busy Home Depot lot. I
had managed to add some distance between us and pulled into the lot, quickly
parking the Camaro. Before we could climb out of the car, the boys had pulled
in and parked in the stall to the right of us.

They began taunting. "Good afternoon, constables," they sarcastically yelled.
"Having a good day, constables? Are you lost, constables?"

At this point, Rob lost his cool. He hit the down-button for the power
window. As it opened wide, he glared at the Russian and yelled back, "We're
fuckin detectives," and hit the window-up button.

Rob wasn't so much incensed that the Russians had made us as cops, but that
they hadn't respected our rank of detective! We weren't merely constables, and
that had to be made clear.

Needless to say, our surveillance was shot, but the look of astonishment
on the faces of the bros and the pregnant pause that followed Rob's shocking

revelation was a surreal yet comical moment in the fight for justice against one of the most violent gangs to ever operate in our city.

I'll have more to say later in the book about the Russian gang, of which the four principal members were all murdered in the ensuing battle for gang supremacy. But I want to change gears now and chat about the work that the police do in partnership with family-crisis social workers.

BEER, SMOKES, AND DRUGS
BEFORE MILK AND DIAPERS

IT'S CALLED CAR 86, AND IT BRINGS TOGETHER A PLAIN-clothed police officer, in this case me, and a social worker specially trained in family crisis intervention. While I was never permanently assigned to car 86, I enjoyed performing relief work when one of the assigned officers was on leave. Car 86 mostly operates after regular office hours, responding to homes where families are in crisis and kids are at risk. They are most typically called to a home by patrol officers that have responded to a family dispute where they've found children that have been abused, are at risk, or in need of care. One heartbreaking case I recall involved a mom with three kids, ranging in age from an infant to a preschooler.

They lived in a rundown basement suite. On this particular evening, there was a drinking party going on with maybe a half-dozen drunken louts. The patrol officers who had responded originally to a fight call at the suite became aware of the kids, all located in the same bed, but clearly not being cared for. No one in the unit was sober enough for the officers to even contemplate leaving the kids in their care. Car 86 was notified.

We were there within minutes. Our role at this point was simply that of child welfare. I looked through the kitchen, the fridge and cupboards, for signs of nourishment. None. Beer, smokes, and drugs, that's where the welfare cheque had gone. No baby formula, no cereal, and no milk. Not even clean diapers.

We bundled up the hapless brood. It was obvious that they had not been bathed in a long while. It also became obvious that they had lice infestations. Normally when children are seized by the Ministry of Families, which is technically what we were doing, they are transported to a temporary foster home in an undisclosed location. The following day, social workers generally formulate a plan for return of the children to the family. Alternatively, the ministry may head to Family Court seeking the removal of the children until the parents get their act together, or extended family members take over guardianship—usually grandparents. In this particular case, our first stop was Children's Hospital to have the kids medically examined for malnourishment and to have the lice infestations treated. Several hours later, we were en-route to a temporary foster home that would take all three for the time being. It was important to keep them together.

While working in Car 86, I found it troubling and disheartening how frequently kids had to be removed from their homes due to parents who were far too blotto to care for them, or prone to violent parenting. Yet somehow, those same parents typically had money for smokes, beer, and drugs, but not the necessities of childrearing. As a cop, you want to protect and save every child who's a victim of mistreatment, but the best you can do is start the ball rolling and hope that the appropriate social agencies successfully alter a path that may otherwise lead to family destruction. The cyclical nature of dysfunction is a trend that long-serving cops see up close. Many of us have dealt with abusive parents only to deal with the criminality of their offspring later in our policing career. Of course, the opposite is true as well. Against the odds imposed by poor or abusive parenting, some youngsters rise above it all and thrive.

The Vancouver Police Department has established a number of youth-related programs to support young people, such as those fighting to beat the odds described above. The undertakings include the School Liaison Program (which at the time of writing was cancelled by the Vancouver School Board), the Soccer Program, the Night Hoops Basketball Program, the Student Challenge Program, and the department's Cadet Program, among others. The latter four are heavily funded by the Vancouver Police Foundation. It's doubtful that the suspects involved in the next incident I'm about to describe participated in such programs as teens. If they had, this call may not have existed.

A SHOT IN THE DARK

WHEN NOT ACTIVELY ENGAGED IN A FAMILY CRISIS CASE, CAR 86 can roam the city and respond to any high-priority call. One clear, moonless night, my social-worker partner and I responded to a take-over robbery at Trader Vic's Polynesian Restaurant and Bar, located waterside in Vancouver's Coal Harbour next to the upscale Bayshore Hotel. The longstanding restaurant had opened in 1961 and would later, in 1990, sadly close its doors. The dining room was housed in a huge, A-frame building meant to resemble a Tahitian hut with tiki torches and palm trees. It was the place movie stars frequented when they were in town. The most popular drink was the Mai Tai. Since the demolition of Trader Vic's, much has changed along the stretch of shoreline that runs to the east. The shipbuilding yards are gone, and so is the industry that thrived on the waterfront, replaced by high-end condos, coffee bars, and a beautiful shoreline walkway.

My social-worker partner that night was Carol. At fifty or more years of age (who really knows a woman's age?), she remained energetic and not one to shy away from action. It was one a.m. or so. The restaurant had closed for the night. The patrons had departed, but the staff remained inside, dealing with the evening's receipts. Three armed suspects forced their way into the large waterside building that housed the restaurant. They tied up the employees and made off with the money from a busy evening in the bar and dining room. Fortunately, one employee managed to avoid the suspects and didn't waste time calling 911 as the robbers headed for the door.

Carol and I were roving the West End, not more than a couple of blocks from Trader Vic's, when the call came across the police radio. We responded immediately. Updated information confirmed that the suspects had just departed. We sped into the lot, headlights out. I had expected to see a get-away car given how quickly we were on-scene, but no car. We were greeted by complete blackness along the train tracks that ran east from our location. Before jumping out of the car, I gave Carol my heavy metal flashlight as a weapon of sorts, and as something to give her legitimacy when we made it into the restaurant. As we jumped out of the car into the darkness, Carol switched on the flashlight, shining it toward the tracks, in the only direction the suspects could've run. I instantly realized that I had made a mistake handing Carol the flashlight.

"Turn it out," I said. As I did, a loud crack came from exactly the direction I assumed the suspects to have fled.

I grabbed Carol, and we both jumped down beside the front stairs for cover. I pulled my gun and pointed it into the inky darkness but could see nothing. I radioed that I believed a shot had been fired our way. Turns out that several residents living in homes above the tracks also reported a shot in what was otherwise the still of the night. I'm quite convinced that the fleeing suspects saw the flashlight shining in their direction and decided to discourage us from heading after them—and it worked. Once I felt enough time had transpired, we made our way into the restaurant and helped free the staff as other patrol officers were arriving. The night-running bandits were never caught or identified, nor was a bullet or shell casing recovered. Nonetheless, the incident left me with real-world insight into how instantaneously and unpredictably lethality can unfold.

But while police work has its perilous risks, it also has the ability to entertain in the most unexpected ways as seen next.

A HAPPY LITTLE HEIFER

THANKS TO A CHAP NAMED ROBERT CHARLES KIELING, A SAS-katchewan wheat farmer, I spent an entire evening on stage with Canada's signature musical voice: Anne Murray. When he should've been farming wheat, Mr. Kieling was traversing Canada from east to west in order to attend all of the venues on Anne Murray's Cross Canada Tour. Obsessed with Anne, and not of sound mind, the delusional farmer wrongly believed that Anne loved him and secretly messaged him in the lyrics of her songs. His delusion was so powerful that he had spent time in jail for disobeying court orders to stay away from Anne. No amount of reasoning or legal restraints were going to prevent him from a life of misperceived love.

It was the late eighties; Anne was finishing her Canadian tour with a final concert in Vancouver at the regal Queen Elizabeth Theatre. There was reliable information that Robert was driving frantically to Vancouver from the preceding tour stop in Alberta, intending to rush up on stage at some point during the concert, cradling a bouquet of roses, and physically carry Anne away to a life of bliss as his bride. With a man of such determination, there was credible fear that he would do exactly as he intended, or at least make an overt attempt, the "art of seduction" not being a farming strength.

The promoter and theatre management were truly worried about how the night would shake-out and the degree of risk they were exposing Anne to by allowing her to take the stage bearing in mind the strength of the information. Despite the concerns for her safety, "the show must go on" was the evening's credo. The police were consulted, and a plan was soon put in place to keep Anne safe. It would require readjusting the stage lighting and curtains, and discreetly inserting two police officers onto the stage in between the band and the front of the stage where Anne would primarily perform.

I got the call on a day off and so did a colleague of mine. We donned our uniforms and attended the theatre well ahead of showtime. We met with key folks, including the lighting engineer, promoter, and stage manager. The plan was reviewed and green lit by all, including Anne. My partner for the evening was John. He would be seated on the left side of the stage, and I would be seated on the right side. The stage curtains would be fractionally closed at each end, just enough to conceal us. The stage lighting would be re-aimed, so that it always left us in the dark (literally—not figuratively). From our concealed perches, our combined viewing angles enabled John and me to observe the entire audience. The band performed a few feet behind us, while Anne sang and danced a few feet ahead of us.

I really wondered how the audience would react if Mr. Kieling burst onto the stage, forcing us to reveal ourselves and swing into action. How goal-oriented would the farmer be? How forcefully would he resist being arrested before an audience of three thousand Anne Murray fans? Would he be armed? What if he made it past us and got to Canada's Songbird? We'd forever be the losers that allowed a Canadian treasure to be harmed. With these thoughts swirling in my head, it was difficult to enjoy the performance, despite having the best seats in the house. Fortunately, Mr. Kieling never appeared. We learned later that he was unable to arrive in Vancouver in time to make the concert. Anne safely completed the final concert on her tour and was whisked away to safety before any harm could befall her, or our reputations, the audience none the wiser to the evening's peril.

As a side note, Anne drew a sizable laugh from the audience with a corny comment that also made its way into the concert's review in the morning newspaper. Prior to the show, John and I happened to be chatting with the promoter. He asked if there was anything funny with a local context that Anne could use on stage to connect with the audience. Around this time, the municipality of Surrey, a nearby suburb of Vancouver, had been on the receiving end of many jokes and jibes. Morning DJs were perpetuating the "never having to say you're Surrey" idiom at every opportunity. I pointed this out to the promoter.

"That should do," he said. Later, while the band played filler music between a couple of songs, Anne danced a little jig. Then it came: "I'm just a happy little heifer from Surrey."

I almost fell out of my seat. The crowd loved it though—well, perhaps not those from Surrey. It definitely connected her with the audience; it also made its way into the newspaper the next morning. The music critic playfully mentioned Anne's "happy little heifer" remark in his review of the concert.

CHIEF, THIS MAN CALLED ME A HUN!

KEEPING WITH THE ENTERTAINMENT THEME, HERE'S HOW I was accused of calling another of Canada's greatest talents, the late Leslie Nielsen, a "Hun."

Yes, I did call one of Canada's finest comedic actors a "Hun." Well, sort of. To get to the "Hun" reference, we need to travel back to June 16, 2005. The Odd Squad that I described a few chapters back held its annual gala fundraiser, which was the talk-of-the-town. Entertainment was topnotch and the guest list was the who's who of the Vancouver business community. The event was the principal source of income to fund the drug-awareness programs and video productions of the Odd Squad. Many of North America's best musicians contributed time and proceeds to the cause, including Bruce Springsteen and Vancouver bluesman Jim Byrnes, a decades-long member of the Odd Squad Board of Directors.

The keynote speaker for this particular gala was the now-late Leslie Nielsen, who sadly passed away in 2010 at the age of eighty-four due to complications with the flu. Leslie acted in a hundred films and 150 television programs during his extensive career. He's most notably remembered for starring in the hit comedy movie *Airplane* in 1980 and the hilarious series of *Naked Gun* movies during the late eighties and early nineties, which were a spin-off of his earlier television series, *Police Squad*. Nielsen's on-screen police persona was that of Detective Frank Drebin, a handsome, silver-haired, bumbling cop, who in the end always managed to inadvertently save the day, and the damsel.

On the afternoon before the gala, I was among a small cadre of senior police members invited to a social with Leslie Nielsen in the officers' mess, which was hosted by Chief Constable Jamie Graham. I had been appointed as the tour guide that would later take Leslie Nielsen, his wife, and a couple that had been travelling with them on a tour of the town in the department's antique police car.

Upon meeting Leslie at the afternoon social, I joked with him (never joke with a comedian; they're always better than you!) by saying, "Listen, Leslie, if I call you hon (short for honey) this afternoon, it's because my wife's name is also Leslie, and I'm bound to get mixed up." Without so much of a nanosecond wasted, Nielsen shouted over to the chief in his Detective Drebin persona, "Chief! Chief, this man just called me a Hun!" And the chief's response? He shook his head and chuckled, knowing that I had just been upstaged by one of Canada's finest comedians.

Naturally, I had to call Leslie "hon" at least once during our drive, which was a most amusing tour of the town. The old squad car is a 1947 Mercury reproduction of the patrol cars in use by the Vancouver Police Department in the late 1940s. It is black with white doors and displays the "Vancouver Police" graphic of the era on its two doors. On the roof is a single red light that flashes. Mounted on the flat plane of the left front fender is a huge chrome mechanical siren from the time period. It produces the classic, slow to build, low-to-high frequency wail that was most associated with firetrucks of yore. Powered by its original flathead V-8 engine, the car emits a satisfying rumble through its dual exhaust that elevates to a staccato as the engine revs its way through a "three on the tree" manual gearbox.

It was a beautiful spring day when I wheeled the Merc to the front of the police station to pick up the two couples. The two women climbed into the couch-like rear seat of the vintage coupe while Leslie made his way into the front, followed by the second husband. Both couples were in a jubilant mood. They got a real charge out of being in a police car from an era when they were in their late teens or early twenties. If they had been arrested back then, they would have been taken to jail in just such a car.

Leslie was banging his hand on the rigid steel dashboard of the old Merc, joking about how solid yet unsafe it was. As we made our way through the busy streets of Vancouver, I was winding up the old siren at every opportunity, which the two women in particular thought was a hoot. We drew quite a crowd at stoplights in downtown, with bystanders trying to figure out who was in the vehicle with me. Those who recognized Leslie Nielsen must have thought it was another *Naked Gun* sequel. The laughter in the car was non-stop, as was the hilarity of Leslie's impromptu commentary.

And that's the story of how one of Canada's greatest and most revered comedic actors alleged to the chief of the Vancouver Police Department that I had called him a "Hun."

Before leaving town, Leslie signed a framed poster from the gala, which he left for me. This is what he wrote:

Rob— ("Mr. Daisy")
Thanks for driving!
Richard Cranium
*   AKA*
Leslie Nielsen

The man was a true gentleman and a heck of a lot of fun.

So absurd is the next story that it would make a great file for Detective Frank Drebin!

Me in Grade 12 with neighbour's dog Duchess on the hood of my 1959
Austin A40 that I drove to Surrey to meet an RCMP officer friend of
his for the ride-along that sparked his desire to become a cop.

My I.D tag day-one in the B.C. Police Academy, looking a little tired.

Receiving my graduation handshake from Chief Constable Winterton of the VPD in 1980.

B.C. Police Academy Class Sixteen. I'm back row, 1st from left.

My mother and I on graduation day at the B.C. Police Academy, 1980.

Me as a junior constable on patrol.

Me after my first promotion, becoming a corporal, a rank that is no longer used in the VPD.

"Do you know this man?" Me working undercover as a detective in the
Drug Squad, heading out to make some drug buys 1992.

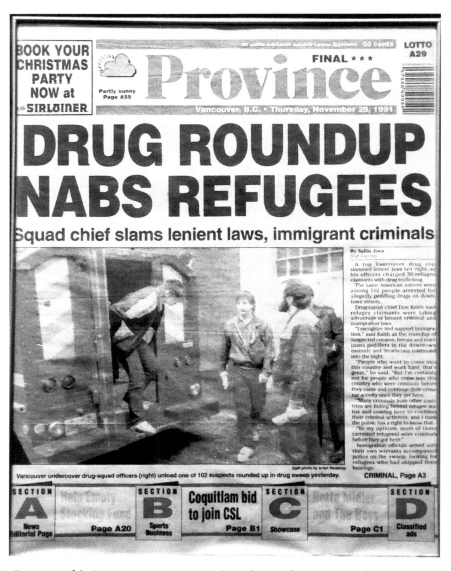

Front page of the Province Newspaper November 28th, 1991, featuring news of the drug dealer round-up arising from the long-term undercover project situated in Vancouver's drug-ridden Downtown East Side (DTES). I'm in foreground as an arrestee emerges from the police wagon.

I'm immersed in a dense grow op, taken down thanks to the suspect's jilted girlfriend and her call to Crime Stoppers cementing an end to the abusive relationship.

My Drug Squad cohorts. Me second from the right.

My colleagues and I amid the industrial-sized grow op operated by the Russians.
It was from this building that Alexander and Eugene Alekseev were tailed
by Rob and I, eventually arresting Alexander several blocks later.

Me working in the DTES as a bike patrol officer on a rainy
evening in the late 1990s. Photo credit Al Arsenault.

Members of the VPD's bike patrol taking a break on my front
lawn during a full-day of endurance training.

Outside the VPD's Granville Street community office. It was here that I met the young
man that had been causing havoc at the HMV store several weeks before due to a
mental illness. Now stable, the young man apologized to me for his outrageous conduct
and expressed appreciation for being treated respectfully during his psychosis.

Members of the VPD bike patrol on-stage for the presentation of the
1997 Vancouver Tourism Award. I'm fourth from the left.

Thanks to the clandestine efforts of my bike team, I rode out of the hotel on my festively decorated police bike following the Vancouver Tourism Award Banquet.

Colleagues and I escorting singer, entertainer, dancer,
Mitzi Gaynor during her visit to Vancouver.

Here we are on-stage during the Mitzi Gaynor show, in which she briefly interviewed each bike member. I'm third from the left. (Note – the picture depicts the emcee, not Mitzi.)

Cst. Glynis Griffiths and I on police bikes on Robson Street in downtown Vancouver, late 1990s.

Patrol officer Cst. Bruce Rhode and I apprehend a male attempting to immolate himself while wrapped in a Canadian flag to protest Canada's immigration policies.

Members of the VPD bike team on a crisp morning in downtown Vancouver. Me in dark jacket.

Receiving a generous donation of $5,000 from Jacqui Cohen, president of the *Face the World Foundation,* in support of youth outreach programs operating out of the Granville community police office. Singer, entertainer, Tom Jones standing next to Jacqui with his arm around her.

Cst. Jamie Munroe and I meeting with members of the Vancouver Ambassadors program operated by the Downtown Vancouver Business Improvement Association.

Promoted to a superintendent commanding the VPD's Investigation Division.

Me as an inspector attending my son's elementary school to chat with the kids while bringing along a supply of police shirts for them to wear.

Wolds colliding. My brother John (wearing green vest) confronting Black Block protestors that were rioting and causing damage during a protest march opposing the 2010 Winter Olympics. CBC TV interviewed Chief Chu regarding a slow police response to the rioting on the other half of the split screen.

John picking up a paper box toppled by the Black Block while Chief Chu answers questions posed by a CBC reporter during the split-screen reporting.

Me with classmates Chief Chu and Cst. Al Arsenault
enjoying a laugh together at a social event.

In my inspector's dress uniform showing-off
my tiny "pipes." Photo credit Al Arsenault.

VPD's Honda-supplied anti-street-racing sports car. The P.A.C.E.R. Program (Police and Community Educating Racers) discouraged street racing by encouraging drivers to join autocross clubs and compete in sanctioned time trials. The P.A.C.E.R. car was a quick one on the autocross course, and it generated plenty of earnest discussion with young folks about road safety. I brought this program to the VPD through my connections with Honda Canada.

At the wheel of the 1947 Mercury police car after dropping off Leslie Nielsen and company at their hotel following a tour of the city.

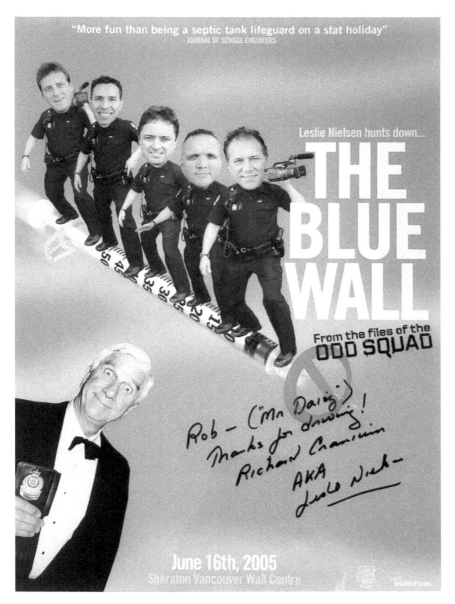

The signed poster I received from Leslie Nielsen: "Rob, ("Mr. Daisy")
Thanks for driving! Richard Cranium AKA Leslie Nielsen."

Youth touring the DTES with the Odd Squad's *On Track* program. Me next to cameraman.

Former biker Joe Calendino leading a session with vulnerable
youth. The slides depicting Joe's spiral downward.

Chief Jamie Graham with H.A.D. (Bert) Oliver Q.C. at a VPD Mess dinner
where Bert and I reconnected many years after a fierce cross examination.

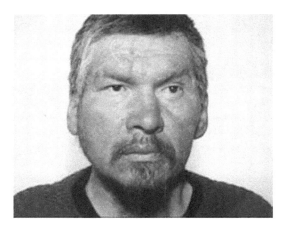

Mr. Frank Paul, the man with two first names, whose tragic life of neglect left a legacy
in the form of British Columbia's Independent Investigations Office. Thereby removing
from the police, the role of investigating incidents of serious injury or death in which
police actions, or inactions, may have played a contributing role. Photo credit CBC.ca

With a couple of engineering colleagues checking out the flying bridge on the
R.G. McBeath police boat. One of the perks of being the fleet manager.

John Rothwell, to whom this book is dedicated,
and his lovely wife Diane on a better day.

127

My final automotive review. The hedonistic, twin-turbo V12-powered Rolls Royce Wraith in black. Nothing like going out in style...and speed.

28

GOING FOR SMOKES, BACK SOON

THAT'S WHAT HE TOLD HIS GIRLFRIEND AS HE DEPARTED THE small suite rented by her. Susan lived in a modest basement suite in a corner house in an upscale neighbourhood of Vancouver. She was the timid sort, so when the property owners who resided upstairs asked her to look after the place for the weekend while they were away, she had her boyfriend Brad stay with her. It was a relaxing Saturday night. After watching a movie together, Brad announced that he had to get smokes at the local 7-Eleven, and he left Susan alone.

Not more than a few minutes later, Susan heard footsteps upstairs. She was freaked out. No one should have been up there, and of course, as luck would have it, Brad wasn't there to comfort her as she called 911 to report a possible break-in. The communications centre held Susan on the phone while the police were en-route. This provided her with a sense of safety and reassurance but also allowed the responding police units to be updated in real time. The footsteps continued to be heard, so it seemed clear that someone had broken into the main-floor residence.

It was a dry, pleasant evening as I raced silently to the call, hoping not to alert the suspect to my arrival. I parked several houses to the east and approached quickly on foot. It was about eleven p.m., and the neighbourhood was quiet. I was the first officer on-scene that busy evening. I positioned myself along the west side of the house, which gave me an unobstructed view of the west-facing second-floor windows, including the dining-room window. Through that window, I clearly saw the suspect looking through cabinets with the use of a flashlight. He had a black balaclava pulled over his head. I updated the responding units, which assisted in containing the house while we awaited the arrival of a police dog.

There's no sense in moving in too early and risk losing the suspect. Plus, the presence of a snarling, white-fanged shepherd generally encourages a surrender rather than "fight or flight." With the house contained, I knocked on the basement door and entered the suite to obtain a key to the upstairs from Susan. She was frantic. "I wish my boyfriend was here," she lamented between sobs. I met the dog handler and passed him the key to open the front door.

"Vancouver Police! Show yourself," the dog-man ordered while restraining his raging K9. Suddenly, a loud smash of glass breaking was heard from the east side of the house. Then a struggle as the officer containing that side of the property grappled with the suspect. There was yelling, barking, and commands to cooperate being shouted; it was a chaotic, violent arrest. The suspect had jumped through the glass window and down about three metres to the ground. He had no intention of giving up, for which he had good reason.

Once the crook had been safely secured in the waiting prisoner van, my thoughts turned to Susan. I worried about how panicked she would be hearing all the commotion outside her basement window. She was literally shaking with fear and shock as she sat on the couch. I tried to comfort Susan by letting her know that the suspect was in custody and on his way to jail. She had performed admirably by calling the police and staying on the line to provide a play-by-play of what she heard from upstairs. I was hoping her boyfriend would be home soon to take over, and then it hit me, and it likely just hit you as well.

"What's your boyfriend's name?" I asked.

I stepped outside and returned a moment later with news, bad news.

"Susan," I said, "the guy we arrested is your boyfriend."

"There must be a mistake!" she madly protested. "He's at the 7-Eleven getting cigarettes." But I could hear the reality begin to set in as her voice tapered off.

"I think you need to phone a friend, Susan, that can sit with you tonight while you process what happened." I left Susan's suite and headed to the jail to interview Brad. He was in his early twenties, long and lean, as most young construction workers are. He was fortunate to have had such a caring girlfriend, which he knew was now over.

Brad confirmed for me that, knowing that the occupants were away for the weekend, he had concocted the story about heading out for smokes to buy him the time needed to break into the upper residence. He hadn't counted on Susan being so diligent in her role as part-time caretaker. I asked him why he wore a balaclava over his face during the break-in. He said that he didn't want the neighbours to recognize him.

I charged Brad with break and enter and wondered how the court case would unfold with Susan being the primary witness. Because they weren't married, or living common-law, she would be a compellable witness for the Crown, whereas if they had been married, she wouldn't be. But Brad did the last honourable thing he could and pled guilty, saving Susan from testifying about being duped by "B&E Brad." Hopefully, she found a non-smoker she could trust to share her life with.

While Brad's plan was deeply flawed, some opportunists operate at their own peril without a plan.

CRIME DROPS IN

THE FORMER BRITISH COLUMBIA FILM CLASSIFICATION OFFICE
was located in a single-level commercial building in the Mount Pleasant area
of Vancouver. Prior to 2007, it would screen all new movie entertainment and
assign classification ratings, such as: General, Parental Guidance Advised, Over
14 years, Over 18 years, Restricted, and Adult.

It was well into the wee hours of the morning when a silent alarm was triggered in the building. I responded in my patrol car, parking close by and walking
to the address in question. Although it was a single-story building it was fairly
tall, thanks to an attic, which pushed the height of the roof to something more
in line with a two-story building. Work had been taking place during the day
to install new roof-top air-conditioning units. The techs had left a tall ladder in
place at the side of the building, which gave access to the roof.

A young opportunist by the name of Billy had been prowling the neighbourhood, hoping to make a quick buck through crime. He spotted the ladder and
up he went. Instead of enjoying the expansive view of city lights, he discovered
that the workers had not yet fastened an air-conditioning unit to the ventilation shaft upon which it sat. Billy managed to shove the AC unit off of the
shaft without the need for tools. The exposed shaft was approximately eighteen
inches square, wide enough, thought Billy, that he could lower himself into
the building like a character from a James Bond movie. Without a flashlight to
examine the shaft's routing, he jumped in feet first.

I arrived on-scene five or so minutes after the silent alarm had been triggered. It was a busy night, and I was the only car available. While checking the perimeter of the building, which was all intact, I could have sworn that I heard a faint voice in the distance calling for help. I was having difficulty localizing the muffled pleas. Were they emanating from a neighbouring building, or perhaps a car in the area? I had no idea. Eventually, I climbed the ladder to check the roof. The cries for help became louder but remained weirdly muffled. Once on the roof, my flashlight picked up the displaced AC unit and the open shaft. I headed that way, noticing that the voice was becoming stronger. Shining my light down the shaft, I saw the top of Billy's head about six-feet below. His arms were extended above his head. He was clearly stuck.

Billy had failed to realize that the shaft made a ninety-degree bend, enabling it to run parallel to the ceiling inside the BC Film Classification office. He was fine for the moment. He told me that he could breathe and wasn't hurt.

How to get him out? I mused. I decided that it was time to wake-up the Vancouver Fire and Rescue Service from their slumber.

Once they arrived, even they were perplexed for a few minutes. Do we force our way into the building and deconstruct the ventilation system? Can we lower ropes and a sling? A plan was formulated. The firefighters would attempt to haul Billy up the shaft with ropes. After a few bouts of trial and error, Billy's ascent to short-lived freedom was in progress. Once extracted from the shaft and checked over for injuries, his freedom was again constrained, this time by metal handcuffs.

Arresting Billy was easy. It's not often that a crook calls out for help from the police mid-crime. More challenging are those cases in which the hairs on the back of your neck guide your investigative actions.

COP INTUITION NETS A KILLER

I ARRESTED A COLD-BLOODED, VIOLENT MURDERER FOR BEING drunk shortly after he viciously beat an elderly man to death. "How does that make sense?" I hear you asking. It was the early nineties in Vancouver's Shaughnessy neighbourhood, home to the city's elite. A retired, widowed physician had just been brutally murdered in his home. It was too early in the investigation to know anything about the suspect, other than that he had departed the residence a short time prior to my encounter with the noted drunk.

I was patrolling slowly in the area, looking for any sort of clue or sign of a suspect in the murder. There was not yet a suspect description to guide the responding officers. As I cruised not more than two blocks from the doctor's home, I saw a somewhat inebriated male clumsily making his way along the sidewalk. He didn't know I was there. I watched him for a bit to get a further sense of his purpose in the area. This guy was rough looking, like he had a history of hard living and drinking to forget. He was scruffy, shabbily dressed, unshaven, and totally out of sync with the residents typical of the neighbourhood. I knew that he didn't belong but had little other than his drunkenness to use as a wedge for further investigation. It was a warm summer's evening when I pulled up close to him and got out of my marked Ford Police Interceptor.

I wasn't sure how the suspicious character would react to my presence. I was in uniform, so there could be little doubt in his mind that I was a cop and obviously suspicious of him. Would he fight? Did he have weapons? I made the approach. Despite being clearly intoxicated, he played it cool. He acted somewhat dazed and confused, claiming that he didn't know where he was or how he got there. Call it "cop intuition," but I knew there was more to his story, and that I couldn't just let him depart. Though I had no articulable evidence to support it, my senses were telling me with crystal clarity that he had been involved in the homicide. At this point, there still wasn't a suspect description to go on, as the homicide was no more than forty minutes old, and there were no witnesses of value.

The symptoms of drunkenness that the suspect exhibited, combined with his real or manufactured disorientation, supplied me with the legal grounds to arrest him for being in a state of intoxication in a public place. Generally referred to by cops as "SIPP," for short, this power of arrest isn't a criminal charge. However, it does authorize the police to take into custody an individual that is unable to care for themselves due to intoxication. In layman's terms, it's a trip to the drunk tank to sleep it off. I handcuffed my suspect and called for a prisoner wagon to transport the male to jail. At least this would give us an opportunity to verify his identity and either clear him as a suspect or investigate further. The arrest got really interesting when I was helping the subject into the rear compartment of the prisoner wagon (once colloquially referred to as Paddy wagons, but this terminology was deemed derogatory to folks of Irish decent—go figure).

While loading our suspect, I noticed a thick, gold ring on the baby finger of his right hand. I thought to myself, where did this character get such a nice ring? If you just guessed that it came from the murdered doctor, congratulate yourself. That's exactly where he'd obtained it from, and it was the lynchpin to the charge of murder, and his eventual conviction.

During the ensuing court proceedings, I gave evidence on my actions and observations from that night. When defence counsel asked if I had provided the accused with his "Charter of Rights" warning for murder, I said "No." That set off a few fireworks until I explained that I had arrested the suspect for being intoxicated, which is not a criminal offence to which a charter warning was required. At the time of his arrest, I had no meaningful evidence other than cop intuition to even consider arresting the suspect for murder. If I had done so with insufficient grounds, I could have jeopardized the entire case. Yet, arresting him for being drunk in public was a lawful action that was uncontested by the defence. I suspect it went uncontested because defence counsel didn't want to preclude the use of "drunkenness" as a defence to murder; however, the trial didn't play out that way. In the end, the suspect was convicted of second-degree murder.

It was very sad to see the life of a retired physician so brutally cut short. After all of the patients he'd treated and all of the lives he had likely saved, it was nothing short of cruel for him to be violently deprived of the retirement he'd so justly earned. You could say he was an angel, but not the motorcycle-riding type that roars into my next story.

FROM HELLS ANGEL TO TRUE ANGEL

I GRADUATED FROM EAST VANCOUVER'S TEMPLETON HIGH School in 1976. It was a tough school of 2,400 students, some of whom were simply warehoused from nine a.m. to three p.m., but there were many who prospered academically, beating the odds that defined the East End.

I returned to the school seven years later as its police liaison officer. One of those not prospering when I returned was a scrappy, young Italian kid named Joe Calendino. Fearless Joe had an attitude as big as a Buick and a chip on his shoulder, just as heavy, that darkened his world. Despite his oft-misplaced bravado and penchant for fisticuffs, there was something exceptionally likable and honest about this iconic East End rounder. That "something" was respect. Joe respected authority, which I suspect was drilled into him by his traditional Italian father. As a cop in uniform, I was a target for those wanting to publicly display their disdain for authority while bolstering their "tough guy" image among peers. But that wasn't Joe. He always responded to me respectfully and without animosity. Don't get me wrong; we weren't friends, and though he was respectful, he didn't drop by to chat (which in hindsight, I wish he had). Joe was often in trouble for his bullying and disruptive behaviour, yet underneath his veneer of "tough guy," he was a kid trying to find his way in a world that didn't warmly embrace him.

I recall speaking with a grade twelve class, answering their questions about law enforcement, the typical "what if" questions that teens like to pose with an air of defiance. Near the end, Joe's hand shot up. He was slumped in his seat near the back of the class, emphasizing the importance of his question with several grunts and "Sir... Sir..." to ensure that I would see him and respond.

"Yes, Joe, what do you have?"

I'll paraphrase Joe's question as best I can:

JC: Sir, like are the cops allowed to hit a teenager?

RR: Good question, Joe. What happened?

JC: The cops had me in the back of their car, and I was mouthing off pretty good. Then the cop in the passenger seat turned around and smacked me across the face, not that there's anything wrong with that; I deserved it. But I just want to know, is he allowed to do that?

Of course, the room lit up with stifled giggles and laughter, including Joe's. But that little exchange gave me unfiltered insight into his character. Sadly, he believed that he deserved to be hit, and that there wasn't anything wrong with it. That defining moment stuck with me long after Joe was eventually transferred out of the school due to his combativeness.

Years passed, and we both moved on with our lives with very little expectation of our paths crossing in any meaningful way again, but we (or at least I) were very wrong.

I'd occasionally read Joe's name in a police report over the next few years, usually as a suspect in an assault, or as a "hang-around" with the Hells Angels. It wasn't long after that Joe found himself a full-patch member of the Hells Angels Nomad Chapter. Tough as nails, Joe was clearly an enforcer for the gang, among his other illegal HA-related activities. One of his high-profile assaults was captured on the surveillance system of a casino in Kelowna, British Columbia, resulting in criminal charges against Joe and a lot of bad press for the HA club. The Angels despise bad press and are intolerant of drug use by their members, both of which Joe was now guilty of. Joe's chosen lifestyle and destiny didn't surprise me, though it did disappoint.

As the inspector in-charge of the Criminal Intelligence Section (CIS) 2000-2003, I sat on the National Outlaw Biker Committee, which met regularly to share intelligence on biker criminality and formulate coordinated national enforcement strategies. Within my CIS office, I had two detectives assigned to outlaw-biker intelligence gathering and enforcement. Detective Larry Butler knew motorcycles. In fact, he enjoyed racing them. He was a smart, congenial detective who knew his way around covert operations and the field of intelligence gathering. Larry's partner was Detective Kevin Torvik. Young, with movie-star good looks, Kevin had actually been a student at Templeton High School when I was the liaison officer and Joe was the problem child. It was a near-unbelievable twist of fate that would later have both Kevin and me working to put bikers, including Joe, in jail.

Around the time of the assault committed by Joe in the Kelowna Casino, it became apparent to us that Joe had become addicted to drugs and that his life as a potent member of Canada's notorious biker gang was falling apart, as was his social life and family life. Joe would soon be hitting rock bottom, strung-out on crack and mired in the despair and filth of Canada's epicenter of addiction: Vancouver's Downtown Eastside. Over the few short years that marked Joe's decline, Kevin had always tried to reach out with the goal of extricating Joe from his gang lifestyle and addiction. The approaches of Kevin, Joe's "one-time school buddy," were firmly rebuffed by Joe, until Joe was near death in a hospital bed. His addiction had literally pulled him into the gutter.

Joe's life had been surrendered to the chemical cocktails that were making his former brothers-in-arms rich. The next step for him was certain death. In jail for selling crack to an undercover cop, Joe was visited by Detective Kevin Torvik, who brought him a burger and fries, knowing that Joe would be hungry and thin as a rail. Joe's rapidly declining health had replaced his muscular frame with shocking frailty, leaving him gaunt, looking like a corpse warmed over. The bikers whom he had served with loyalty had long abandoned him, stripping him of his membership and misplaced self-worth.

Kevin managed to get through to Joe, touching a nerve that still held a kernel of respect for authority. Deep within Joe was repentance. His choices had left a trail of destruction—a trail that was now destroying him. He swore to Kevin that, if he survived, he would commit himself to a life of helping others, youth in particular.

Sure, thought Kevin cynically, yet there was sincerity in Joe's weakened delivery that gave Kevin hope. If Joe beat the odds of addiction and severed himself from criminality, Kevin would be there to support him all the way.

Detectives Torvik and Butler briefed me on Joe's condition and his desire to help prevent young men and women from falling into a life of gangs and addiction.

"We want to support him," they insisted. Despite my concern that Joe could relapse and bring discredit to the police department, and any program he might be connected with, I cautiously gave the green light. It was my recollection of Joe as a troubled student at Templeton, who had always been respectful of my role, that underpinned my decision. I briefed the chief and the department's management team on the developments with Joe, and the fact that we wanted to engage with Joe in presenting his story to students in high school. Naturally, there were pockets of well-intended resistance within the VPD, believing "once a biker, always a biker" and that we should never align ourselves—past or present—with such a lawless element of society.

Despite the clarion calls for caution that emanated from within the VPD, those of us connecting with Joe wanted nothing more than for him to succeed in his mission to deter youth from making decisions that could lead to gang affiliation, criminality, and eventually jail or death. (It's a well-established decree that the only two ways out of gang life are jail and death.)

We were of the view that Joe's message to our youth was powerful, compelling, and that it must remain the singular objective for all of us embarking upon his meritorious journey. We believed that the value Joe brought in dissuading young members of society from falling for the lure and easy money of gangs and drugs held immeasurable untapped potential, which I emphasized during an interview with a reporter for the city's main newspaper. In doing so, I wanted to effectively message the Hells Angels, making it clear to them that Joe's exclusive focus was on his commitment to work with "youth at risk," and that his efforts were proving enormously beneficial to a broad cohort of youngsters headed down a darkened path. In fact, I'm not aware of any other similar program that has consistently delivered such hard-hitting, authentic messaging and generated the results that Joe has achieved through his Yo Bro and Yo Girl organizations, which grew out of his indomitable efforts to reach kids. Joe's ability to firmly connect with youth, especially troubled teens, is rooted in his unquestionable credibility. Joe isn't the typical preachy adult trying to tell the kids "the way it is." He's lived it, and barely survived. His delivery is direct, raw, and chilling. He pulls no punches, despite a history of delivering them.

As he vowed during his most somber moments, Joe has steadfastly pursued his goal of diverting young men and women from engaging in illicit drug use and all of the attendant risks, including violence and potential gang membership. Joe's life as a member of the Hells Angels and his drug addiction are chronicled in outstanding detail and accuracy in the book *To Hell and Back,* written by Joe and his former high school counsellor and educator Gary Little. (2017 L&C Press.)

I'm always touched when connecting with Joe. His energy is infectious and his commitment to his mission relentless. I'm incredibly proud of him for turning his life of "Hell" into a life of redemption. He has evolved from a Hells Angel to a true angel. The incorrigible scrapper of Templeton High School has turned out ok. Oh, and no, Joe, the police are not allowed to hit you for mouthing off. Even if you think deserved it, which you didn't.

The role of school liaison officers (SLO) has become highly topical of late, so I want to take a moment to share my insight, having spent three years as an SLO in an east-end high school. School liaison officers within the VPD must apply for the position and face a fairly intensive selection process to get there, the essence of which means that they want to work with young people and support them on many non-authoritative levels. The role of an SLO is not one of enforcement. These officers are not the school's private police force. In fact, I had that discussion day one with the principal of my assigned school. We both acknowledged and agreed that enforcement against students should optimally be the role of patrol officers in the area. That doesn't mean that a school liaison officer would abdicate their duties in any kind of emergent situation requiring intervention. In the worst-case scenario, think of an active shooter at a school. While we most associate these horrible events with our American neighbours, our schools are also vulnerable to life-threatening events, with or without a gun. (Being Canadian, we see knife attacks most frequently).

The argument against the presence of police officers in schools seems to focus on a small cohort of students that have expressed fear of the police in general, not the specific officer in their respective schools (as I understand the concern to be). Fear of the police is a problem, I agree. However, the "fear" isn't resolved or dealt with by removing the officers. Doing so only deepens the mistrust by driving a wedge between those who legitimately fear the police and the police who reach out to serve and protect all. It also denies the preponderance of students who benefit from the ear of an officer from that relationship. In my three-years of being an SLO, students confided in me concerns such as: being subject to incest at home, being sexually assaulted by a boyfriend, being bullied by other students, and being the victim of robbery by thugs in the area. These were reports that would not have come forward, and had remedies implemented, without the students trusting me—period.

Removing the police from high schools has left students vulnerable to gang recruitment in the very halls of the institutions dedicated to protecting them. Both male and female students get attracted by the lure of well-monied and powerful gangsters, especially if these kids have a dysfunctional home life. In a short time, they often become "owned" by the gang and have no means of extricating themselves. As examples of what happens, young girls may be forced into prostitution for the financial benefit of the gang, while young men will be forced to courier drugs. The VPD has documented youth as young as twelve couriering drugs for gangsters. With an SLO assigned to the school, the likelihood of gangsters recruiting at these vulnerable facilities is far less likely. The SLO can engage services such as the area patrol officers and Gang Squad members to apply enforcement against predators. In their zeal to be "woke," I have no doubt that the Vancouver School Board has rendered students less safe in their respective schools by terminating the SLO program. And in doing so, it has shortchanged students from many beneficial programs that were delivered by the SLOs and underwritten by the VPD. Wouldn't it be wiser to retain the school liaison program and have the officers reach out to those students who fear the police and work collaboratively to gain their trust? There may be many historical factors that feed into such fears, but there could also be occurrences in the lives of these students that our Youth Services Section could assist with. No one should live in fear, irrespective of the cause. We should feel safe and protected in our communities, and the police are an integral piece of that fundamental right. While the police are far from perfect, by working together, not against each other, we can remedy fear—be it fear of the police or others.

If I had not been a school liaison officer, I would never have known Joe as I did. Without the benefit of that history, I may have dismissed his claim of wanting to help youth-at-risk as meaningless hyperbole intended to get the cops off his back. Fortunately, that was not my assessment, and from it, immeasurable benefit has flowed. Thanks to Joe's immutable determination and courage, he survived his many dark days—days which made my darkest days seem bright by comparison. Nonetheless, there were days in which my sun failed to rise.

Chronicled next is one of those days.

THE DARKEST DAYS

CHIEF CONSTABLE JAMIE H. GRAHAM LED THE VANCOUVER Police Department from 2002 to 2007. Graham came to the VPD after thirty-four years of service in the RCMP, his last posting as chief superintendent of the Surrey Detachment in British Columbia. Prior to his appointment in 2002 as the VPD's new chief, I had never met Graham, a tall, imposing man, looking somewhat like an amalgam of Clint Eastwood in *Dirty Harry* and Christopher Lloyd, who played Jim Ignatowski in the sitcom *Taxi*. From my perspective at the time, Graham was an outsider, and I wondered how his RCMP culture would fit within a municipal police service. I knew that we'd have to work closely together, so it wouldn't be long before the question would be answered.

I was the inspector in-charge of our Internal Investigation Section (IIS), and by delegation, the department's discipline authority, which meant that the chief and I would be collaborating on police-misconduct files. Shortly after a formal introduction, I saw Chief Graham depart headquarters in an older Ford Taurus sedan that he had been temporarily assigned. I emailed him, writing, "Hey, Chief, you're really stylin' in that Taurus." I figured it would be good to test his sense of humour. He got a good laugh out of the email, and at that point, I knew it was all going to work out; however, the next day, the chasm between federal policing and municipal practices became abundantly clear.

I had popped by his seventh-floor-view office in the headquarters building to review a conduct complaint with him that may have had some serious under-tones. As a municipal police agency, all conduct complaints are investigated pursuant to regulatory legislation contained within the BC Police Act. Every step in this fairly complex process has to be followed precisely and within certain time limits. Documents are to be served and update reports submitted to the complainant and the Police Complaint Commissioner every thirty days.

Jamie listened intently to my brief explanation of the case at hand, then exercised his authority. "Bring him up here; I'll give him both barrels and send him home."

Whoa. "Not so fast, Chief," I stammered, and explained that, as municipal cops, we're subject to the arduous terms of the Police Act, and there are critical steps to execute beforehand. With that, I told him, I'd get the investigation rolling.

The BC Police Act was new to Chief Graham, but he caught on immediately. My investigative team and I met with him every Wednesday morning to update him on the files under investigation and seek his counsel and direction. He always remained cool-headed and could synthesize a barrage of information rapidly. There came a day, though, in which I thought his unruffled demeanour would vaporize.

I had received an early morning call from Tom Stamatakis, the president of the Vancouver Police Union. He asked me if I was sitting down. I knew this wasn't going to be good . . . and it turned into my darkest day as the inspector running the Internal Investigation Section.

The preceding evening, a newly recruited officer had been a peripheral part of something involving his teammates that he knew was corrupt and criminal in nature. The information I received had been bravely reported to the union by the rookie officer. The details shocked me. The allegations were that, on Granville Street in downtown Vancouver, six VPD officers had arrested three individuals who were believed to be persistent drug traffickers. These individuals were placed into a prisoner van and transported to an isolated area of Stanley Park, whereupon each of them was beaten to some degree by the officers, after which they were abandoned in the park. The so-called "purpose" of the beatings was to discourage the traffickers from conducting their illegal activities in Vancouver.

After extracting the details from Stamatakis, I attended Chief Graham's office to brief him. Having been the chief of the Vancouver Police Department for less than a year, a crisis of this magnitude was the last thing he needed.

Nonetheless, Chief Graham remained his cool-headed self as I rolled out what I knew of the incident so far and what my response plan would be. Graham agreed that the officers involved needed to be removed from duties immediately and placed on an administrative suspension while an investigation commenced. I knew that the group of officers, later dubbed the "Stanley Park Six" by the media, would be appearing that afternoon for the next shift in their rotation. As they showed up, I had two Internal Investigation investigators escort them to a boardroom. There I advised each of them of the allegations that were now under investigation and administratively suspended them from duty. They were escorted out of the building shortly after.

While I lived through many "less than bright and cheery" days during my term as the head of the Internal Investigation Section, this was by far the darkest. It was now all hands-on-deck as the detectives in the Internal Investigation office launched into the investigation, sparing no horsepower to uncover all possible evidence. A special prosecutor was assigned and eighteen criminal counts were eventually laid against the respondent officers. They all pled guilty, with a range of sentences handed down by the judge in criminal court. Following the criminal proceedings, a discipline hearing was convened by Chief Constable Graham in which he fired the two most aggressive officers implicated in the assaults while demoting the remainder and handing them each a lengthy suspension without pay.

This rendering, while somewhat controversial, has proven over time to have been just and correct. Chief Graham saw the true potential in the four young constables whose jobs he saved. All four continue to serve the citizens of Vancouver with distinction and pride. Their service records being exemplary and their personal and professional achievements being exceptional. I feel confident in saying that these events were a rare and isolated anomaly for the individuals involved and for the organization they serve. Nonetheless, all of us within the Internal Investigation Section were shaken and profoundly troubled by the evidence procured during the difficult investigation. We benefitted greatly throughout the ordeal from the steadfast and reassuring leadership of Chief Graham. There's no doubt that this event shook the organization to its core, and that we came out the other end stronger and more committed than ever to excellence and to exceeding the expectations of the pubic we serve. This sense of pride and professionalism, underpinned by integrity and accountability, was led and fostered by Chief Graham, and those ideals continue today as our guiding principles.

Perhaps Graham's strong leadership skills were inherited from his father, a colonel in the Canadian Army, or perhaps, they were they honed while living in New Delhi, or Quantico, Virginia. However he may have come by them, as chief, he knew how to inspire his organization and support the men and women, sworn officers and civilians, who did the heavy lifting 24/7.

I recall one early morning when a couple of patrol officers responded to a serious car crash. The chief, using his radio callsign of "Car One" attended the call. The scene was chaotic as morning commuters were lining up, unable to proceed safely through the intersection.

From "Car One" came a broadcast over the radio. It was Chief Graham, advising that he'd direct traffic in the intersection, freeing up the constables to complete their investigation. Word spread quickly through the patrol division that the chief had performed the thankless task of directing traffic at a messy collision. Some could hardly believe that the chief would undertake this belittling role on his way into work, but that was pure Graham. He was there to support his people, even if it meant directing traffic, so that the officers on scene could process the collision and get the road open ASAP.

Graham never missed an opportunity to connect with those in the organization, irrespective of their level of responsibility or prominence, always asking, "How's it going?" We learned a lot from Chief Graham. He was the right guy at the right time, building the VPD into a modern, forward-looking police agency that became a leading model for law enforcement globally.

After his role with the Vancouver Police Department, Graham spent five years as the chief of the Victoria Police Department on Vancouver Island. He later retired on the Island with his "main squeeze" (as he puts it with the glint in his eye of a teenager in love) Gail. He now spends much of his spare time restoring vintage Volvo P1800s. We remain in regular contact.

Not sure if this next event met the lofty threshold of the professionalism that Graham had established for the VPD, but it was innovative, creative, and wildly effective.

33

DRIVEN TO DISTRACTION

SOME DRUG DEALERS PREFER TO REMAIN IN THEIR FORTIFIED residences and let the customers come to them. So it was on West 4th Avenue in Vancouver when I was a member of the Drug Squad. Let's call our dealer "Bud," based on his primary commodity.

Bud resided in a suite on the third floor of a three-story walk-up. His presence as a drug dealer brought many undesirables into the building, prompting a series of resident complaints that were the catalyst to our enforcement action. He also lorded over the walk-up like some kind of evil genius, which served to intimidate the other tenants.

The main stairwell of the building led directly to the front door of Bud's suite, which was a rear-facing unit overlooking the laneway. In addition to being a drug dealer, Bud was a techie-freak, meaning that he knew how to wire-up the building in a manner that would give him the ability to monitor activity out front of his building and up the entire stairway to his front door. Video screens in his suite displayed the activity continuously, with motion sensors adding further security by activating alarms to alert Bud to friend or foe headed his way. I'd like to think that we fell into the friend category, but I knew better.

Getting to the drugs before Bud did would be the challenge of the evening. After making an undercover buy of drugs, we obtained a search warrant and then went for dinner in Chinatown to plan our approach over plates swimming in sauces with colour too vibrant to be real. Somehow, we had to create a distraction sufficient enough to redirect Bud's attention away from his TV-type

147

monitors, allowing our Emergency Response Team (ERT) to blow the fortified door off its hinges with the use of breaching rounds, sometimes called master keys. These are shotgun rounds specially designed to destroy door hinges without causing dangerous ricochets. As a frangible, the rounds immediately disperse into minute particles upon delivering a destructive impact, greatly reducing the risk of shrapnel-related injury or unintended damage.

Bud's suite featured a large, south-facing living-room window, giving him an unimpeded view of the laneway below. Clearly, we needed to draw him to the window and hold his attention long enough for the ERT gunners to take their pre-determined positions and blow the hinges into the ether. A number of "Scorsese-style" scenarios were discussed. The action had to be relentless, compelling, and loud enough to be heard. Fortunately, it would be all of that and more.

We met with a couple of uniformed patrol officers in the area and briefed them on their starring roles. The "hats," as uniformed cops are occasionally referred to disparagingly by detectives, would chase an undercover car down the lane behind Bud's building with full lights and siren active. The covert car would pull to a screeching halt directly in line with Bud's picture window. The two patrol officers would use their car's PA system to deliver loud verbal commands to the two scruffy drug cops in the covert car. They'd be directed to exit the vehicle and lay prone on the pavement. But to make the whole event more riveting from a spectator perspective, our scruffy "bad guys" would be less than quiet and respectful. Some expletives and upright fingers would keep the show entertaining for as long as needed.

The scenario played-out like a TV drama, with plenty of yelling and resistance from the drug cops acting as crooks. A spotter in the laneway watched for Bud's mug plastered in the window observing the showdown taking place below. At that moment, a green light was called and two ERT members rushed the stairs and blasted the door, one shooting the lower hinge and one shooting the upper. *Boom Boom* was heard in quick succession, followed by "Police, don't move." The plan was executed flawlessly. We were inside before Bud and his two guests could get their butts off the couch. As dynamic and intense as the entry was, those acting out the distraction had more fun and hilarity to enjoy than the rest of us. Despite all of the manufactured aggression and hostility, the distraction ended rather humorously when the hats and detectives bid each other adieu and simply climbed into their respective vehicles and drove away, leaving a number of bewildered spectators to rationalize what they had just witnessed.

With Bud having no opportunity to flush drugs or otherwise destroy evidence, the full scope of his criminal operation was documented and presented in court. The story of distraction was also told in court, where it played out like a Siskel and Ebert film review. Definitely two thumbs up!

While accessing Bud's suite as quickly as possible eliminated his ability to dispose of evidence, response times can literally be the difference between life and death, as we'll see next.

RESPONSE TIMES MATTER

I WANT TO PRESENT TWO SERIOUS INCIDENTS IN ORDER TO highlight the importance of response times. These events were remarkably similar in nature, though dramatically different in their outcomes. In both cases, a speedy police response may well have saved lives. The Vancouver Police Department takes response times seriously, reporting on them regularly and adopting strategies to shorten them.

It was six a.m. or so. I had just taken over as the dayshift duty officer from the nightshift duty officer. The duty officer in Vancouver is the on-street manager of police resources and all serious calls and incidents. While each of Vancouver's four patrol districts have supervisors on the road all day and all night, it's the duty officer that has overall command city-wide.

This particular Sunday morning turned out to be exceptionally busy. Many of the calls received early on Saturday and Sunday mornings emanate from incidents that have their origin in the events of Friday and Saturday nights. A good example is the drunken husband who stumbles in at five a.m., setting off a domestic dispute that escalates to violence. Whether such an event triggered this particular call, I don't know, but the radio broadcast said that a woman was being beaten with a hammer by her partner and that there was a three-year old child in the basement suite in which the family lived. Normally, a number of patrol units would be immediately available to attend a serious "in progress" call such as this; however, on this busy morning, there wasn't.

I was nearby and immediately started racing to the address in question. Anytime someone is being beaten with a weapon, the response must be of the highest priority. The next officer to respond on the police radio was Chief Constable Jamie Graham. Never one to shy away from a call, the chief was headed full-tilt to the address to cover me. Patrol units would also break away from other calls, but their arrival would be delayed. En-route to high-risk calls, cops must formulate a plan, which is exactly what was going through my mind. What would I do if I heard a woman and child screaming as if being beaten? The answer was clear. Boot the door in and do my best to confront and contain the suspect. The risk, though, which has to be factored-in, is the possibility of the offender taking a victim (in this case, his partner or child) hostage. That event would trigger a whole new dimension to the call, and likely result in hours of negotiation if successful and tragedy if not.

The house in question was on the east side of town, but in a fairly good part of a working-class neighbourhood. It was an older home sitting on a typical thirty-three-foot-wide city lot—not rundown by any stretch but not a well-cared for property. I quietly parked my unmarked patrol car a couple of houses away and ran to the property in question, locating myself next to a basement window between the subject house and the neighbouring house to the south. The basement curtains were closed, so I had no visuals to absorb. I listened and heard nothing. That was unusual. None of the yelling and thumping around that you'd expect. I quickly relocated to the rear basement door. Just as I was about to knock, I heard the sound of heavy footsteps approaching the door from within. I pulled my pistol, held it at the ready, and stepped back and to the side. I needed to move off the potential line of attack and gain additional reactionary distance. Just as I did, the door flung open.

The suspect exited the suite enveloped in an air of hostility. It was clear that he wasn't on his way to church that bright Sunday morning. I pointed my pistol at centre mass and forcefully ordered him to get on the ground. In these particular situations, a suspect must clearly understand that you mean business. There's no room for ambiguity. The suspect, a rough-looking character, thirty or so years of age, thought about it for a split second, then dropped to his knees. I can hardly describe the sense of relief I felt. Pulling the trigger, regardless of how justified, is a cop's worst nightmare. It typically sets in motion a litigious traumatic journey in which criticism, second-guessing, and rhetoric is espoused by self-declared experts pursuing anti-police agendas.

I held the suspect at gunpoint for a few moments until the chief ran around the corner, pistol in his hand, to assist me. With the chief providing cover, I holstered my weapon and engaged in contact, affecting the arrest and handcuffing the suspect. Though I hadn't been inside the suite to check on the victim and her daughter, based on the information relayed over the police radio, I had reasonable and probable grounds to believe that the suspect had committed a serious assault, thereby giving me the grounds to arrest him.

With things soon under control, I wasted no time entering the suite and assessing the need for medical treatment. Fortunately, neither mother nor her child had sustained any serious physical injuries, though I'm certain they were emotionally affected, especially the child. The suspect had used a large hammer to smash-up the suite, including dishes and the kitchen furniture. I doubt that there was much money in the kitty to replace the destroyed items and repair the damage. The patrol officers assigned to the case arrived and took over. Their investigation would lead to charges against the suspect and protection orders for the victim and her daughter. The Ministry of Families would be notified and engaged in formulating a safety plan, which would likely include relocation of the mother and daughter into a safe house, at least for the time-being.

It was clear that the suspect's actions had been mitigated by his knowledge that the police were on the way. Fortunately, he didn't count on us being there so soon, which enabled me to take him into custody before he could escape or return to cause more carnage in the future. And while this case turned out better than the initial information in the call would have suggested, it wasn't so in the next incident I want to review.

It was about four a.m. My partner and I were winding down our nightshift with a coffee at an all-night doughnut joint not far from the hammer call I just presented. Another two cops had joined us in the shop. (I guess the old cliché about cops and donuts has some validity.) We were chatting about the evening's events when a call came over the police radio reporting that a woman was being attacked with a knife in her home and that a child was also present. So much for winding down. That's the nature of the beast in policing. The transition from fatigue and drowsiness to panic and turmoil takes place in the blink of a weary eye. All four of us were now in hyper-mode as we raced to the scene in separate cruisers, lights flashing, sirens wailing.

The house was a higher-end property divided into three suites, which is often the case with large, majestic pre-war houses in parts of Vancouver that had been rezoned for greater density. Our victim occupied the main level, which had a set of stairs leading to a wide veranda and a large wooden front door. As we climbed from our cars, the suspect saw us arriving and smashed out a living-room window through which he accessed the veranda. He then leapt to the lawn below, got to his feet, and had just begun to hotfoot it when he was tackled by the two officers who had been with my partner and me at the donut shop. My partner and I ran up the front stairs and into the house through an unlocked front door.

Prone on her back on the hardwood floor of the living room was an immensely obese woman, clearly in shock and rapidly bleeding-out from multiple severe lacerations. She wore only a thin nightie, which had provided no protection against the implements used to stab and slice her. I want to be factual, not gratuitous, in describing the depth of her lacerations, some of which splayed open her abdomen, revealing a massive, thick layer of yellow, gelatin-like fat. Punctures and bone-depth gashes were located on her arms and thighs. My partner began addressing the wounds that were bleeding the heaviest. Fat doesn't bleed, so it was the arm and leg wounds that were of greatest concern. I knelt at the victim's shoulders and gently wiped her clammy forehead while speaking with her in an effort to reassure her and keep her from slipping into unconsciousness, but she was fading. By this point, other officers arrived and took the child, a girl, five years of age, into the kitchen to comfort her and remove her from the chaos. There's little doubt that she had witnessed the vicious attack on her mother. I told the victim that she had a beautiful daughter, which brought her back, and I truly believe gave her the strength to fight impending death due to the loss of blood.

"How old is she?" I asked. "What's her name?" I kept our victim focused on staying strong for the young girl while gently rubbing her forehead. I feared that she would slip away before the paramedics could arrive and start an IV and life-saving treatment.

Fortunately, our young mother survived the brutal attack, largely due to our rapid response time and the application of immediate aid. I have little doubt that the attacker would've killed his common-law spouse had we not arrived when we did. Upon searching the home, we found five knives and a blade from an electric hand mixer, all coated in dried blood, all of which had been used to attack our victim. I clearly recall a serrated steak knife that had been driven into her body with such force that the blade had a series of sharp bends in it, from striking bone, resembling a lightning bolt. Even at its very tip, the blade had a ninety-degree bend.

Information from the attending emergency physician was relayed to us. It was his opinion that our victim's obesity had saved her life by shielding critical organs from the plunge and slash of the weapons used to mercilessly attack her. Again, our rapid arrival likely prevented the certain death of our victim and possibly even her young daughter. The suspect, the victim's partner, would in all probability have continued the attack had he not seen our black-and-whites scream up to the front of the house or heard our approaching sirens.

So, yes. Response times matter.

I periodically think of this woman and wonder how she and her daughter are doing. As a cop, it's disconcerting how you suddenly find yourself so critically invested in someone's life, and then are just as suddenly gone when the next call comes in. The volume of calls in a city as diverse and layered as Vancouver seldom leaves time for meaningful follow-up. Maybe it's simply better to close the book on a case and keep moving forward. As much as any cop wants to make the world a better place, there's a limit to one's capacity for grief. What if she and her daughter were not doing well?

While it's clear that the police are duty-bound to deal with tragic, highly emotional incidents, there's also plenty of opportunity for fun and high-spirited antics. My days riding a police bicycle in Vancouver's gridlocked downtown was the ideal antithesis to the gut-wrenching side of policing.

POLICING BY PEDAL

WHO KNEW THAT RIDING A BIKE AS AN ADULT WOULD REQUIRE such intensive training followed by certification? But if you want to ride a police mountain bike in downtown Vancouver, such is the case. I was assigned as the sergeant in charge of the downtown bike unit from 1996-2000. Despite having been an avid cyclist for years, I learned a lot about bike control, maintenance, and rider physiology during the two-week training program.

After passing both a medical examination and a timed qualification ride, I was a student of the bicycle at thirty-eight years of age. "You need to walk before you can run," was the mantra repeated by the instructors as we practiced our slow-speed riding skills, which included a number of challenging exercises repeated over and over until perfected. One of these was a slow-speed race in which the last person across the finish line was the winner. Riders had to keep moving in the same direction (no track stands!) and could not put a foot down or have contact with a rider beside them. Winning a race by crossing the finish line last is counter-intuitive and was a little more difficult than expected.

With slow-speed skills under our spandex, riding down staircases and over obstacles was next, followed by emergency high-speed maneuvers and dismounts along with emergency braking. With our riding competency meeting the established benchmarks, we were off to the outdoor gun range to practice rapid dismounts followed immediately by a challenging session of shooting at various targets within prescribed time limits. To make things more realistic, riders had to sprint a kilometre of dirt road on their bikes before dismounting.

This maxed-out heart rates and breathing, making fine motor skills almost impossible to control with any degree of accuracy. The overarching goal of the gun range was to replicate reality in our training as much as possible. It's unlikely that a police officer would be relaxed and both mentally and physically prepared for a sudden gunfight on the street, and the gun range should be no different.

After passing the training and certification process, I was outfitted with police riding gear and given a slightly used "Rocky Mountain Stump Jumper" mountain bike as my patrol vehicle. This was the early days of mountain biking, prior to the popularization of bikes featuring dual suspension and hydraulic disc brakes. Over time, I felt exceptionally well-suited to the hardtail Rocky, spending many hours in its saddle wearing a uniform and packing a firearm. My role as the sergeant was to lead my team of bike patrollers, responding to calls with them, and as time permitted, taking calls of my own.

There's a vulnerability that comes with losing the security of two tons of steel and glass to protect one from the peril of downtown traffic. The absence of a patrol car also exposed us to the vagaries of Vancouver's weather, unpredictable as it is. Lastly, sitting atop a bicycle leaves an officer physically unprotected from those who may pose a threat to either the police or the public. I felt this in a most visceral manner the first time I headed to meet up with my teammates over the bridge that connects with Vancouver's busy downtown. I was riding alone, and as I mentioned during a radio interview later that day, "I felt naked," as though everyone was looking at me, and I had no clothes. This paranoia only lasted a short time before I learned to embrace the barrier-free openness between me and the entire world. It's this unimpeded contact with the police that is foundational to the success of the bike patrol program, and the public's love of it. Waving down a cop car in a time of need, or even to ask for directions, can be challenging at best in the busy downtown core, but call out to a bike cop, and you'll be heard.

Tourists were particularly enamoured with the program and often wanted their photos taken with us. In fact, in 1997 the Vancouver Police Bike Patrol Program won the Vancouver Tourism Award, which recognized the safety and security we brought to areas popular with tourists. This is not to mention the interaction we shared daily with curious travelers seeking lodging or a recommendation for a restaurant. The award was highly prestigious, normally going to a tourism-related business or non-government organization (NGO) that went the extra mile for tourists. I was notified ahead of time that we had won; however, it would be kept confidential until announced at a banquet planned around the presentation in a downtown hotel. I worked with the Vancouver Tourism folks to plan a dramatic arrival in which twenty bike officers in uniform would cycle into the darkened ballroom from each side of the large hall, riding to the stage with their red and blue lights flashing. The officers would then dismount their bikes and take to the stage in an orderly manner at which point the house lights would return.

The event went off without a hitch. The lights were lowered, allowing our bright-red and blue police lights to twinkle with maximum effect. The ballroom was full, and the guests taken by surprise with our arrival. I'm sure that no one expected the cops to show up! It created a different and unconventional award presentation, but one that definitely entertained the attendees. I accepted the award on behalf of the men and women who rode police bikes, engaging day after day with tourists and the public alike. While I was tied up with media interviews, my teammates decided to accessorize my bike with streamers, balloons, and other festive décor that had been used to set the mood in the ballroom. I had a good chuckle as I rode my way out of the hotel and onto the mean streets with my "party" bike.

One of my first days riding with my new team came to a crashing end. Robson Street is lined with high-end retailers with designer labels. The sidewalks are always busy with shoppers, some of whom choose to take their chances running across the busy street mid-block rather than walking to the corner. It was raining heavily this particular afternoon. I was riding with fellow officers Jamie and Glynis, both of whom are highly-skilled cyclists. We were riding single-file. I was the lead bike with Glynis and Jamie following close behind. We had a good clip going when three umbrella-carrying young women decided to make the mid-block dash. Their quick glimpse confirmed a break in car traffic but not bike traffic.

The three jutted out directly into my path. I braked hard. *Bam!* Glynis rear-ended me. *Bam!* Jamie rear-ended Glynis. It all happened in a heartbeat. None of us were hurt physically, though that couldn't be said about our individual and collective pride. With sidewalks full, our double-header was seen by many. Hopefully, what they also saw was our laughter as we waved arms and madly accused each other of causing the collision, just as you would expect to see from drivers when three cars collide at an intersection. It was really quite hilarious and emblematic of the fun we had working together, even when things went sideways.

Due to a not-so-harmless crash a couple of years later, we had to escort Glynis to the hospital to have road-rash treated, for which I felt a sense of blame.

Back on Robson Street again, a robbery had just occurred at the London Drugs. The suspect fled on foot. I was riding with Glynis. It's fair to say that Glynis is far more athletically coordinated than I am. This was not only evident on our police bikes but also on the ski hill, where she adeptly snow-boarded through densely treed descents that had me flailing like a fish out of water on my skis during our ski-club nights.

We saw the suspect. He ran east on Robson Street and turned north on Thurlow, which happens to be a one-way street running southbound.

The sidewalks were too crowded for our bikes, so Glynis and I stood on our pedals and headed north in a southbound lane of Thurlow, dodging cars as we went. We were closing in on the suspect when the handlebars of our bikes suddenly locked together as we rode parallel to each other, squeezing as far as possible to the left in order to minimize our exposure to oncoming traffic. Unfortunately, our bull-bar extensions met and became fused as one, meaning that neither of us had any real balance or ability to control our rides as we sped against traffic. I knew immediately that an unpleasant outcome was inevitable, and so did Glynis.

Probably due to my greater weight, I managed to remain upright as we tried to disconnect our entangled bars, but Glynis didn't. Before we could gently slow our bikes, the bars suddenly freed themselves, sending Glynis into an unavoidable meeting with the pavement. It was a warm summer day, so shorts and a short-sleeve jersey meant that plenty of unprotected flesh would suffer the wrath of the road as Glynis came to a tumbling halt on the asphalt. In hindsight, it was probably unwise to chase the suspect by cycling against the flow of traffic on a one-way street, but it hadn't looked busy when we'd started our perilous pursuit. Needless to say, the suspect made good his escape while we made good at the hospital.

I certainly felt bad for the pain that had befallen Glynis. It wasn't superior riding skill that kept me from being the individual who wouldn't survive the entanglement; it was simply mass— mine being greater than hers. Stretches of white gauze adorned Glynis's extremities as we departed the hospital, leaving me to wonder if I had unintentionally, and perhaps recklessly, jeopardized our safety by engaging in the dangerous pursuit. That said, I'm sure any cop would back me up on how difficult it is to break off from a pursuit, even if it's using a bike to chase a suspect fleeing on foot down a busy road against the flow of traffic.

"Dog with a bone," comes to mind.

When not responding to 9-1-1 calls, or patrolling a given area, police bikes are often dealing with protests and large-scale public-order events, the Celebration of Lights fireworks show being a good example of the latter. Fights and drunkenness were prevalent during the early days of the fireworks, which the cops often referred to as the "Celebration of Fights" for reasons quite obvious. Through public education and police "meet and greet" tactics, along with zero-tolerance for liquor, the fireworks have slowly evolved into the family event that they were always intended to be.

Police bicycles enable officers to immerse themselves in crowds yet move rapidly if need be. These same attributes are effective when dealing with major protests and public marches. I spent four years on a police bike dealing with a multitude of "anti-this" and "anti-that" groups, getting to know the players and those who always showed up irrespective of the cause. (A note of clarity: I don't include in these protest elements, non-violent protesters lawfully exercising their right to protest. Much social progress is attributable to the power of the people.) Their playbook was usually the same: agitate the public by blocking roads, occupying political offices, or damaging buildings and smashing windows of businesses that represent capitalism. These are all tried-and true tactics intended to compel police intervention. The only caveats to such strategies seemed to be these: Make sure that the media is present with cameras rolling to catch the action; if the police engage in arrests, don't assist law enforcement by voluntarily moving. Force them to take physical custody and be certain to scream in non-existent pain. The goal is always to portray the police as fascist bullies and agents of the capitalist state.

Once I fully understood the playbook, I adjusted our response, which at times became no response at all if there wasn't an imminent concern for public safety. Without the police, the media typically had little interest in attending and wouldn't be prepared to hang around awaiting a dramatic clip that wasn't forthcoming. This tactic didn't mean that we were abdicating our duty, only exercising it from around the corner where we could watch and observe but not be baited into a response. No cops, no media—nothing to gain. That point was driven home to me in 1997.

The University of British Columbia hosted the Asia-Pacific Economic Cooperation (APEC) Conference of 1997. Although the RCMP took the lead in policing the event, the Vancouver Police Bike Squad assisted, largely dealing with the multitude of protests that targeted world leaders in attendance from countries with questionable track records around human rights. The most deplorable of these was considered to be President Suharto of Indonesia. He became the flashpoint for protestors. Suharto was the leader they wanted to publicly send a loud, clear message to, and frankly, for good reason. Our role, however, was not that of judge or critic.

World leaders are Internationally Protected People (IPP). All host countries are required to provide IPPs with defined levels of security based upon a numerical threat rating. The highest level of security includes police-escorted motorcades. For safety reasons, these motorcades must keep moving. A stationary motorcade can expose an IPP to tremendous risk and trigger an international incident. On the afternoon in question, Suharto was scheduled to leave UBC in a police-escorted motorcade on his way to the airport. UBC sits at the westerly point of Metro Vancouver. It is surrounded by ocean, with only four main routes in and out of the campus.

The protestors were well organized. Their runners were gleaning intelligence on possible routes to be used by Suharto's motorcade. This information was being shared electronically with a large body of protestors that intended to stop the motorcade by sitting across the road and linking arms. I'm not sure what the plan included once the motorcade was halted, but it would definitely lead to chaos and worldwide news coverage. The intelligence-gatherers knew the building Suharto would be leaving from and the approximate time his motorcade would depart. What they really needed to know was the intended route.

Disinformation can be an effective tool to redirect the forces of your opponent. I imagine that disinformation in boundless forms has been used since the evolution of Homo sapiens to gain an upper hand against competitors. While we obviously weren't at war, the principle was relevant just the same. As a ploy, the police in charge of Suharto's security purposely let slip a fabricated motorcade route just as a decoy motorcade pulled up in front of the building from which Suharto would soon depart. A Suharto decoy got into the limo. The hook was set and bait taken.

The incorrect route was transmitted by the protest organizers, leading the larger group to quickly assemble at a critical juncture along the erroneous route. My bike team and I joined the protest group, adding credibility to the ruse. As the tension grew and the moment of departure neared, the protestors took to the roadway, sitting down and linking arms. They were determined to stop the motorcade and make their grievance loudly known. As planned, the media were there, cameras mounted on shoulders. This would be it: the final big showdown, in which APEC 97 would close, carrying the vociferous message of the protestors worldwide.

I had conversation with the protest organizers. They were hardened in their positions and not about to negotiate a truce of any sort. I listened to police communications and knew that the decoy motorcade was headed our way. I also knew that Suharto's real motorcade had discreetly departed from the rear of the building. Before reaching the road occupied by the protestors, the decoy motorcade broke off and returned to the university. I knew this, but the protestors didn't. With Suharto safely en-route to the airport, I wished the protestors a good night and told them that we were leaving.

"But you can't," replied an organizer.

"Sure we can," I assured him. A look of bewilderment came over the faces of the tightly linked protestors.

"But what about the motorcade and Suharto?"

"Gone," I said. "You missed him."

The protestors were confounded by the news of Suharto's discreet departure, and not entirely ready to believe it. Had they been duped? Or was I duping them with false news as a strategy to have them leave the area? They decided to wait it out a little longer to be sure. I sincerely encouraged them to pack up. I couldn't very well leave a group of protestors sitting in the middle of a road, even though it was a route closed to the public. In time, they realized that a motorcade was, in fact, not on its way to their Alamo. Puzzled and confused and without an audience to play to, the protestors' ranks grew incohesive and splintered. With no likelihood of arrests or news-worthy theatre, the press lost interest and departed, leaving an aimless group to ponder what had gone wrong. This outcome reaffirmed in my mind the notion that, without the police and media as integral participants, protests are largely neutered. I'd see these results many times over during my days on a police bike dealing with protests large and small.

While some might argue that the police violated the rights of the protestors by engaging in subterfuge, the strategy enabled Canada to meet its obligation to protect Suharto without the need to have the police physically confront a group of well-meaning protestors. Overall, I'd say that the actions of the police that afternoon were reasonable and proportionate when balanced against the unequivocal duty to protect internationally protected people. Reasonable and proportionate has long been the legal yardstick used to measure the appropriateness of a police response. While we may not like everyone we protect, Suharto a prime example, we are not empowered to pick and choose, nor should we ever be. Though I felt bad about the deception undertaken in the transport of Suharto, I was grateful for not having to employ the alternatives. These were idealistic university students sincerely offended by the decision to host individuals they viewed as murderous dictators on their campus, and I can't blame them.

While there exist many legitimate causes for protest, the police must balance the right of the protestors to voice their concerns with the right of the public to go about their business relatively unimpeded. This is a bit like marriage counseling, in which neither spouse is willing to compromise. Motorists fume when an intersection is taken over by protestors, and protestors are outraged when the police seek their removal.

The role of the police in these circumstances is that of public safety, i.e., everyone's safety. Generally, the police will try to work with protest leaders to develop a plan that will serve the needs of the protest group while also establishing an agreed-upon duration for contentious activity, which may be occupying a public building or taking over a roadway. When a protest group chooses to block a road, there are a number of variables that the police must consider before taking enforcement action. For example, can motorists be easily diverted around the blocked road without a great deal of aggravation or risk? Generally, within a city's network of roads, this can be accomplished. While it may be highly annoying to those affected, it's part of balancing the right to protest with the right to freedom of movement. As an aside, this balance is often applied outside of law enforcement, and to the detriment of "freedom to move" for quite legitimate non-protest reasons, such as when a city work crew digs up a street, as they are prone to do in the summer, or when roads are blocked for parades and public celebrations. But what about when the road being blocked by a protest group is a critical link with no viable alternative for the movement of traffic, including emergency vehicles? For example, blocking a bridge. In such circumstances, the police must act swiftly, in my opinion, to restore the freedom of movement due to the absence of suitable alternate routes.

There are other fundamentals that may demand immediate police action to remove a protest group. Taking over private property or subjecting the public to possible harm will force the hand of the police, requiring them to pursue enforcement action if a negotiated resolution is rejected by the protest group. Chaining the doors to an office tower housing an oil company or the US Consulate is an example of endangering the public and will trigger a firm police response. A well-used strategy of protest groups to frustrate the police in securing a negotiated resolution is to deny that the protest has any form of leadership, thereby circumventing any opportunity for discussion, negotiation, or accountability. Was it simply happenstance that so many people showed up at the same place and time with similar signs to protest the same perceived injustice? Highly doubtful.

Logistics, resources, and capability are additional variables which the police must weigh when determining appropriate responses to "take-over" tactics so often employed by rogue protests groups. If such a protest doesn't present any immediate danger to the public or protestors, the police may await the production of a court-imposed injunction, accompanied by an enforcement order, prior to taking any steps beyond negotiation to end an occupation. There's a delicate balance the police must strive for between enforcing the rule of law and accommodating, or in fact facilitating, protest, and to some degree civil disobedience.

The "reasonable and proportionate" test that I raised applies beyond the scope of policing protests, as it did when I fractured a suspect's wrist in a matter completely unrelated to protest. Before we get there, I want to wrap-up this chapter on "policing by pedal," with an anecdotal observation about cycling in the city by contrasting the difference I experienced between cycling in a police uniform and cycling in my own tattered gear.

On the police bike, motorists were remarkably obliging and courteous as I and the other bike cops stitched our way through downtown streets choked with cars, trucks, and buses. It made cycling vastly safer for us and far more enjoyable than when I would cycle home from work on my own bike, dressed in my unlaundered riding togs. In fact, I occasionally forgot that I was on my personal bike and immersed in the "kill, or be killed" arena that road-riding was before the emergence of cycle lanes and an increase in cycling's popularity. Despite the sudden loss of respect for my non-uniform presence, I continued to apply many of the same tactics when riding my own bike that we applied on police bikes to negotiate traffic. Probably the most basic of which was that of replacing traditional hand signals for left and right turns with a simple practice of pointing where you planned to go, using whatever arm corresponded with the direction of your turn. Trying to indicate a right turn with the use of a left arm is less than effective, and intended for use in cars. Point and shoot is what works on a bicycle, especially when combined with eye contact and receiving a nod or verification from a motorist to go ahead.

I would often wish that motorists treated every cyclist as if he or she were a bike cop. If so, the mean streets of Vancouver could be a far more tolerant and welcoming environment for cyclists. Of course, cyclists have a corresponding duty to operate in a safe, predictable, and lawful manner. Even so, collisions can be unavoidable as I discovered when a motorist ran a four-way stop while I was cycling home from work one afternoon. I entered the intersection on my bike when I saw the vehicle approaching on my right dip as the driver applied his brakes. I wasn't expecting him to be back on the throttle as I crossed his path. To my horror, he had performed the classic "taxi" stop in which a driver slows for a stop sign but jumps on the gas well before the vehicle is motionless. In doing so, the driver in this case was cognitively blind to the fact that I was mere feet from his front bumper. He had scanned for cars but failed to comprehend the presence of something in front of him that wasn't what he was looking for.

His bumper passed just ahead of my right shin and connected with the downtube of my road bike. It's often said that time slows down during a near-death experience. I clearly recall being pinned to the front of his massive Chrysler sedan and wondering when he was going to hit the brakes. I could hear his engine continue to accelerate prior to the driver reacting and stomping on his brakes. The latter action catapulting me into the intersection. I landed on my back and felt my head strike the roadway. Fortunately, I was an early adopter of helmets for both cycling and skiing. My hard-shell yellow lid kept my cranium intact, limiting my injuries to scattered bruising and a swollen knee. My bike didn't survive as well as, looking more like a pretzel. The young driver was shocked and apologetic. He was also kind enough to load my twisted Italian steed into his trunk and give me a ride home. At least I didn't have to take the bus and be subjected to the harassment that defines the next case.

WHAT WOULD YOUR MOTHER THINK?

STILL WORKING ON THE POLICE BIKES, MY PARTNER AND I responded to a bus that had an unruly passenger onboard. It was a fairly full bus, carrying shoppers and commuters home in the late afternoon. The subject in question was reportedly loud and obnoxious, using the "C" word to hatefully refer to women on the bus, and generally telling everyone to "fuck-off." He clearly frightened many of the passengers and exhibited aggression well beyond the scope that the bus driver was prepared to deal with.

We met the bus at one of its regular stops, where it awaited our arrival. After a quick chat with the driver, it was evident who the offender was and why the driver wanted him removed from the bus. I approached the suspect, who was seated alone. He was an older male, probably in his sixties. Despite his age, he was large, and there was no reason to believe he wasn't prepared to back-up his filthy mouth with physical violence. I asked him to leave the bus. He steadfastly refused. This obviously wasn't going to be an incident resolved with heartfelt negotiation. My partner and I pulled him up off the seat by his jacket, at which time I quickly applied an arm-lock to gain control of the resistive subject. The arm-lock uses pain compliance through the wrist as a come-along tactic. You walk with me as I ask, and there's no pain. You struggle and resist, the bent wrist will tighten and cause pain. This rudimentary but effective technique was taught in the police academy. I applied it often to combative subjects. It eliminates the eventual fight that otherwise is likely to erupt in such scenarios.

Even with the arm-lock properly applied, our senior pugilist was aggressively pushing back and trying to free himself in the narrow aisle of the bus. Clearly a fight here between the suspect and two cops would also endanger the passengers seated in the proximity. I applied greater pressure to the back of his hand, thereby increasing pressure on his wrist while telling him to stop fighting. With enough pressure, I managed to maintain control of the suspect and get him down the stairs of the rear door and off the bus. My partner and I were then able to handcuff the subject. At no point during our interaction with the senior scrapper did he complain of an injured wrist, though I doubt he wasn't feeling much pain in his heightened state of agitation. The fighter was taken to jail for breaching the peace, which empowers the police to securely hold someone in custody without criminal charges for a few hours until they regain their composure and can be safely released. That was the end of it for us, or so we thought.

The suspect filed a complaint with the Police Complaint Commissioner of British Columbia alleging that I broke his wrist in the altercation and that the police had no authority to remove him from the bus or use force against him. An investigation was launched. My partner and I wrote statements outlining the event and explaining our actions in response. The incident was fully investigated by the Internal Investigation Section of the Vancouver Police, which included interviewing the bus driver. The investigation found that our actions were justified, given the conduct of the suspect, and that the alleged fracture of a single tiny bone in the complainant's wrist was unfortunate but had occurred as a direct result of his resistive conduct.

The Office of the Police Complaint Commissioner (OPCC) is a body of the British Columbia legislature that performs civilian oversight of police investigation of complaints related to police conduct. The commissioner can order additional investigation in cases that he chooses. Alternatively, he can order a public hearing into events in which he opposes the findings of the police investigation. Our case was headed to a public hearing. This is a judicial proceeding replete with lawyers for the Office of the Police Complaint Commissioner, the complainant, and the respondent police officers (us). Based on evidence presented by the complainant, witnesses, and the respondent police officers, the accused officers can be found guilty of offences laid out in the BC Police Act's Code of Conduct. Penalties can range from written reprimands to suspensions without pay, and ultimately, dismissal.

While having one's actions in the "heat of the moment" scrutinized and analyzed *ad nauseum* is part of the job, it's never a pleasant experience. Such was the court case that would form the substance of our public hearing. As a respondent officer, one is essentially being put on trial, most often for actions believed at the time to be just and appropriate. Unlike a criminal trial, in which a conviction requires certainty "beyond a reasonable doubt," a finding against a police officer in a public hearing is based on a less rigorous yardstick known as the "balance of probabilities." This is a sliding scale; the higher the intended penalty, the higher the "balance of probabilities" threshold must be.

These hearings can become quite contentious, as ours did. The complainant, now portraying himself as an older, more dignified man, was either not being truthful or his memory was grossly failing him. I took the stand and began my evidence. Clearly at question wasn't so much the allegation that my arm-lock caused the fracture of a small bone in his wrist, but whether our actions that day were reasonable and proportionate to the circumstances.

A zealous lawyer representing the OPCC demanded to know on what basis I concluded that the complainant's conduct justified his removal from the bus. I shared the information provided to me by the bus driver, which included the threatening disposition of the complainant at the time and the profanity he had been directing at women on the bus. He then asked how I knew that the alleged conduct had offended anyone on the bus. I went on to say that I noted elderly women on the bus, not unlike my own mother. And while my mother had plenty of tolerance, having raised three rambunctious boys and two girls, I was using her as my guide. I felt that if she had been on the bus, she would have been frightened and offended; accordingly, went my reasoning, so would the other women on the bus irrespective of age.

Counsel for the OPCC went ballistic. Whether a theatrical ploy on his part to rattle me or a sincere reaction to my testimony I can't say. He bellowed in response, "This is not about your mother!" He angrily insisted that she wasn't there and had no part of this.

I agreed. She wasn't there. "But if you're asking me how I knew women on the bus were offended, that's how," I retorted, all the while thinking what absolute scum he was for admonishing me in the way he did. Of course, his berating of me only meant that I had obviously delivered an answer to his question that he wasn't anticipating and that undermined his courtroom strategy.

The adjudicator, a retired judge, was not swayed by the lawyer's combative cross examination of my evidence. He went on to find the actions of removing the hostile passenger from the bus was more than justified, and that no passenger on a bus should ever be subject to the verbal abuse that our suspect had delivered from his seat aboard the most public of conveyances. The force used to remove the suspect was found to be proportionate despite resulting in a minor injury to his wrist. Case closed. The findings of the public hearing effectively quashed the complainant's hope to sue for injury.

It was a long, difficult slog, but in the end, the actions of my partner and I were justified by a formal tribunal following a hearing that felt no less serious or intimidating than that of a criminal proceeding. I was truly grateful that justice had prevailed. And I know that my mother, though no longer with us, would agree.

The yardstick of "reasonable and proportionate" can also be used to measure inaction, which is what happened one afternoon during the 2010 Winter Olympics in Vancouver. The results of this thrust my oldest brother into the global media and put Chief Constable Chu on the defensive.

37

WORLDS COLLIDE ON AN
OLYMPIC SCALE

I HAVE TWO OLDER BROTHERS. THE ELDEST, JOHN (WHOM THIS book is dedicated to), passed away in 2019 following a brave and sustained battle with cancer. Saying that John had a fiery streak for what he viewed to be "just and fair" in this world would be like describing a category F-5 tornado as a gentle breeze. John wouldn't hesitate to jump into a fracas on behalf of the underdog. Soon after I became a police officer, he told me that if anyone were to come after me or cause me a problem, he'd take care of it. I know that his heart was in the right place. The pledge meant a lot to both of us, although I think we both knew that it was a little unrealistic. That said, his older brother role of "protector" knew no bounds.

It was February 13, 2010, the first day of competition for the 2010 Winter Olympics held in Vancouver, Canada. Protests had dogged the build-up to the Olympics despite the overwhelming support for the world-class event held by the preponderance of Canadians. Coinciding with day-one of competition was a protest march calling itself the Heart Attack March. The majority of protestors in the march wished to peacefully express their opposition to the games; however, their message was hijacked by a radical group of anarchists claiming to be part of a global anti-capitalist movement called the Black Bloc. These individuals dressed entirely in black. They masked their faces to conceal identities and carried knapsacks containing projectiles such as rocks, and balloons filled with red paint. The paint was intended to simulate blood when thrown against a business thought by the Black Bloc to represent capitalism, consumerism, or whatever "ism" they capriciously opposed at any given moment.

The Black Bloc element was approximately fifty or more strong. They led the march as it progressed north along Vancouver's Granville Street in the heart of the downtown shopping district. As the group approached Georgia Street, all hell broke loose. The Black Bloc thugs embarked upon acts of violence and destruction. They openly smashed store and bank windows, threw newspaper boxes into the middle of the road, and generally caused havoc, which frightened and intimidated law-abiding citizens enjoying the morning. There was, however, one law-abiding citizen that wasn't prepared to cower and allow the thugs to destroy a city that he loved and grew up in, and that was John.

The police at this point in the havoc were re-assembling after dealing with other similar squirmishes in the downtown core before assessing the latest threat and embarking upon a response. But from the perspective of the public amid the carnage, the police were failing to react with adequate speed and force. As a cop who has dealt with violent protests, I understand the need for a planned, measured response, and the desire to apply winning tactics rather than a provocative knee-jerk reaction. Still, it felt disconcerting to see the damage being inflicted upon our city and the fear it infused in our citizens.

John and his delightful wife, Diane, had been enjoying a lovely morning downtown, which was to include lunch and some Olympic-related festivities. Through happenstance, they found themselves at the epicenter of the chaos. That night, John appeared on every TV news report in Canada and around the world. Amid the violence and destruction wrought by the anarchists in black, John's fearless sense of self-justice kicked into overdrive. If the cops weren't going to fight the anti-capitalist mob of thugs, he was. With regional, national, and international press capturing every moment on video, John threw himself into the fray, pushing some of the Black Bloc agitators away from their targets of destruction. And at one defining moment, played over and over on the nightly news, John looked back and boldly motioned to the silent majority of cowering citizens doing their best to keep out of harm's way, saying, "C'mon, let's get them. Let's get them." John knew he couldn't turn the tide of destruction by himself, so why the hell weren't others jumping in to help?

While other citizens on the street may have been exercising greater caution, or common sense for that matter, I was proud of the fact that the person who had balls big enough to jump in on behalf of all of us who love this city was my brother John! Of course, John's "one-man battle against evil" made for a great TV news clip, but it also lit a firestorm of criticism against the police for what was being characterized as a lethargic, delayed response to the chaos. As a member of that very police agency, I almost blindly support its actions when criticized by the media and self-proclaimed armchair experts. Having thirty-plus years of policing experience to draw upon, I typically understand the issues and the dynamics that underpin complaints against the police, but this was different. This was personal, yet public on a global scale; this was worlds colliding in Olympic proportion, personal and professional, as I'll explain.

I was watching the CBC evening news the day after the Black Bloc attack on Granville Street. Under scrutiny by CBC was the lagging response of the Vancouver Police to the destructive actions of the anarchists. CBC was live-interviewing Chief Constable Jim Chu on the street, seeking from him some kind of explanation for what was seen as a partial policing failure. To emphasize this point, CBC used a split-screen approach, placing my brother John on one side of the screen and the chief on the other. While the chief spoke, John's "let's get them," segment was looped, playing over and over as contrast to the chief's comments. Seeing my brother juxtaposed with the chief on CBC's National News broadcast caused me more than a little concern. As a member of the department's executive committee, I met every morning with the executive officers, including Chief Chu, to review the events of the preceding evening. We'd strategize on how major cases would be handled to ensure that public safety was addressed first and foremost. Just how the next morning would play out in the chief's office after CBC's critique on the VPD's response to the Heart Attack March weighed on me.

Chances were, my brother's identity would become known. Heck, he'd played on the VPD's hockey team for a few years as a guest player, so many members of the department knew him. I wondered whether I should inform the chief and executive members or just let it slide and allow things to unfurl without my intervention. I knew that I wouldn't be held responsible for anything that my brother did or said that was ill-advised, yet there could be a shadow if it was presumed that his "heroic" actions impugned the reputation of the department in this event. In the end, I was proud of John's one-man war against anarchy and decided that I would speak up with pride, not humility, at the morning meeting. And that's exactly what I did, being careful not to exhibit criticism of the police members that had been in attendance when the Black Bloc riot broke out.

As I had hoped, the split-screen contradiction was, for the most part, laughed off by the chief and executive team with no lasting repercussions. Nonetheless, the surreal picture emblazoned in my mind of my brother John upstaging my boss, Chief Chu, on the national news will not soon fade.

38

TEA TODAY, INK TOMORROW

IT'S INEVITABLE THAT OVER THE COURSE OF A THIRTY-THREE-year policing career, things will occasionally hit close to home, such as finger-printing your mom's dearest friend.

I'm not judgmental, at least I try not to be—how successful I am is debat-able. Nonetheless, I understand that good people sometimes do bad things. There may be deeply hidden issues acting as a catalyst to behaviour incongruent with one's values and beliefs, which I'm certain applies here. Until now, this story has never passed my lips out of respect for the person involved. You'll understand why.

I was a young cop, and as all young cops in the department were required to do in the era, I was serving my six months of inside time by working in the city jail. Although the jail was staffed by full-time jail personnel, regular patrol officers were assigned six-month stints to augment the resources needed to properly run the jail, which served as a pre-court holding facility. My preferred position during my term inside was that of assistant jailer, which required me to photograph and fingerprint subjects charged with criminal offences. The printing and photography work were both done the "old way." The camera was a 35mm SLR mounted upon a tripod. The offender stood behind a signboard bearing the relevant details applied with magnetic numbers and letters. After the Kodachrome moment, the officer would use a small roller to apply a thin layer of black viscous ink onto a flat block mounted on the counter.

The officer then rolled the tip of each of the offender's fingers, one at a time, onto the ink block. The trick was to obtain a consistent layer of ink on the ridges of the fingertips without the ink seeping into the valley between the ridges. Getting it perfect was a bit of an art form, especially when your client was not a team player. Some prisoners strongly objected to being fingerprinted, knowing that doing so would eventually reveal their true identity had they chosen to lie about their name. It might also bring to light any number of outstanding warrants for arrest that the subject was hoping against odds to avoid.

The explanation I most often delivered in persuading the less agreeable to cooperate was this: "You can only be released from jail by the court, and you can't *go* to court, until you've been fingerprinted, so let me know when you would like to be fingerprinted." This ultimatum, while no longer lawful, was generally fast-acting, though some hardened cases would play the long game. Eventually though, the daily slice of baloney on white bread became more torturous than anything the court could impose, thus making the option to be printed and photographed far more palatable.

In addition to fingerprinting and photographing those lodged in jail, due to the severity of their criminal charges or the need for court-imposed release conditions, I spent a couple of hours per day photographing and fingerprinting subjects that had been released from custody prior to being transported to jail. These were individuals accused of less serious crimes who had agreed to attend the police station for fingerprints on a specified date followed by a court appearance several days later. They were issued a document referred to as an Appearance Notice, which contained instructions outlining the criminal charge and the dates for fingerprinting and a first appearance in court. Appearance Notices (mockingly referred to by some officers as Disappearance Notices, based on the rate on non-compliance) were largely issued to shoplifters who had been arrested by store security. If the attending officer in such a case was satisfied that the offender met the provisions of the Bail Reform Act, the subject could be released at the scene to be dealt with later. This legal arrangement eliminated the need to incarcerate low-level offenders, thus allowing such individuals to remain free, provided they made the necessary appearances.

Candidates for Appearance Notice fingerprinting and photographing represented every social stratum, income level, and demographic of the Canadian population: male and female, young and old, rich and poor. They were most often contributing members of the community that had—for reasons many and varied—lost their moral compass for a phase. One emotion most shared when I printed them was a deep sense of humiliation. I often felt bad for them, especially when it was apparent that they were going through a terribly difficult time in their lives and had (allegedly) committed a crime that was entirely out of character. But imagine the exponential increase in humiliation when you arrive for fingerprints and a photo only to discover that your best friend's son is the cop that will be inking and clicking.

She lived down the block from my parents, who were still living in the house that I and my four siblings grew up in. In her mid-fifties, Mrs. B. visited often, as neighbours in our corner of East Vancouver did. She and my mother shared pots of tea while also sharing many family tidbits and local gossip. It wasn't that long ago that Mrs. B. had been sitting at my parent's kitchen table when I had dropped over to the house. She had seemed pleased to see me then, and proud of my policing career. But on this less social and far more difficult meeting at the police station, Mrs. B. appeared bewildered and distraught, hurt and confused, and so very deeply ashamed. Not allowing anyone else in the waiting room to sense our connection, I called her into the printing room. Once in the privacy of the printing room, I told her that I wasn't judgmental and didn't think any differently of her than I had that afternoon in my parents' kitchen. Good people sometimes do things that are completely out of character, I told her. Why she had shoplifted, or what she had stolen, I didn't know, but I knew instinctively that this incident wasn't a reflection of who she was, and it most certainly wouldn't affect my respect for her. Most importantly, I assured her that I would never reveal any of this to my mother or others. I kept that promise through to the end of both of their lives, and I share the story now for the first time.

You might ask, "Why reveal this event?" I share it as an example of the confidentiality a police officer must be prepared to maintain, and of the likelihood that, as a cop, you'll encounter incidents and events that hit close to home. These may involve relatives, friends, or the kids of your friends and relatives. And possibly even matters concerning members of your own family. It's inevitable, but it's also critical that the confidentiality of such information be protected. I could cite other instances wherein I received information of a sensitive nature that I could not reveal. For example, I can't tell a friend or associate that their adult child was a victim of a sexual assault, or alternatively, is a suspect in a such an incident, despite the importance the information may hold for the parents, unless of course the parents retain formal guardianship of the adult. This usually applies when the progeny is developmentally still a child.

In BC, improper disclosure by a police officer is a serious breach of the Code of Conduct under the authority of the BC Police Act. It could also be a criminal offence. Dismissal from one's police agency and the potential for criminal charges are very real consequences for improper disclosure of police information. It's a serious breach, which could result in violence or death, if for example, leaked information threatened the safety of a confidential informant or an undercover police officer.

The Vancouver jail, where I held Mrs. B's trembling hand and rolled her fingers one-by-one in ink, may seem a throwback in such a modern city. Nonetheless, it serves a legal necessity and can be credited with helping keep the city safe for residents and tourists alike, who fill Vancouver's many parks and sidewalk cafes year-round.

But the jail's iron bars and slamming doors doesn't mean there's never any fun.

STICKIN' IT TO DUTY COUNSEL

EACH INDIVIDUAL CHARGED WITH A CRIMINAL OFFENCE AND locked-up in the city slammer is legally entitled to a visit from duty counsel prior to heading to court. Duty counsel is a legal-aid lawyer who represents each accused person during their initial appearance in court, if they do not have a lawyer of their own. Duty counsel is granted access to each prisoner in advance of court, in order to acquaint themselves with the circumstances of the respective cases. To do this, duty counsel will attend the city jail daily and set up at a table in a small room. Jail personnel will escort prisoners to and from the room for their private meetings with duty counsel.

The entrance to the duty counsel room was partway down a hall that extended from the booking counter to the cells. Counter staff had a clear view of the hall, including the wall phone used by prisoners to contact specific lawyers. The proximity of the duty counsel room also enabled a quick police response should a prisoner take a dislike to the lawyer *du jour*. The lawyer performing the role of duty counsel rotated fairly often, giving opportunity to pull a few quick pranks on a newbie. One of the favourites, and I suspect the most juvenile, was to glue a one or two-dollar coin to the floor just in front of the door into the counsel room. Inevitably, the newbie would casually reach down to pick it up but not be able to. This would elicit cheers and laughter from the expectant audience, and the newbie. Ice broken. Welcome to jail!

Comical remarks from prisoners were often heard by jail staff during the booking process. These were largely off-the-cuff comments, many of which were priceless, such as when a prisoner speaking on the wall phone with his lawyer, yelled to the counter staff asking, "What am I here for?"

An officer at the counter yelled back, "PSP Over," which means possession of stolen property over $5,000 in value. Now, possession of stolen property is one of the most common charges laid by the Crown. It's a bread-and-butter charge that every defence lawyer knows inside out. Or so I thought. The prisoner repeated the charge of "PSP Over," to his lawyer. A moment later, the prisoner yelled back, "My lawyer wants to know what 'PSP Over' means." Without missing a beat, the booking officer yelled back, "It means get a new lawyer!" Not sure if the message echoed sufficiently through the hallway and into the phone for the lawyer to hear, but it was certainly good advice at the time.

Spontaneity can turn something that sounds indifferent into something hilarious, such as the following deadpan retort to a prisoner's smart-ass answer. The chap being booked into the jail was a rough sort and older than your typical arrestee. He had been around the block more than a few times and wasn't intimidated by the process. Throughout the entire booking procedure, he was impatient and generally sarcastic, clearly becoming annoyed with the personal questions asked in order to ensure that medical concerns could be addressed while in custody. Also, that Stats Canada got their tidbit of data as well. One such question pertains to marital status. The booking officer must check one of four potential answers listed on the booking sheet. The officer asked: "Are you married, single, widowed, or divorced?"

Our hostile client replied rather belligerently, "Well, I jack off once in a while, what does that make me?"

"Married, I guess," replied the straight-faced booking officer as he checked the corresponding box and moved on without so much as a pause. Those of us present for the exchange nearly hit the floor. Even the arrestee chuckled before he caught himself and reacquired his nasty disposition.

While many of the subjects in the Vancouver jail are there due to serious charges of assault, not all fights result in charges; some result in indigestion, as we'll soon see.

40

FOOD FIGHT—SORT OF

THIS PARTICULARLY VICIOUS FIGHT BETWEEN TWO THIRTY-
something males living the high life on Point Grey Road, one of Vancouver's
most expensive streets, didn't result in anyone going to jail, though one of the
combatants went to the hospital. The two were pals of some sort that, during an
evening of drinking and getting high, decided to tumble down the back steps in
a full-on case of fisticuffs. What they were fighting about, I do not know, and
I'm not sure they did either; however, upon my arrival they had settled their
differences and were again on speaking terms. After some initial investigation, I
deemed the battle and bloodshed to be consensual. Neither adversary appeared
to be more of a victim than the other, and despite one contender holding a cloth
to his bloodied ear, neither wanted anything to do with charges.

"Let me see your ear," I asked.

Off came the bloodied cloth. To my astonishment, there was a bite taken
out of the subject's right ear. And it wasn't just a nip; it looked like a bite out
of a sandwich. It was a perfect crescent-shape positioned above the area of the
earlobe, which was now missing. The wound was bleeding profusely and in
need of medical attention.

"How did that happen?" I asked

"I think he bit me," was the reply.

An ambulance arrived and transported our mutilated man to the hospital.
Given that peace had now befallen the household, combined with the reaffir-
mation of friendship between the battle bots, I concluded the call and departed.

Roughly twenty to thirty minutes later, I received an urgent message to call the hospital. The attending nurse asked if I could retrieve the portion of ear that had been severed; the doctor was hoping to reattach it, but it had to be done quickly. I raced back to the house in question, rustled up Ear Man's adversary, and asked him for his help in locating the chunk of ear so that it could be reattached. The brawler stood stone-faced for a moment, then sheepishly stammered, "I-I swallowed it."

Oh . . . good God, I thought. "Really?"

"Yup."

I had our communications centre relay the results of my inquiry back to the hospital. The ear would not be forthcoming, at least not quickly or in a condition that would lend itself to reattachment. I had been prepared to race this human tissue to the O.R. for a little needle and thread work, and it wouldn't have been the first time that I transported human tissue in a race against time.

THE HEART OF THE MATTER

I WAS WORKING ROUTINE PATROL ONE RAINY EVENING. IT WAS dark, just past the dinner hour, when I was dispatched code-three (lights and siren) to the Vancouver International Airport. My destination was not the terminal but a gate that would enable access airside. At the gate, I was to connect with airport security, in order to be escorted onto the runway to meet an inbound flight. Speed in this case was essential.

A patient on the operating table in a major Vancouver hospital was awaiting the arrival of a donated heart from outside the province. The heart was on a commercial flight full of passengers, and its shelf life was rapidly diminishing. The airliner's arrival had been delayed, but it was now closing in on Vancouver's airspace and would soon touch down. My run to the airport was exceptionally quick despite the heavy traffic. With my emergency lights in full bloom and the siren wailing, I parted the traffic and kept the wheels turning. At the airport, I raced to the noted gate and met with airport officials that were driving a white truck with a yellow flashing light.

We watched the airliner on its glide path, saw a puff of smoke as its wheels grabbed the asphalt, and waited for the jet to come to a stop at the end of the runway. "Stay behind us," instructed the security team as we drove onto the taxiway and out to the jet with our emergency lights flashing.

The forward cabin door opened as a mobile stairway pulled up to meet the open hatch. A member of the flight crew quickly stepped out carrying a white Styrofoam picnic cooler, the type you might pick up at Canadian Tire for a few bucks to keep a six-pack cold on Canada Day. She handed me the cooler. Inside was a human heart on ice, and no, I didn't peek.

I knew the importance of this mission and the fragility of the item being transported, but the non-descript white Styrofoam cooler seemed remarkably cheap for an undertaking of such gravity. Nonetheless, it was fulfilling its job, and I had to fulfill mine. I placed the cooler on the floor of the car. This was going to be an aggressive run to the hospital, and I didn't want the cooler toppling over and spilling its contents. I updated the police communications supervisor, advising that I had the "package" and was en-route.

"Please update the hospital and have a nurse meet me in the Emergency Ward."

I followed the airport truck to the exit gate then pushed the V8-powered Ford Police Interceptor to its limits. It's a fairly long run from the south side of the Vancouver airport to Vancouver General Hospital, especially in late rush-hour traffic, but I'd like to think that my practice in the rain on the high-speed training track back in the academy paid off. That heart and I never missed a beat, arriving quickly and safely. The organ was delivered to O.R. staff and prepped for implant into a waiting chest cavity. And while I hoped it would beat for many years within its new recipient, I certainly knew that my heart was beating . . . and rapidly.

A few years later, I had the opportunity to again deliver the essence of life to a recipient; however, this time it was more personal. I had long been registered in Canada's Unrelated Bone Marrow Donor Registry, having joined the registry some time previous when the police department had sponsored a campaign to encourage its members to sign up. I had long forgotten about the commitment when out of the blue I got the call. Could I come in for additional testing? I was a provisional match.

Of course. "I'll be right there," I said. Testing, paperwork. More testing, more paperwork. Soon I was declared a match. Once I committed to donating my bone marrow, there was no turning back. The recipient's white blood cells would be killed in preparation for my bone marrow. Without it, the patient would most certainly die.

Within a couple days, I was in the O.R. about to receive an epidural that would eliminate any feeling below my lower back. I wasn't giving birth, but I was about to have four holes drilled into my pelvis in order to suction out life in the form of bone marrow: 906 millilitres of it. The surgeon and O.R. nurses were amazing. The first question I was asked by the surgeon was what genre of music I'd like played in the O.R. It was my pick, he insisted. I was into blues at the time, and soon the room, which was full of talented medical experts and sophisticated machinery, was alive with guitars, smoky vocals, and 4/4 time. The procedure was flawless, and I was soon in a recovery room itching to get home. The pain that followed wasn't as severe as I was led to believe it would be, and I was back at work within three days. Climbing stairs was a challenge for a week or two, but overall, the experience was a very positive event in my life. I received a commemorative wristwatch from Blood Services Canada along with a framed certificate of appreciation.

Of course, one can't help but wonder how the recipient is doing. Who they are? Young? Old? Prior to the procedure, I signed a release form that would allow the recipient to connect if he or she so chose. I never heard anything and actually made an inquiry myself a few months later. I learned that the female recipient had not survived the ordeal. Her organs had begun shutting down, and there was nothing further that could prevent her impending death. It was a sad outcome that put a pall over the jubilance of having had the possibility of saving a life. I wish I knew more, but just as it was in my account of the woman nearly murdered by her knife-wielding partner, sometimes it's best to just move on and simply hope for the best, knowing that you contributed in some meaningful way.

Despite the heartbreaking outcome, some folks feel that karma rewards selfless acts. Presumably, the opposite is true, as we'll see next.

42

KARMA AND MERCEDES-BENZ

IN A CASE OF MORE MONEY THAN BRAINS, OR PERHAPS MORE booze than sense, I responded to a severe collision in the wee hours of the morning, in which two new Mercedes-Benz vehicles had collided with each other. The two demolished Mercs sat in the middle of an intersection where a quiet side street intersected with a semi-major corridor in the city.

Clustered around the crumpled German marques, one a sports coupe and the other a full-size sedan, was a group of fashionably-dressed twenty-some-things—the stock-promoter types, who often live larger than their incomes permit. As I started my investigation to determine who the drivers were and which occupants were in which vehicle, I got the sense that something wasn't adding up. It was clear that everyone had been drinking and that they were doing their best to obfuscate the facts. I managed to figure out a few things, though: The occupants of both cars were all friends, and they had been partying at a nearby bar, closing down the venue. Then they'd decided to relocate to the home of a member of the group. They split themselves between the two high-performance Bavarian machines, and the race was on to see who could arrive at the new location first.

The exact route taken by the two cars was unclear to me, except for the last block before impact. One vehicle clearly took the noted side street as, I presume, a faster route. Who knows if the driver saw the stop sign before flying through it and colliding at a ninety-degree angle with the second Mercedes that was shooting up the main road? I informed the group that, without the drivers identifying themselves, they were violating a term of their insurance policies and would likely invalidate any claims pursuant to the collision. They didn't seem to believe me. Despite their arrogance, karma eventually paid a visit.

One of the vehicles belonged to the girlfriend of one of the guys at the scene, whom I suspected to be a driver though he denied such at the scene. I called the girlfriend at her home and confirmed that her boyfriend was using the car that evening. I explained to her what I was investigating. Needless to say, the relationship may have sustained more damage than the cars. The other Mercedes was leased to the boss of one of those in attendance. The female employee seemed devastated by the damage but denied being the driver. Fine. I figured that there were no innocent parties involved, so I recorded all of the evidence, including the fact that every member of the uncooperative group had been drinking and that no one would comment on who was driving. The demolished vehicles were impounded and my report, which documented the circumstances, was submitted with a copy directed to our provincial insurance provider.

A week or two later, I was contacted by a senior agent for the Insurance Corporation of British Columbia (ICBC). He had read my report and wanted to discuss my findings. Following our conversation, he verified that ICBC would not pay out the claims for the two Mercedes-Benz vehicles due to the breaches of contract pertaining to the pervasive use of alcohol and the refusal of the drivers to identify themselves. That was a $200,000+ lesson for all involved. Had someone been seriously injured or killed, there were investigative techniques open to me that would likely have identified the drivers, but it would have been a long, expensive investigation.

Here's how that complex investigation would probably have unfolded: In the event of airbag deployment, which was the case in both cars, the driver's face would almost certainly have left skin cells on the deflated steering-wheel airbag in each vehicle. The cells could be collected with a swab and analyzed. If the driver's DNA profile is on file in the National DNA Registry, the driver's identity would soon be established. If, however, the driver's DNA was not included in the registry, undercover techniques could be applied to surreptitiously obtain a DNA sample from all those suspected to have been a driver in the collision. The samples would then be compared against the airbag samples. A match would enable the investigator to apply for a warrant to compel the tentatively IDed driver to provide a "known DNA sample," to be compared against the airbag sample. A match would provide compelling evidence of who the driver was, which would inevitably lead to criminal charges and a high probability of conviction. Other evidence, such as statements, video, and forensics would further corroborate the findings.

There were no truly innocent victims involved in this particular incident, or serious injuries sustained that would justify the expense and resources required to pursue an exhaustive investigation as described. Instead, I allowed karma to be judge and jury. I have no idea whether debts were ever settled for the destruction of two premium automobiles, given ICBC's refusal to pay any claim related to the collision. As they say, karma's a bitch, and based on this crash, can be expensive too.

One of the interesting aspects of a motor-vehicle collision is the randomness of such an incident. The Mercedes-Benz case excluded, occupants of the involved vehicles don't generally know each other, despite coming together in an unplanned manner, the outcome of which could hold some interesting coincidences, such as those described next.

CAR CRASH COINCIDENCES

I'M GOING TO PROVIDE A QUICK OVERVIEW OF A FAIRLY SERIOUS car crash from the late nineties, in which the investigation revealed a number of headshaking coincidences.

The crash occurred on Vancouver's leafy West Side at a four-way stop between two intersecting roads in a quiet neighbourhood. I arrived to find two mangled cars and a group of elderly seniors milling about, dazed and confused. An elderly woman was lying on the rear seat of one of the smashed vehicles, clearly in need of medical attention. An ambulance soon arrived. Paramedics examined the woman and decided to transport her to the University of British Columbia Hospital for further treatment.

I began my investigation by identifying the two drivers. No witnesses were located. The drivers blamed each other for the crash, each saying the other had run the stop sign. I examined the driver's licence of driver number-one and compared the picture to the individual to confirm authenticity. This is something the police must always do when taking enforcement action against a driver. The image was a satisfactory rendition of the elderly driver, but I was confused by his date of birth, which was noted on the licence in pairs of digits representing day, month, and year. Except in this case, the year indicated was "99." I thought perhaps that "99" was a code for some category I was unfamiliar with. I asked the driver his date of birth. He replied, stating the year of 1899. I was dumbfounded. I had never in my career dealt with a fully-licenced individual that had been born in the nineteenth century. Once I got over the fact that the gentleman was approaching his hundredth birthday, I got to work taking statements and figuring out the sequence of events, which revealed these coincidences:

(We'll call the vehicle driven by our driver born in 1899 as vehicle #1.)

- Both drivers accused each other of running the stop sign.
- Vehicle #1 was driven by Mr. Brown, accompanied by his wife, Mrs. Brown, who was also in her nineties.
- Vehicle #2 was occupied by an elderly couple of similar ages to those in vehicle #1.
- The rear seat of vehicle #2 was occupied by an elderly woman in her nineties, also with the last name of Brown, though unrelated to Mr. and Mrs. Brown in vehicle #1.
- Before the collision, vehicle #1 was on its way to the UBC Hospital to pick up a patient that was being discharged.
- Vehicle #2 was on its way back from the UBC Hospital after picking up a discharged patient (that being Ms. Brown in the rear seat).
- As a result of the collision, Ms. Brown from vehicle #2 was now on her way back to the UBC Hospital by ambulance for further medical attention.
- Following the collision, the elderly couples from both vehicles headed to UBC Hospital in separate taxis. The Browns were going to pick up a discharged patient; the second couple to check on the formerly discharged Ms. Brown.

As I was unable to determine which driver had disobeyed the stop sign, and frankly I wouldn't be surprised if they both had failed to stop given the scope of damage and absence of skid marks, I wrote my report and allowed the insurance company to determine liability. Fortunately, all of the elderly participants in this calamitous event, save for backseat Ms. Brown, weathered the incident like troopers despite their advanced ages. It left me shaking my head, though. As the coincidences emerged during my investigation, I felt like a character in a sitcom, which was not unlike how I felt the afternoon I ran into a building I thought was on fire, intending to rescue its occupants from impending death.

44

BROTHER BERNIE

THIS SHORT STORY STILL MAKES ME CHUCKLE SO MANY YEARS later. It's often the unexpected comedic moments amidst chaos that serve as bright sparks in one's memory. I was an inspector at the time, working in uniform as the City's duty officer, which is essentially the on-road police manager overseeing all police activity within the city.

I was driving along Powell Street through an economically challenged area of Vancouver's Eastside, when I saw smoke billowing from an open third-floor window of a rooming house. The building was antiquated but relatively well kept. It served as home to many older members of the community, who survived largely on meagre pensions and government programs. The black smoke churned out of the open window like a plume rising from a volcano eruption. I didn't see flames but knew that it wouldn't be long before they appeared as oxygen flowed through the open window to feed the smoldering embers. One thing about policing, you attend a lot of active fires. And thanks to many nightshifts, police officers are often the first to spot fires, be they houses, commercial buildings, or dumpsters that light up the night sky. Succinctly put, cops are professional fire spotters, after which alarms sound in nearby firehalls, rustling firefighters from their restful slumbers. Cops working nightshift have always felt a little good-natured animosity toward firefighters, snoring the night away. But cops concede that, when responding to a blaze, firefighters earn their pay and more. And with the emergence of fentanyl poisoning the illicit drug trade, some firehalls respond to overdose calls multiple times per evening. They also respond to other medical emergencies and automotive collisions, sometimes employing the "Jaws of Life" at life-threatening crashes. Nonetheless, when the cops are pushing through an exhausting nightshift while all is dark and quiet at the firehall, it can sow seeds of first-responder discontent.

Well, that was a bit of a diversion! Back to the rooming-house fire.

I radioed my observations and requested the fire department's attendance. Then I bailed out of the car and ran into the building through its front door. This was not one of our problematic buildings that see near-daily police responses, but a quieter facility that was unaccustomed to the urgent arrival of police officers. The front entry gave way to a common lounge area for the building's residents. My sudden appearance in uniform caught everyone's attention, especially that of an elderly chap who seemed most pleased to have me drop by. His false teeth weren't in his mouth, but I had no problem understanding him as he asked what was going on. I replied that something was burning. His eyes lit up and a smile shot across his weathered face as he excitedly asked, "You know my brother Bernie?!"

The kindly chap seemed so delighted that I knew his brother Bernie that it stopped me in my tracks. Sitcom humour strikes again. I felt bad having to say no, but my mission was to determine the source of the smoke and to evacuate the building if necessary. I ran up the central stairway to the third floor, where smoke was now filling the hall. Several elderly live-ins had opened the door to the unit that was spewing the smoke. To my utter amazement, the billows of smoke had been produced by food in a frying pan that had been left unattended on the electrical element of a stove. It had burned for a long duration before the smoke was noticed by any of the residents. The occupant of the offending suite had left the building, inadvertently leaving his dinner to carbonize.

I was glad that nothing more serious had occurred. Life for the elderly living in rooming houses can be perilous at best. In this case, no harm was done that a few large fans from the fire department couldn't correct. Still, to this day I chuckle about "knowing brother Bernie," and wish I could've brightened the old-timer's day by saying, "Yes, I know Bernie, and he's a wonderful chap."

INVESTIGATING DEATH

BY THIS POINT IN THE BOOK, THERE'S NO DOUBT THAT YOU'VE noticed the connection between policing and death. The police are tasked with investigating deaths, the majority of which are not murders but rather death by accident, misadventure, or suicide. And of course, death by natural causes, such as heart attack, disease, and all other ways in which our bodies succumb to Mother Nature's call.

Unlike the smoke-filled rooming house of Bernie's brother, this house fire rapidly consumed a turn-of-the-century, three-story Kitsilano home that had been divided into three suites. Regrettably, the fire also consumed the lives of the two basement tenants, in addition to injuring three firefighters early on a frosty winter morning. An unexpected backdraft forced the firefighters to jump from the second floor to escape a blast of flames and intense heat. They suffered a variety of sprains and bruises from landing on the grass but no serious burns or debilitating injuries. Nonetheless, they were sped off to hospital to be treated and checked over for medical issues less visible.

Unfortunately, the couple that had been asleep in the basement suite never managed to escape, although based on body positioning, they had certainly tried. His charred corpse was found lying on the bedroom floor directly beneath a window that was a potential portal to safety if time and oxygen had been on their side, but they hadn't. Her body was found on the floor, on the opposite side of the bed to where the window was situated. It's believed that both victims had been asleep in the bed when the fired erupted. Before having any real

192

chance of escaping the inferno, the couple were overcome by toxic smoke and crippling heat. The fire then burned their bodies, leaving remains that appeared similar to heavily charred wood in a fireplace. The fire was traced back to an electrical overload due to space heaters used to heat the chilly basement suite. It was a preventable tragedy of immense proportion, and one in which smoke detectors, proper electrical wiring, and circuit breakers might have saved the lives of two occupants and prevented the potential deaths of firefighters caught in an inferno.

While the fire was accidental in nature, unexpected death can occur any-where, at any time. I was called to investigate a grisly death at a residential construction site one sunny afternoon. The victim drove a small dump truck, the type used by landscapers more-so than those used to haul full loads from excavation sites. The driver was a man in his mid-thirties, clearly a hardworking individual with a young family to support.

After dumping a load of gravel alongside a house under construction, the truck's bed became stuck in the up-tilted position. While it was jettisoning the load of gravel, several of the stones had found their way onto the vehicle's frame at the pivot point between one of the rails of the cargo bed and the chassis of the truck. In order to clear the rocks, the driver held a hammer and large screw-driver as he knelt down next to the truck's chassis. He leaned into his work, placing his head between the cargo bed and the truck's frame. As he knocked clear the debris, the cargo bed suddenly freed itself and collapsed downward without giving the driver time to remove himself. Sadly, his neck became wedged between the rail of the cargo bed and the frame of the truck. The gap that ensnared the driver's neck was no more than an inch wide. The bed's weight compressed the driver's neck to the same thickness, quickly killing him. While this fatality didn't involve a child directly, it did take the life of a hardworking father that had been issued faulty equipment. Sadly, he had been doing his best to overcome workplace obstacles in order to keep his job and source of income, but his diligence cost him his life.

It's tragic workplace events, such as this death, that underpin the rigorous rules, employment standards, and practices that apply to industrial work sites. While the police investigate workplace deaths to determine if there is evidence of criminality, such incidents are also investigated by government agencies that regulate workplace safety. Depending on the outcome of these investigations, tribunal hearings may result in fines and other penalties being imposed against the company responsible for the job site.

Sometimes, death strikes when we're having fun, such as volunteering one's time as a track worker at an international automotive event. Vancouver's first Championship Auto Racing Team (CART) Indy Race ran September 2, 1990. It was a beautiful, warm, late-summer day as the Indy cars screamed their way around Vancouver's False Creek and the former lands of Expo 86.

I was working at the track as the sergeant in-charge of the crew assigned to police the day. Fans were excited for Vancouver's first Indy race, and frankly, I was excited to be assigned to the event. The Indy cars would reach 330 km/h on the straightaways. It was a high-speed mix of sights and sounds—very loud sounds as we discovered. Hometown hero that year was Ross Bentley, and partway through the race, his car stalled mid-point of a tight chicane meant to reduce the speed of the race cars. Bentley's vehicle had come to rest against the far wall of the track. The yellow caution flag flew, and the chicane was closed to race traffic. Rather than entering the chicane, which is a tight, U-shaped section of track, race traffic was directed to pass it by staying on the racetrack proper and not making a sharp left into the chicane. Believing the chicane was now safe to enter, three track workers left their place of safety behind the track-side wall, climbing through the portal in the wire fence to dash over to Bentley's open-wheel Indy car. They got behind his vehicle and gave it a short, hard push forward, which was enough for Bentley to re-fire his Lola/Cosworth engine and re-enter the race, managing to place eighteenth despite the stall.

As the three workers turned to run back to their safety zone, a race car driven by Willy T. Ribbs incorrectly entered the chicane, travelling at high speed. The three track workers were unable to make it across the track before Willy's car was upon them. Two workers were badly clipped by the rear wing of Ribbs' car, while the third worker, Jean Patrick Hien of Quebec, was caught under the left rear wheel of the car and violently spit out like a rag doll. Despite emergency surgery at hospital, Mr. Hien did not survive. The two other track workers were hospitalized with non-fatal injuries. Following the accident, the race resumed. While it was underway, I consulted with the duty officer in-charge of policing for the city and our Collision Investigation Unit to strategize on how to proceed with an investigation of the incident. I spoke with CART officials, explaining the need for me to conduct a preliminary investigation into the collision immediately following the race. Contact was made with management for the Willy T. Ribbs' race team. It was agreed that I could interview Willy T. Ribbs following the race; however, his lawyers wished to be present. This was fine with me. It wasn't a criminal investigation, but it was certainly a serious matter, which had taken the life of an innocent track worker living out his dream of working with the CART Indy Race Series.

Immediately following the race, in which Ribbs' finished in tenth place, we convened in the leather-lined A-class motorcoach that served as Ribbs' mobile home and office. It was an opulent RV on wheels in which I sat with Willy, his lawyer, and a lawyer representing his race team. Willy was clearly upset by the incident. There's no doubt that it appeared accidental; however, an investigation was necessary and answers needed, such as why Willy was in the chicane when flaggers had waved him off. Was this gross negligence? And most importantly, was the death a case of culpable homicide?

Willy T. Ribbs was cooperative with me as I obtained a detailed statement from him. While I can't publish those details, I can say that despite the presence of lawyers, there was no attempt to withhold information on Willy's part, though some inconsistencies were noted between his description of the incident and what was captured on video by several TV cameras broadcasting the race. Slight deviations in one's memory of a traumatic event are not unusual or conclusive of deception. The human brain tends to fill in gaps with what the subject assumes or hopes to be true, when it isn't. Eye-witness statements often don't align with incontrovertible evidence such as video, despite the witness's earnest sincerity.

As disturbing and tragic as the accident was, the investigation carried out post-race was reviewed by the Vancouver Police Department's Collision Investigation Unit, which found that the death of Mr. Hien was accidental within the parameters of a high-risk sporting event, notwithstanding Willy T. Ribbs' improperly entering the chicane. There would be no criminal charges arising; however, I understand that a civil action was launched by the family of Mr. Hien. The incident also generated much controversy over CART's decision to continue the race with the participation of Willy T Ribbs, undeterred by the fatality. I'd like to think that track workers today are kept safer and better protected as a legacy to Mr. Hien.

Other activities can increase one's risk of death, as in the sudden death of an older Italian man, which I investigated. It seems that this "Romeo" had a much younger paramour that he visited weekly. The ensuing activity elevated his heart rate and blood pressure, which given his state of physical fitness, was not a good idea—though an enjoyable one. He expired in a labour of passion, which may not be such a bad way to go as long as it doesn't involve an adulterous accord.

I attended the rented house where Romeo's life had ended. The ambulance had already transported him to hospital where no medical intervention would be successful. I spoke with his twenty-something female companion, obtaining details of what happened. Seems the extra dollars paid for her services helped offset the cost of rent. When death is unexpected, it's the job of the police to deliver a notification of such to the next of kin. No doubt, we've all seen this reflected in one cop show or another. It can be a tremendously difficult knock to make. I knew what I had to do as I climbed into my patrol car and started over to the family home. I thought about what I would say. The man may have been engaged in an illicit affair, but even the dead are entitled to privacy. *Well, I'll play it by ear,* I thought, not knowing who would be at the house or their level of shock.

I pulled up to the modest 1950s two-story family home in a part of town with a sizeable Italian population. They saw me coming. I was met on the stairs by the adult daughter of the deceased. She was teary-eyed but composed. She knew why I was there. I offered her my condolences. I needed to ask a few questions to complete my investigation. She answered them frankly. She also intimated that they knew of the weekly dalliance engaged in by her father. Though his death came as a shock, that part of it didn't, for which I breathed a sigh of relief.

While time is critical in successfully treating many catastrophic health emergencies, such as heart attacks and strokes, we don't normally associate this type of event with young, healthy teens. Unfortunately, even with the miracles modern medicine has delivered us, death among the young can't always be predicted or prevented. One of the more difficult cases I handled involved the loss of a sixteen-year-old lad who would've made any parent proud. He was both an excellent student and athlete. After a basketball practice one evening, he arrived home complaining of a mild headache. He decided to go to bed early, saying goodnight to his parents at nine p.m. or so. When they went to check on him a few hours later, he had slipped away due to an aneurism.

It was a heartbreaking file to investigate. As with all first responders, calls involving children take the greatest emotional toll on police officers. Often, police and first responders can't help but connect deeply with circumstances involving children, especially if they too are parents. Not being able to make a difference in the lives of the family, losing their only son to an aneurism, left me feeling helpless and frustrated. There are, however, occasions when a difference is easily made.

I recall my partner, who was a father of two young boys, telling me a heartwarming story when I returned to work after a Christmas break. He had attended a call on December 24th, in which a single mom was being harassed by her ex. She had two young tots and lived in a sparsely furnished basement suite. The family of three had no Christmas tree, gifts, or festive accoutrements. Just before heading to the call, my partner had stopped at a gas-station convenience store. The store had a fully decorated Christmas tree on display. After dealing with the call and reassuring the family, my partner returned to the gas-station convenience store. Following a word or two with a compassionate store manager, the tree and all its adornments were loaded into the back seat of the patrol car, along with whatever Christmas-like gifts could be purchased from a gas-station convenience store.

That evening, Christmas was delivered by a police car and a man in blue rather than a sled and a man in red. And while it was a modest Christmas, it was more gracious than the Christmas many others in the city would experience, especially those burdened with poverty and addiction. For them, the best gift may well be a shot of Naloxone at a critical moment in time.

46

BACK FROM DEATH

DEATH BY OVERDOSE TAKES MANY LIVES IN THE CITY OF VAN-couver, as it does across the province, the nation, and the globe. In 2019, 245 deaths were attributed to illicit drug toxicity in Vancouver, which was down remarkably from 2018, when a peak of 395 deaths was recorded. Regrettably, 2020 saw the loss of 408 individuals in the City of Vancouver due to illicit drug overdoses. And it just gets worse. The B.C. Coroner Service recorded 1,011 overdose deaths in the province in the first six months of 2021

Without the broad distribution of Naloxone (colloquially referred to as Narcan), the 2020 overdose death rate in Vancouver would have been much higher. If administered within the survival window, Naloxone reverses the effects of an opiate, pulling an individual back from certain death. I've watched this in action, and it's mind-blowing for those that haven't witnessed a life restored in this manner. I was working in Vancouver's Downtown Eastside and came upon a red-haired male sprawled out on the sidewalk. He appeared to be a drug-user in his thirties and little more than skin over bones. From every indication that I, as a seasoned cop, would use to judge whether an individual is dead or alive, this chap was dead. His lips were blue, his pulse non-existent.

The paramedics arrived and got straight to work preparing an injection. The needle's plunger was rapidly depressed, sending a dose of Naloxone into the subject's muscle mass. Within moments, he sat bolt upright and was mad as hell. Anger upon being reunited with life is a common response when Naloxone is administered. Our man had no idea that he had been shaking hands with the

Grim Reaper moments before opening his eyes to find a cop and a paramedic team hovering over him. Did he think we were responsible for his near-death experience? It took some firm talk to convince him that the paramedics had just saved his sorry ass, and that he might want to thank them. Once he settled down, the gravity of the situation crystalized, and he became teary-eyed and emotional. He didn't wish to be transported to the hospital for a check-over, so away he aimlessly wandered, once again becoming part of the ever-worsening sordid street scene.

While this lanky, old-before-his-years, street-level addict survived, many of the illicit drug deaths involve recreational users rather than the hard-core addicts we tend to associate with overdosing. The "more at risk" cohort are individuals who choose to use heroin in secret while living a life that appears completely normal on the outside. They may be coping with physical or emotional pain, or they may just be in the mood to party and be relieved of the week's stress. Their tolerance for opioids is likely far less than that of an addicted user. A "hot spot" of fentanyl in the heroin mix may be enough to cause death in a recreational user while not doing so in an addicted user. And that's one of the problems with street drugs. There isn't a level of quality control to provide a user with an assurance of the drug's purity, consistency, or potency. It's a crap shoot each time. Dealers cut (mix) heroin with fentanyl to extend its profitability. Unfortunately, their rudimentary methods of mixing fentanyl fail to produce a homogenous product of any verifiable potency. I compare it to an auto-mechanic performing brain surgery. Sure, auto mechanics know how to use tools, but what do they know about the intricacies of the brain and its many regions once the bone saw has been switched off?

Vancouver was an early adopter of supervised-injection sites and needles exchanges. These were, and still are, strategies of a Harm Reduction philosophy that generated plenty of controversy politically and within various social demographics. Those opposed to the concepts enveloped under the banner of "harm reduction" often referred to the strategies as "enabling" drug addiction rather than preventing it. I've looked at it from both perspectives through the lens of a street cop, but I continue to fall in favour of harm reduction at the user-level as a guiding principle over that of harsh enforcement.

Every time a user fixes in a supervised injection site or receives a bundle of clean needles at a needle exchange, there's an opportunity for intervention—intervention that may lead to participation in a treatment and recovery program. Or simply intervention that may prevent an overdose death. There has been notable success in harm-reduction practices, but that doesn't mean we should give up on enforcement. Selective enforcement against drug dealers is best targeted above the survival street-level traffickers. These targets are non-addicted dealers that are in it strictly for the money. They use and abuse the addicted population for profit in ways most cruel and inhumane. They deserve, in my cop-hardened view, the harshest of penalties when convicted.

There are, however, circumstances that justify zero-tolerance enforcement against street-level traffickers, addicted or not. These include trafficking to youngsters, or targeting locations where youngsters are likely to be found, such as schools, parks, and community centres. The exploitation of our young for illegal purposes is never ok, and should carry with it a high degree of deterrence upon conviction. Children are entitled to our protection. This is a non-negotiable tenet, yet it's not uncommon for traffickers to see dollar signs in lunch money. When I was assigned to the Granville Street strip in downtown Vancouver, we knew of a strategy employed by crystal meth dealers in which they would target young runaways surviving homelessly on the street. The dealers would befriend such a child or teen and get them started with a few free hits of highly addictive crystal meth. These hits were enough to create a dependence on the powerful chemical concoction due to physical changes the drug makes to the brain. From that point on, the dealer would own the lost waif and would force him or her to hit the street as a sex worker. The money earned would be turned over to the dealer in a desperate exchange for the next shot of "crystal," as it was euphemistically known.

Many well-intended advocates argue that decriminalizing all drugs would eliminate this sort of exploitation and take the profit out of the black market, especially if the government established a "safe supply" distribution network. Under this model, those needing drugs could be confident that the government-supplied product met the highest standards of purity and consistency, thereby greatly reducing the risk of unintentional overdoses. It's all a bit Pollyanna in my mind. I don't think the government could ever fully replace the black market city-wide, province-wide, or nation-wide. Think of the logistics of supplying Canadians with their drugs of choice irrespective of their location in this vast and sparsely populated land. Would it be delivered by courier? If so, how would the homeless with no formal address receive their doses?

Logistical challenges aside, I have come to conclude that lives would be saved with the adoption of "safe supply" distribution, at least on a localized scale; that being Vancouver's epicentre of addiction, the DTES. It's time.

While I support achievable, realistic harm-reduction strategies, there's also a place for enforcement. Though a number of years have flown by since I participated in a major undercover drug-enforcement operation in Vancouver, the drug-dealing environment has changed little despite the many publicly-funded non-government organizations pursuing a mandate to help those in Vancouver's drug-ridden Downtown Eastside. Here's a peek into life undercover.

MONTHS UNDERCOVER IN THE DRUG WORLD

WORKING UNDERCOVER IS A CURIOUS THING. IT'S AN ACTING gig without a script, cameras, or a paying audience. That said, it's exhilarating. It keeps you on your toes with your brain engaged, even when projecting exactly the opposite. And the stakes are high—deadly high. The undercover (UC) project I'm about to describe netted more than a hundred drug dealers in Vancouver's Downtown Eastside (DTES) in the early 1990s. Cocaine from South America was ravaging the community, fueling a crime wave of violence and death. The UC project operated for a number of months, during which evidence was gathered to support 180 criminal charges against 102 suspects.

I was not one of the two UC operators who immersed themselves in the drug world posing as addicted users, but rather part of the cover team that had their backs every night as the undercover duo engaged with street-level and mid-level dealers. My role, as that of cover team member, was to always have an eye on our UC operators. We needed to know where they were every minute that they were face to face with dealers, and we needed to ensure their safety. If the proverbial "shit hit the fan," we were there to jump in and extricate our undercover operators.

Our UC operators were specially trained police officers brought in from elsewhere in Canada specifically for this role. They had both been trained in the art of undercover work and were eager to put their skills into action. The plan was for them to arrive in town as Marc and Chloe, a boyfriend and girlfriend down on their luck. The officer playing the role of Marc was handsome, charismatic, and never lost for words. He was small in stature but scrappy and tough as nails with a quick-fire temper. Now in his early thirties, he was a little older than Chloe and played a much wiser street-educated "rounder." Chloe was in her mid-twenties, petite, pretty, and blonde. She portrayed herself as shy and new to the street scene. Their boyfriend/girlfriend relationship was played as shaky, and somewhat day-to-day in its permanence.

The operational plan called for (I'll use their character names) Marc and Chloe to arrive in the DTES in a beat-up van, penniless and in need of work and drugs. They would spend the first week simply being part of the bar scene, where they'd play pool for a few bucks and drink with the locals. This would allow their back-story to become known and build credibility among the DTES inhabitants and the dealers who serviced them. This is an important step before asking to buy drugs and climbing the distribution chain a level or two, which was the project's main goal.

To prepare for their introduction into the street scene, our UC operators needed to dress down. In her real life, Chloe enjoyed designer labels and regular salon visits. She definitely didn't fit into the seediness of her new work environment. In defiance of every standard of fashion she once lived by, Chloe was on her way to the thrift store to buy someone else's discards. It was a blow to her psyche that required assuaging by the rest of us.

"Don't worry, Chloe; it's all been laundered," we insisted. What a change. The metamorphosis of Chloe from attractive and sophisticated to a penniless "plain Jane" waif was astonishing. She wore her coat of humility with pride, adjusting and adapting in the week before her introduction into the "skids," as the area is colloquially known to Vancouverites. Marc, on the other hand, felt a sense of comfort in the thrift store togs while he let his stubble darken with length. A ripped t-shirt and worn-out jeans were all he needed to become "one with the street."

It's important in any undercover project to avoid the police station and anywhere cops might hang out. You never know who within the criminal element may spot a UC team member entering or leaving the police station. Nonetheless, office space is needed for the daily administrative tasks involved in running a major undercover operation. In our case, this was accomplished by renting an apartment in a Vancouver suburb to serve as the project's field office and home base. It would be from here that we would start and finish each day. With our UC operators acclimated to their roles and the field office stocked with computers and the necessary documents and paperwork, it was time to roll into town.

We would launch each day with a loose game plan of which bars to hang out in and which known targets we would be looking for (a target being a prolific drug trafficker who we planned to make a buy from). As part of the cover team, my compadres and I would hit the bars in advance of the operators, assessing the action and being in place before Chloe and Marc wandered into the degeneracy of a skid-row bar. It was important to fit into the squalor of these rundown establishments and all-night businesses, in which our UC operators would find themselves night after night.

On the first foray, Chloe and Marc entered one of the problem bars and sat at a small, terrycloth-covered, circular table that had probably been holding glasses of beer for decades. They ordered: Marc going with the bar's cheapest domestic draft beer while Chloe ordered a bottle of import, something she was accustomed to doing in her more polished existence. The night went well. Chloe and Marc had a few drinks and managed to meet and chat with a number of the locals. They were getting their names and backstories out there, and that was good. In the debrief that followed though, it was pointed out to Chloe that as penniless down-and-out strangers, ordering a pricey import bottle of beer was out of character.

"But I'm not drinking out of those glasses," she exclaimed. Oh, yes, you are! And from that night forward, nary a bottle would touch her lips.

Over the course of the multi-month project, there were many comical moments that a scriptwriter couldn't possibly envisage. There were also many high-risk scenarios and moments of great tension when our UC operators were out of our sight and having their UC personas challenged by thugs that ruled the streets and drug trade. As the cover team, we had to make quick decisions about whether to jump in or not. Doing so would likely expose the project and bring it to a sudden end. A lot had been invested, and none of us wanted a premature wrap. Fortunately, the project ran its full term and was record-breaking in its number of charges and eventual arrests. Along the way, Chloe and Marc acted with Academy Award excellence. They would have domestic spats in the middle of a bar and stomp off on their own. Chloe played the role of a lost waif with such artistry that every creep wanted to befriend her and take her under his protective wing, and more. Many of those wings were attached to the drug dealers we were targeting; how serendipitous!

Over months in the skids, Marc and Chloe showed a continual decline in their health thanks to theatrical make-up that slowly replaced their healthy glows with ashen-coloured skin, and white smiles with yellowed teeth display-ing paint-on cavities. In spite of Chloe's immaculate dress and deportment in her real life, like a chameleon, she adapted flawlessly to wearing thrift store togs that were seldom changed and never washed.

Though they rolled into town broke, over the term of the operation Marc and Chloe not only bought drugs from a wide array of street-level dealers but managed to work their way up the distribution chain to mid-level traffickers. Their infectious smiles and air of sincerity enabled them to gain the confidence of these higher-level distributors, who in turn sold them larger amounts of illegal drugs, which they believed Marc and Chloe were breaking into smaller packets and re-selling. This was exactly what the operational plan had been structured to do.

Working undercover as a member of Marc and Chloe's support team was an amazing and extraordinary policing experience. I have many wild memories of spending nights in Vancouver's worst bars and hiding in the squalor of DTES laneways in order to keep Chloe and Marc in sight as they worked the streets and bar scenes. On one occasion, I was hunkered down next to a dumpster in what can only be described as the most putrid, malodourous of laneways on the continent. I couldn't move at the moment without drawing attention to myself. As I crouched low and out of sight in the shadows, an amorous drunken couple decided that the opposite side of the dumpster would serve as a good backstop for rather raucous copulation. I guess it's true, love is beautiful even if the location isn't.

It's amazing how close all of us assigned to the project became during the course of its duration. Yes, we had differences and the occasional squabble, but overall, the team dynamic was incredibly strong and the commitment from everyone overwhelming. The fun factor, though, is what I'll remember most, such as when Marc came to pick me up in the beater van he and Chloe used as their transportation. I lived at the bottom of a cul-de-sac in a quiet residential part of Vancouver. Anyone driving down my street that wasn't a neighbour got a hard look, not just from me but from all of us living on the block. I'm not sure how many of my neighbours knew at the time that I was a cop. I certainly didn't look it during the course of the UC project, thanks to scraggly hair, a beard, and a jean jacket. But here came Marc, shooting down the hill to pick me up mid-afternoon in the wreck of an old panel van. As only crazy Marc could do, he pulled a tire-squealing 180-degree hand-brake U-turn in the cul-de-sac and stopped at my toes. The image of a "druggie" in a beater van pulling a smoky 180 and picking up a similarly unkempt man amid the manicured lawns and pulled curtains must have been a sight. I'm surprised that no black and whites gave chase after what I'm certain would've been a flurry of calls to 9-1-1.

Over the course of the project, evidence was gathered to support 180 criminal charges against a total of 102 DTES drug traffickers. After reviewing the totality of the investigative files, the Crown issued arrest warrants for all of the suspects. This kicked-off one of the largest criminal round-ups in the history of Vancouver. Every beat officer and patrol officer in the area was given a package containing photos of each suspect and a copy of each warrant. All of the cops on the street and the members of our undercover project spent the next few days scouring the DTES for each of the wanted individuals. Word of the round-up hit the street quickly, driving all manner of traffickers and criminals into hiding, or prompting them to vacate the city to avoid arrest. None of them knew who was and was not on the round-up list, but if they had trafficked narcotics recently, they opted to assume their names were listed. I actually had several individuals in the area ask if their names were on our list. I guess, if it was, they wanted to get the ordeal over with. If not on the list, they could rejoice and get back to whatever legal or illegal activities they relished.

The near-inexhaustible rate of crime and drug trafficking on the streets of the DTES subsided for a period of time, bringing an eerie calm to the area that was greatly appreciated by its elderly and law-abiding citizens, many of whom had been confined to their rooming houses, for fear of attack, for a very long time. I wish that the positive effects of such an enforcement project could be sustained, but that's a little too utopian given the harsh realities of the neighbourhood, which is often referred to as "Canada's poorest postal code." The three main drivers of the area's turmoil were, and continue to be, homelessness, drug addiction, and mental illness. Enforcement by the police is but one of many coordinated strategies needed to affect long-lasting change.

More recently, a social movement under the hashtag "Defund the Police" has gained momentum. Variations on exactly what is meant by defund the police exist, but it generally refers to reallocating funding from police agencies to social-service agencies dealing with the trifecta of urban dysfunction: homelessness, mental illness, and drug addiction. The concept presupposes that the need for police services will vastly diminish if these alternate social agencies are adequately funded, thereby reducing the trifecta's destabilizing effect on society and the corresponding need for police services. While somewhat quixotic and over-simplified, I think most police executives would agree with me in finding that the notion of reallocating funds from the police to other necessary social services has merit. That said, there's a chicken and egg argument that must be resolved beforehand. Do you immediately defund policing and allow crime to escalate and public safety to erode while changes are made to deal with the trifecta? Or do you deal with the trifecta first, and when demand for police services diminish, defund the police accordingly? As it is now, demand for the services of the Vancouver Police Department far outstrip its ability to respond during peak hours. For example, on any typical evening, there may be seventy or more 9-1-1 calls awaiting a police response. These are serious events considered by the callers to be emergencies. They may be assaults in progress, break-ins underway, violent domestic disputes erupting—you name it. (Think back to "Response Times Matter.") How can defunding the police be justified until the public's demand for emergent police responses has been suitably reduced? It's funny how no one needs the cops until they need the cops, then they better get there in twenty seconds or less!

I fully support adequate funding for social services that have a track record of success in housing the homelessness, treating the addicted, and caring for the mentally ill; those agencies have long been underfunded. We are now paying the financial, ethical, and moral price for turning a blind eye to these needs; however, defunding the police is not the answer. At least not yet.

The absence of robust social services over the years has thrust upon policing all of the failures noted above. The cops are the social safety-net of last resort, and they shouldn't be. But until society places greater value and urgency in treating the trifecta of social failures, the cops will remain the agency burdened with the fallout. The police are legally bound through an Oath of Office to respond to every emergency call, every crisis, and every public safety concern.

No other social agency has such an all-encompassing broad-ranging mandate. Defunding the police without a commensurate reduction in society's demand for its services will exacerbate the trifecta of social dysfunction, taking us further down the rabbit hole of failure. This can only result in greater violence and social disorder.

Hopefully, that won't always be the case. I look forward to a day when police funding can be safely reduced. It'll mean that we've got a handle on homelessness, addiction, and mental illness, but we're not there yet. Not even close. At least that's the way I see it.

Oh, back to Marc and Chloe. They both left town at the conclusion of the UC project, returning to their policing careers outside of British Columbia. Chloe later married and became a mom. Marc, well, he pursued his passion for hockey, becoming a senior-level coach in his retirement. No doubt that his scrappy attitude and quick mouth continued to serve him well on the ice and off.

A crime group with scrappy attitudes taken to the extreme is up next.

FROM RUSSIA WITHOUT LOVE

I MENTIONED THAT I WOULD HAVE MORE TO SAY ABOUT THE notorious Russian gangsters that attempted a violent and bloody take-over of the Vancouver drug trade in the early nineties. Well, here we go.

We knew that the core of Vancouver's Eastern European Organized Crime (EEOC) group was comprised of four principal gangsters we referred to as the "Russians." They consisted of two sets of brothers that were cousins: the Alekseevs and the Filonovs, all of whom are dead today, the victims of murder and/or suicide. The leader of the Russians was Alexander Alekseev. Partnered with his brother Eugene, Alexander was fearless, ruthless, and aggressive. Eugene not so much.

Eugene had studied to be a pharmacist. He was a softer, more sensitive individual, and it seemed he was only in the gang at his brother's insistence. I was a detective in the Vancouver Integrated Intelligence Unit at the time and carried the EEOC portfolio. I had encountered Eugene a number of times by this point, both as a street cop and as a detective in the Drug Squad (a "narc" in the lingo of the day). I had Eugene's pager number from an earlier arrest we had conducted on the brothers for maintaining an illegal marihuana grow op. Eugene knew me as Rob from this event. Following two attempts on the lives of the brothers, presumably set in motion by the Hells Angels, in which the vehicles driven by the Alekseev boys blew up, I called Eugene's pager and left the following voice mail:

"Eugene, it's Rob the cop. If you're still alive, give me a call."

I left my pager number and had little hope that he'd pick up the phone to call me, but to my utter astonishment, he did. His first words to me were, "I only called you because your message made me laugh." Well, I thought, if you can laugh at almost being killed twice, you must have a pretty liberal sense of humour.

My reference to being alive was rooted in the knowledge that the Russians were, we believed, on the Hells Angels hit list, making their mere day-to-day survival somewhat tenuous. The exploding cars I mentioned hadn't killed the Russians, but in all likelihood, could have. On the first occasion, their SUV was parked beneath a popular Vancouver restaurant. When the key was turned after the lads had climbed in, a loud explosion occurred beneath the truck, but the jerry-rigged device failed to fully detonate, leaving the Russians alive, albeit shaken. A second attempt was made to annihilate the brothers with a more powerful and professionally built incendiary device, but the Russians outsmarted their adversaries with the installation of a remote-start mechanism in the vehicle. They had parked on Quebec Street in Vancouver, not far from the luxury-view condo they rented in a nearby tower. While the bomb did what the assassins had expected, the Russians didn't. They started the SUV from half a block away rather than the driver's seat. This gave them front row seats to an explosion that would likely have killed them if they had been seated in the vehicle.

Back to Eugene. We started a series of interesting calls. Our conversations led me to believe that the gangster lifestyle was not for him. He wanted out. Without going too deep into those discussions, I don't think Eugene found the escape key before apparently taking his own life in a luxury hotel in Mexico by shooting himself in the head. There remains some doubt about the suicide theory, with others in the gang world believing that Eugene was murdered pursuant to a contract the Hells Angels may have placed on his life. Sometime later, Eugene's brother Alexander disappeared, and is today presumed dead. Most likely murdered by rival gangsters involved in organized crime who chose to eradicate the Russian cohort and the threat they posed.

I'm barely scratching the surface of the violence and criminality between the Russians and their enemies during this time in history in order to set the context for an arrest of Alexander Alekseev that Rob-one and I performed while we were partners in the Drug Squad. This event preceded my time as an intel detective and my later interactions with Eugene—or Eugeniy as his name is properly spelled.

We had received a tip that a large hydroponic marihuana growing operation was located in a two-story commercial building at 2nd Avenue and Pine Street in Vancouver. In the wee hours of the morning, Rob and I dropped by to have our first look at the building. It was in darkness, but strangely, we spotted a piercing ray of light being emitted from the corner of an otherwise dark, second-floor window. It was atomic in its brilliance, and consistent with the operation of powerful, ultra-bright grow lights.

At the front door, air could be heard rushing out of the mail slot. You could literally feel the flow of air leaking out of the building, driven by industrial-sized fans that were in use to cool the interior of the structure given the build-up of heat generated by the grow lights. But most telling of all was the unmistakable odour of fresh marihuana, a smell that we had come to recognize with science-like accuracy. A colleague of mine was once asked in court by a shrewd lawyer how he knew the smell he detected was in fact marihuana and not something else. While this was a bit of a headscratcher of a question, the officer's explanation was brief, elegant, and unambiguous. It went something like this:

"If I walked into a room in which you were peeling an orange, I wouldn't ask for a bite of your apple."

Olfactory senses aside, while Rob and I stood at the front door, we suddenly heard voices and footsteps approaching the door from the inside. We quickly threw ourselves around the side of the building and kept an eye on the entrance. The two Alekseev brothers exited. We knew we had the grounds to arrest them, but with only two of us and two of them, the odds of getting both into custody were slim. Plus, the likelihood of them being armed was also very high given the size of the grow operation and what we knew about the Russian gang's propensity for weapons and deadly violence.

The brothers began walking south on Pine Street. Because we weren't expecting action, Rob and I had left much of our equipment locked in our car located part-way down the alley that ran behind the building. We did a quick inventory of what equipment we each had on us at that moment as there was no time to head back to the car.

I had a gun, which was a good start. I didn't have handcuffs, but Rob did. One pair. He also had the portable radio in his pocket along with the antenna, which he had removed. I had the battery in my pocket. The radio would have to be quickly and discreetly assembled as we tailed the Alekseev brothers on foot. The portable radios in use in the Drug Squad at the time were very tall. Disassembling them allowed the radios to be covertly carried in pieces slotted into various pockets. While this practice may have mimicked Keystone Cop antics, it was necessary based on the ridiculous size of the radios.

As we walked the dark streets of a mostly commercial district of Vancouver, we had to maintain distance while also keeping pace with the brothers in an effort not to lose them if they made a turn. They looked back several times and clearly sensed that they were being followed. Suddenly they each turned in opposite directions, one choosing to head west and the other heading east. We could only go with one, which would it be? We made a quick decision to go with Alexander, believing him to be more the kingpin than Eugene. Alexander made a few more turns and was soon walking east in a laneway lined with commercial buildings and warehouses. The alley was unlit and very lonely. We saw Alexander slip into a loading bay and managed to corral him and announce ourselves as police. We were not in uniform, and I didn't want Alexander to mistake us for gang rivals.

I had my gun out. I could tell that Alexander's mind was racing as we confronted him. What would be his next move? Fortunately, he slowly complied with our demands and was taken into custody by Rob and handcuffed. We finished radio assembly and called for cover and a police wagon, hoping that attending officers might spot Eugene and nab him for us. Also, we had no idea whether other members of the Russian gang were in the area keeping an eye on the lads. Eugene was out of sight and could be calling reinforcements. We felt vulnerable despite having Alexander in cuffs.

Alexander said very little as he furtively looked around trying to spot additional undercover cops. Once he realized than no other cops were emerging from the shadows, he looked at us and asked in a chilling deadpan voice, "There's just the two of you?"

From that cold, emotionless remark, I took it that he was regretting his decision to be peaceably arrested. Had he also known how poorly equipped we were for a confrontation, he would have been much harder on himself for misjudging the situation and being compliant with our demands.

With Alexander in jail, the long arduous task of obtaining a search warrant and dismantling Vancouver's largest marihuana cultivation to date was to begin.

Inside the building, we counted 1,100 plants. This bust hurt the Russians financially, but certainly didn't put them out of business. Death would eventually do that, which I suspect Eugene knew was coming one way or the other. It's too bad that he never pursued his ambition to be a pharmacist, though one could argue that he was, in fact, a pharmacist, just not a legal one.

Not all drug-based retaliation is attributable to gangsters. A girlfriend scorned can have consequences too.

49

BREAKING UP BY CRIME STOPPERS

BREAKING-UP WITH A BOYFRIEND CAN BE DIFFICULT. WHY NOT let Crime Stoppers help?

Amy had been a faithful girlfriend. So much so that her boyfriend shared with her the locations of his illegal marihuana grow operations. He even toured her through the setups, beaming with pride over the quality of his work and the outstanding crop yields. Despite those pleasant moments, he treated Amy poorly and was an unfaithful, abusive creep. She took control of her life and left him. To solidify the dissolution of the relationship, she picked up the phone and called 1-800-222-8477.

Crime Stoppers is a non-profit registered charity that receives anonymous-tip information related to criminal activity. The information is forwarded to the applicable law enforcement agency. Crime Stoppers is an international organization operating globally through a vast network of local affiliates. Tipster anonymity is guaranteed by Crime Stoppers. The tipster's identity is never recorded or known to the organization. Each tipster is identified with a numerical code. Tipster rewards are paid out in cash by a Crime Stoppers volunteer who will meet the tipster at a pre-arranged location. Rewards are based on the outcome of a tipster's information. An arrest for a serious crime, or the recovery of valuable articles, are files typical of a reward.

Many of the cases I investigated while a detective in the Drug Squad had their origin in a tip from Crime Stoppers, and that's how I met Amy. In her early twenties, Amy was a bright young woman. Petite with dark, shoulder-length hair and an infectious smile, she had more going for her than her pot-growing boyfriend cared to know. Amy related the information about several grow ops her ex-boyfriend maintained to the Crime Stoppers call taker. The information was then routed to the Vancouver Police Drug Squad and assigned to me for investigation. The information Amy provided was of sufficient detail to launch an investigation; however, a Crime Stoppers tip alone is unlikely to provide the credibility required for a justice of the peace to issue a search warrant. Crime Stoppers is aware of this systemic evidentiary impediment. To overcome it, each tipster is asked if they would be willing to meet confidentially with the police if it would assist with their respective case. Amy was willing.

I made phone contact with Amy and verified that she had submitted the tip and that she was willing to meet with the police. She clearly wanted to extinguish all potential for rekindling the relationship with her former boyfriend. My partner and I met with Amy on several occasions over the following weeks. Meeting with confidential informants is tricky business. The safety of the informant is paramount, so meeting clandestinely is essential. One of the most reliable methods of debriefing a source such as Amy is to do it in a vehicle while your partner drives, ensuring that no one is tailing or able to hear the conversation.

In speaking with a confidential informant, or "source," which is the nomenclature I prefer to use, it's important to establish what the source knows to be true from what they may assume to be true. And to separate hearsay from fact. In the case of Amy, not only did I want her to provide the address of any grow ops she was aware of but I also wanted her to describe the exteriors of the houses in question and their interiors, along with a detailed description of the grow itself and the activity taking place to manage it. It's also important to determine recency, as in when was she last at the site? Who was with her? How did they enter the building? Did her boyfriend use a key?

In addition to pulling details from Amy for investigative purposes, I was trying to assess her credibility. Her motive was clear as a sunny day, but how truthful was she being? Investigators must be alive to potential embellishment on the part of a source, or possibly influencing the source to say what the source believes an investigator wants to hear. Sources can be manipulative and treacherous. They come with their own agendas, often wishing to put their criminal competitors out of business or to sweeten a possible plea deal on an unrelated court proceeding. The 1995 movie *The Usual Suspects* features a police interrogation of its main protagonist, Verbal Kint, played by Kevin Spacey, in which Kint subtly manipulates Detective Kujan, played by Chazz Palminteri, telling Kujan what he wants to hear despite it being fiction. It's a brilliant bit of acting and writing, which takes embellishment and lies delivered in a police interrogation to another level.

After debriefing Amy and obtaining all the relevant details, our next investigative tactic was to corroborate her information. Was her description of the house correct? What about the information pertaining to her ex-boyfriend? Once these investigative steps had been completed, and we had amassed as much information as possible to support the existence of an illegal marihuana grow operation at a specific address, we planned to seek a search warrant to authorize forcible entry into the premise. The bar to obtain a search warrant, especially for a residential address, is very high. All of the evidence to support our belief that criminal activity was taking place within must be clearly articulated in a legal document referred to as an Information to Obtain, or ITO for short. The ITO must be suitably compelling to persuade a justice that evidence to support the alleged criminal activity will be obtained inside the premises in question. Once the justice is satisfied with the ITO submission, the affiant officer swears an oath to the integrity of the information contained therein. There are no shortcuts in this business.

With a search warrant in hand for the first grow-op address, I assembled our investigative team and headed to the address, confident that we would find what we were coming for. And did we ever. The basement of this large home was filled with plants that stretched floor to ceiling, with a bush density that would give any green thumber shivers of delight. It took all night, but we managed to eradicate the operation, document its existence for court purposes, and put out a warrant for the arrest of said ex-boyfriend. Further investigations were undertaken into his network of illegal grow-ops as he waited in jail.

We met with Amy afterwards and confirmed that she was doing well and that her boyfriend was none the wiser on how the cops had discovered his green empire. Amy had taken a bold step in dumping her ex and in sealing the deal with a call to Crime Stoppers. Her safety and identity were steadfastly our highest priority. We checked in with her periodically to ensure that she remained safe and was doing well. Her identity was never disclosed by Crime Stoppers, the police, or the courts. My report back to Crime Stoppers verified the accuracy of Amy's information, which qualified her for a reward. How much she received is never shared, but hopefully it helped put some distance between her and her ex.

Not all illegal marihuana grow operations are located with information supplied by a source. Occasionally, they're stumbled upon quite inadvertently. Such was the case during a cycle home in the wee hours following a Drug Squad shift. Riding a bike at three a.m. can be very interesting. Just as I described in the chapter "Go Slow and Listen," sights, sounds, and smells in the stillness of the night seem magnified. Very little escapes the senses when there's no background noise or static to interfere. And once one's senses have been heightened physiologically by a workout, a person can feel as though they've gained super-human powers. While I couldn't leap tall buildings in a single bound during my vigorous ride home, I could smell a marihuana cultivation with canine-like accuracy. The house in question was a post WWII, wood-frame, two-story residence that sat on a small city lot at the end of a block of typical middle-class family homes. Houses in this neighbourhood are often home to families with young children. The houses are only separated by a couple of metres, meaning that a fire could easily jump from one to the next in the middle of the night before anyone was the wiser.

Despite being off-duty and on my way home, I made some mental notes and decided that I would follow up with a proper investigation the next day. One of the strategies for determining if the presence of high-intensity grow lights are present or not pertains to the level of power consumption, which I touched on in the chapter titled "When Cross-Examination Goes Sideways." With the use of a simple mathematical formula, one can quantify the amount of electrical consumption taking place by timing the revolutions of the spinning disc inside the power meter located on the exterior of the structure. High-consumption items typically include appliances, such as a clothes dryer and electrical stove. Electrical heating, if present, is also a heavy consumer of electrical power. Usually, these items are idle overnight, generating a low reading at the meter. A high reading at the meter in the middle of the night with no evidence of any electrical appliances operating is supportive of the presence of a marihuana grow operation. The growers know this.

In order to avoid massive electrical utility bills and triggering a red flag due to excessive electrical consumption, marihuana growers often tap into the electrical service of a house prior to the service entering the meter. This allows unlimited use of electrical power without spiking the utility bill or generating an outlying rate of consumption, but it's also theft. More concerning than the theft of a utility though is the fire risk inherent when an amateur takes a 240-volt line and attempts to hack into it with little or no electrical experience. It can be the ultimate DIY disaster that takes innocent lives with it when the bypass overheats and flames follow. Far too many residential grow ops are discovered by the fire department as they douse a house fire ignited by an illegal grow op. Fortunately, utility companies can quickly determine if the rate of electricity entering a home is the same as that flowing through the meter. A discrepancy would indicate that a meter bypass has been introduced into the line. And so it was in the little house on the corner that had been emitting a pungent, skunk-like odour the evening of my ride.

Indoor marihuana cultivations must be vented in order for plants to survive the heat of multiple metal-halide grow lights. This allows the warm stale air to be replaced with fresh cool air but venting allows the distinct odour of raw marihuana to escape as well. Typically, growers will do their best to vent grow rooms through the main chimney of a house in the hope that the smell will dissipate in the atmosphere rather than fall to the ground. They also prefer to vent in the wee hours when most neighbours are asleep and less likely to wonder why so many skunks have invaded their hood.

Having taken a direct spray from a skunk, I can tell you that it's not unlike being sprayed with a hose. I know this thanks to an evening trip on my bike through the wooded trails near my home. Suddenly, in the beam of my headlight, I saw a skunk by the edge of the trail and braked in time to stop well ahead of the critter. It ambled off the trail and into the undergrowth. *Phew.* I gave it a few moments to add some distance between us before pedaling rather cautiously toward the spot it had vacated. Wouldn't you know it? The little devil was awaiting me. He quickly raised his rear end and let go with a burst of spray that literally soaked a portion of my jersey and cycling shorts. The near point-blank range was deadly accurate and shockingly forceful. If I stopped pedaling, the acrid skunk odour was too much to bear. I kept moving at a good clip hoping to dry out somewhat before arriving home where I threw out my riding gear and bathed, somewhat ineffectively, in tomato juice. Interestingly, my firsthand skunk experience really solidified in my senses the difference between the smell of raw marihuana in full bud and the more chemical-based odour of a skunk's defence mechanism. But back to the smelly challenge of the indoor marihuana cultivators, some of whom have force-fed their vented air into the main sewage pipe of a house as a means of odour-free venting. This method is fairly ineffi-cient, and as you may imagine, introduces other odour and plumbing problems.

Since my days of discovering and dismantling illegal marihuana growing operations, the Canadian government has legalized marihuana possession, use, and production (all within proscribed limitations). Does this "legitimization" of weed propagate feelings of regret or futility when I reflect back on our efforts to eradicate illegal marihuana production? No, not at all. It wasn't the product itself that fired my sense of justice; it was the exploitive and harmful actions of organized crime that fueled my passion to seek and destroy these insidious operations. Any wedge that took the fight to organized crime was worthy in my view, and the drug trade is where organize crime flourishes. Huge sums of cash are generated off of the misery that many families bear when losing a loved one to the chemical concoctions. Drug addiction and overdose deaths start somewhere, and it's usually with weed at a young age. I'm proud of the efforts my colleagues and I put into busting grow-ops; society's nascent acceptance of weed doesn't diminish that in any way. The way I see it, if adults choose to toxify their lungs with harmful chemicals, who am I to judge? I'll be pouring a stiff jolt of single malt tonight, though legally produced and purchased.

Many illegal marihuana cultivators have been taken down by jilted lovers and anonymous calls to Crime Stoppers. And, of course, some by an exhausted cop on his bike. While the cultivation investigations I described relied upon the authority of a search warrant to enter a residence, exigent circumstances can be the catalyst to a warrantless entry under the provisions of Common Law, as we'll see next.

Further information about Crime Stoppers is available at www.solvecrime. ca.

SOMETIMES THE DEAD AREN'T DEAD

THE POLICE ARE FREQUENTLY ASKED TO CHECK ON THE WELL-being of an individual. Most often, the subject of concern is an elderly person living alone that neighbours haven't seen for an abnormally long period of time.

I attended such a call one rainy evening. The house in question was a tiny bungalow that hadn't benefitted from a lawnmower for many months. Neighbours had not seen the elderly gentleman living in the house for nearly as long. It was now the dead of winter; daylight was short, yet no lights had been seen in the old gent's house for days. With my flashlight in hand, I knocked on the front and rear doors and did my best to peer into windows but was unable to raise a response or see any sign of life in the darkness. My mind was settling on finding a corpse as the probable outcome; however, I knew that I had to continue. There could be a chance that he was alive and in medical distress of some sort.

I entered the house through an unlocked back window and loudly announced my presence. No response. I used my flashlight to locate a light switch in the kitchen, but nothing changed when I flicked it. There remained a complete absence of light other than my three-cell heavy-duty Kel-Lite. I gingerly poked my way through the small abode looking for the body I knew I was sure to find. The house was in rough shape. Time and a dearth of general maintenance had robbed it of its livability. The roof had clearly been leaking in more than one place, and it was just as cold inside the dwelling as outside that stormy evening. Using the single beam of light in my hand, I turned into the

220

bedroom. A collection of blankets on an old steel frame bed were covering what appeared to be a bloated human form of considerable size. I had found what I feared I would.

I stepped nearer the bed and let my light settle where the head should be if the blankets weren't pulled so high up. I reached forward and began gingerly pulling the wad of blankets down. Suddenly, with a great cry, the body jerked upward and a head emerged. *Holy shit! He's alive.*

I quickly identified myself as the police and explained that I wanted to check on him. I aimed the light toward me to illuminate my uniform. The man was justifiably paralyzed with fear until he managed to comprehend that I was there to help, not harm. He sat up in bed, and after we had both collected our wits, I began a conversation with a living, breathing being. I was so relieved.

The gentleman was very elderly, and his health was not good. He had no family that I could contact. He told me that the power company had cut his electricity weeks ago due to non-payment. He had not had light, heat, or hot water since. I was furious at this point. I wanted to pull the CEO of the Crown Corporation that supplies electrical power to British Columbia out of what I imagine to be posh surroundings and have him trade places with the old-timer. The roof was leaking and water was dripping into the bedroom with nearly same fury as the rainstorm outside. I was heartbroken that this vulnerable member of our city had been so severely neglected, essentially left for dead save for the concern of a heads-up neighbour who took the time to call.

I notified our dispatch and asked for Car 86 to attend so that the emergency social worker, paired with a police officer, could take over. Their first step would be to find safe, warm lodging for the gentleman. The following day, Social Services could undertake an assessment to determine the best course of action to ensure the ongoing safety and wellness of the corpse that came to life. I hope a lesson that all readers take away from this event is simply this: Don't feel intimidated or reluctant to call 9-1-1 and report that a neighbour or someone you know may be in need of help. More often than not, such a hunch is correct.

And don't be shy about reporting suspicious activity in your neighbourhood. Had some folks in London done so in 2005, fifty-two people may be alive today.

COUNTERING TERRORISM

IT WAS THE MORNING OF JULY 7, 2005 WHEN THREE SUICIDE bombers detonated their vests on trains in the London Tube. A fourth suspect blew up a transit bus above ground. The carnage claimed fifty-two lives while raising a red flag globally around the vulnerability of "soft targets." These are generally locations of high density and low security, enabling terrorists to gain maximum impact with the least resistance. They are also the targets that generate the greatest level of fear in the greatest number of people, thereby paralyzing a city. How many Londoners were eager to ride the tube or a bus on July 8, 2005?

This incident, and the reign of terror inflicted on the US population on September 11, 2001, along with the Madrid transit bombings of 2004, weighed heavily on every chief of police in North America and globally. Chief Jamie Graham in Vancouver was no less concerned for the security of his city and the safety of its citizens.

I was the inspector in-charge of the Criminal Intelligence Section at the time and was responsible for briefing the chief on terror-related threats, which were on the rise internationally and within Canada. It seems these briefings filled the chief with concern, so much so that he declared, on a radio talk show exploring the topic, "If you knew what I knew, you wouldn't sleep at night." Regrettably, the chief took a lot of unjust heat over this statement, which many viewed as inflammatory. Given that my briefings were largely the source of what he knew, I can assure readers of this memoir that his words rang true with me. Canada was on the list of countries targeted by radical extremists and files of substance, requiring immediate investigation, were many.

The mandate for national security falls to the Royal Canadian Mounted Police (RCMP); however, all law enforcement agencies have a role to play, some greater than others. With Vancouver's reputation as a destination city, home to an exceptionally diverse population, we recognized the need to be firmly committed and fully invested in detecting, detouring, and investigating incidents of terrorism and terror threats. We worked closely with the RCMP's local Integrated National Security Enforcement Team for British Columbia (E-INSET); however, given that seventy percent of their files were either rooted in Vancouver, or in some manner connected, we felt more had to be done to generate reliable intelligence that might identify and disrupt a planned terror event at the earliest possible stage. Within this framework, Chief Jamie Graham tasked me with establishing our own counter-terrorism investigative unit and writing its operating mandate. The concept wasn't intended to compete with E-INSET, or undermine its important role, but rather to be complementary and supportive. The manner in which we chose to do that was through the power of our "boots on the street."

The mandate I established for the VPD Counter-Terrorism Unit (CTU) was designed to generate leads and investigate them to determine their level of credibility. If credible, the file would be adopted by the British Columbia's E-INSET team and jointly investigated with the Vancouver Police Counter-Terrorism Unit. There was, in my mind, no value to the RCMP in simply handing over leads that had not been vetted in any meaningful manner; doing so would further overload the RCMP INSET team and potentially allow something noteworthy to slip between the cracks due to an unmanageable workload.

Creating an effective Counter-Terrorism Unit was new to municipal policing. There was no playbook to rely upon, so Mike Purdy, the sergeant that was selected to supervise the unit, and I travelled to the United Kingdom to conduct a best-practices study in advance of establishing our unit. Police agencies in the UK had far more experience in dealing with terrorism than any agency in North America. We started our journey at Scotland Yard. I was shocked by the number of terror threats they were dealing with on a daily basis. These were largely Islamist-extremist-based threats, not unlike those which had markedly altered the Western world's perception of safety and security at home and abroad.

The London Metropolitan Police reviewed with us a number of interesting and effective information-gathering strategies they employed, including the Richer Picture Program. This project leveraged the eyes and ears of public services, such as postal workers and home-visit nurses, who were provided a basic orientation on indicators of potential terror-related activity and products. When they made observations of concern, they reported such to the police through a tip line. These tips have been key to disrupting multiple terror plots that may not have otherwise been identified. This program solidified in me the importance of good intelligence.

Had the Richer Picture Program been in existence prior to the London Bombings, the plot may have been discovered in time to save fifty-two innocent lives. The signals were there, waiting to be detected. All that was needed was someone to report the sight of vegetation dying outside an open window at the suspects' house, or the smell of chemicals being emitted, or perhaps the unusually large purchases of hair bleach by the individuals responsible. Hair bleach contains triacetone triperoxide (TATP), needed to manufacture a high-intensity explosive, which must be kept very cold. A bathtub full of ice was another clue, noted by a public-health nurse but not interpreted as anything of concern.

While the work of Scotland Yard was impressive, I was sorely disappointed by one aspect of their performance. It was three p.m. "Care for a cup of tea?" asked one of the detectives speaking the queen's English. With great anticipation, I awaited what I expected to be a Brown-Betty teapot to emerge from a kitchen cabinet, along with china cups and Murchies loose tea. What I got was a Styrofoam cup with hot water and a Twinings teabag in a paper envelope. No pomp or ceremony. How could this be? I was in Scotland Yard with the world's most famed detectives. Oh well, it was tea, and greatly appreciated despite the less-than-regal presentation.

From London, we took the train north to Manchester and met with the Greater Manchester Police. Their work in the field of counter-terrorism was equally impressive and informative. With its diverse, working-class population, Manchester has dealt with more than its fair share of terror-based threats; however, our next stop arguably had the longest history of domestic terrorism within the Western world. We were airborne over the Irish Sea on our way to Belfast in Northern Ireland. The "Troubles" in Belfast were largely subdued by the time of our visit, but certainly not over.

Mike and I arrived a day early and decided to explore Belfast by transit. The name Ballybeen Estates sounded impressive, so we jumped a bus that made a circuitous loop from our hotel through the Estates, expecting to see centuries-old European castles built of stone. Ballybeen Estates is not what North Americans might think of as estates. Rather they were modest, blue-collar rowhouses with huge murals of their gun-toting loyalist heroes painted on either ends of the blocks of adjoining homes, which were housing families eking out a living at the lower rungs of the financial ladder. Ballybeen Estates is the second largest housing estate in Northern Ireland and not a place for a couple of naive cops from overseas to go nosing around. This was made abundantly clear to us the following day by our high-ranking host from the Police Service of Northern Ireland, formerly the Royal Ulster Constabulary.

Of the many experiences that fascinated me during my policing career, the time spent in Belfast with the Police Service of Northern Ireland may be the top. Learning about the Troubles firsthand from senior members of the police service and seeing the Peace Wall, meant to separate the Catholics from the Protestants, was compelling yet heartbreaking. The violence and murders over decades were nothing short of shocking, and much of it was aimed at the police. As a result, their stations remain heavily fortified and are hidden behind massive walls to this day.

Despite inter-denominational marriages gaining popularity in Northern Ireland, the conflict between Catholics and Protestants, also delineated as Republicans versus Loyalists, simmers beneath a veneer of peace and tolerance, with hostility never more than an insult away. This was most evident when the Counter-Terrorism officers in Belfast hosted Mike and me for dinner in a local pub. The cops are still considered viable targets in the conflict. The machine guns hidden in gym bags at each end of our long table were evidence of that reality. Should certain factions of the IRA become aware of the police presence, social as the event was, deadly attacks could erupt without warning.

Once back on Canadian soil, we distilled all we had learned during our time in the UK and incorporated much of the findings into the mandate and proposed goals of our newly formed Vancouver Police Counter-Terrorism Unit. Any given day, four hundred or more uniformed officers patrol the streets of Vancouver. They take in excess of a quarter million calls per year, and in doing so, generate countless opportunities to receive information from the public about suspicious activity that could pose a terror-based risk to the city, its infrastructure, or its citizens. We trained our officers on the telltale indicators of terrorist planning, teaching them to look for certain clues that could be pivotal. We asked them to seize upon opportunities to converse with the public, and when appropriate, to ask generic questions about suspicious activity. It's well known in policing that the eyes and ears of the public are invaluable in identifying and detouring crime of all genres. As Sir Robert Peel, the father of modern democratic policing, so famously opined: "The police are the public and the public are the police." Once the public become attuned to what should be considered suspicious, the calls start coming in, which is good but also challenging.

We were roughly five-years away from hosting the 2012 Winter Olympics at this point, so every tip required exhaustive investigation. We knew that terrorists are patient. They have been known to plan attacks years in advance, so nothing could be arbitrarily dismissed as not being a threat to the games without adequate investigation.

The following case summaries are typical of those investigated back in 2005 by the newly formed Vancouver Police Counter-Terrorism Unit. You'll no doubt sense the need to scrutinize and fully probe such tips, as any one of these could have been a lead that would prevent a catastrophic tragedy. Fortunately, all of the cases cited were determined to be unfounded, and were subsequently dismissed.

- A letter obtained discussed a religious leader and alleged ties to 9/11 hijackers. The writer of the letter, while possibly having mental-health issues, demonstrated thorough knowledge of world events and sound knowledge of terrorist tactics.
- Information was received that a male was attempting to make a purchase of twenty Scuba re-breather kits at a local dive shop. These units cost approximately $20,000 each and are used primarily by the military for operations. (They do not produce bubble trails.) The alert clerk noted that the male wasn't knowledgeable about the equipment and was nervous. This tip brought heightened concern due to Vancouver's approaching cruise-ship season.
- Reports of suspicious videotaping and photography of critical infrastructures were commonly received. These targets could include water, gas, and electrical infrastructure, as well as structures such as bridges, tunnels,

pipelines and more. Such investigations require significant legwork to determine the motivation behind the reported activity and the legitimacy of the allegations.

- Vancouver receives many anonymous bomb threats. Each such call must be thoroughly investigated to determine if there is a terrorist nexus to the claim. Terror groups have been known to place false bomb threats hoping to determine the response protocols of police and emergency services. And also to identify where to locate a secondary device targeting those responders.

- An anonymous tip was received from a member of the public about a person living in Vancouver who posed a threat to the city through ties to terrorist groups. Dubious tips of this nature may require extensive investigation to firmly identify the subject of the tip and validate or refute the claim.

- As intended when we established the VPD's Counter-Terrorism Unit, patrol officers received training in order to spot possible indicators of terrorist activity. This led to a range of patrol-generated reports, including such concerns as information about individuals possessing terrorist-supportive writings, through to, people possibly involved in the production of explosive devices.

- A tipster claimed that an individual was attempting to obtain several tons of explosives through international sources. A file such as this could easily require Interpol assistance and the investigative services of counter-terrorism agencies worldwide, such as the Joint Terrorism Taskforce (JTTF) in the United States.

The Vancouver Police Counter-Terrorism Unit was highly successful in meeting its mandate of generating and investigating tips related to terrorism. Within a couple of years, a joint decision was made between the RCMP and the Vancouver Police to amalgamate the VPD Counter-Terrorism Unit with a satellite E-INSET team to be co-located within the Vancouver Police Covert Operations building, at 5 East 8th Avenue. I share the address today knowing that the Vancouver Police vacated the building long ago. Anyone viewing the building, which sits on the corner of 8th Avenue and Ontario Street in Vancouver, will notice the advanced security of the building achieved through architectural design. The structure is fabricated with concrete, featuring exceptionally thick buttressing at the ground level. The bullet-proof windows in the two-story building are narrow and set high in the walls. I worked in that mysterious facility for a number of years. It had an amazing, panoramic view of downtown Vancouver and the North Shore mountains from its roof. It's also the building that H.A.D. Oliver QC found so very fascinating the night I drove him home from our mess dinner in his tuxedo, with his chest of medals, including the Order of Canada Cross proudly on display.

The VPD, CTU, and RCMP E-INSET amalgamation was ground-breaking in Canada. Never before had the RCMP agreed to co-locate its national security team with a municipal police agency. Doing so meant also sharing the RCMP's most sensitive database with the VPD. A special fibre-optic cable had to be brought into the building. Sensitive cabling such as this must not be routed inside walls as electrical lines typically are. They must be strung along wire-mesh caging affixed to the walls within the building in order that the cabling is fully visible. This prevents a treacherous subject from secretly tapping into the cable. Unfortunately, when the VPD vacated the building, the satellite RCMP INSET team returned to an RCMP facility. The Vancouver Police Counter-Terrorism Unit was formally deactivated post 2010 Olympics; however, the partnership with E-INSET remains and includes VPD detectives embedded in their offices. And the power of the boots on the street? It continues undiminished despite the dissolution of the VPD's Counter-Terrorism Unit.

Terrorism plots continue as well, as evidenced in 2006 with the Toronto Eighteen terror group that planned to detonate a series of truck bombs at high profile targets, including the Toronto Stock Exchange building, the headquarters of the Canadian Security and Intelligence Service, and a Canadian Armed Forces base. In 2013, two suspects holding radical beliefs intended to blow up a rail bridge outside of Toronto while a Via Rail passenger train passed over it. Also in 2013, two radicalized suspects planned to detonate a pressure-cooker bomb on the grounds of the B.C. Legislature building during Canada Day celebrations. Fortunately, these plots were all detected early enough to prevent them from succeeding. Suspects in all three events were arrested, charged, and convicted, although a stay of proceedings was issued under appeal in the latter case. And let's not forget that the world's deadliest terror attack prior to 911 was planned and executed in Canada by Canadian Sikh militants. Air India flight 182 disintegrated in 1985 when a bomb detonated at 31,000 feet over the Atlantic Ocean killing all 329 individuals onboard.

These attacks are far from the only incidents of domestic terrorism that Canadian police agencies have dealt with, and they won't be the last. It's my belief that detecting, disrupting, and deterring terrorist activity on Canadian soil must remain a high priority for Canadian law enforcement. Geo-political instability, driven by insurgency, climate change, and more recently a global pandemic, among other causes, has the potential to increase the terror threat level, especially as it applies to "lone wolf" operators; those radicalized individuals who harbour conspiracy theories and feel betrayed or deeply aggrieved by government.

Whether an active deadly threat is a terrorist-related event, or more simply a deranged killer at the workplace, there are survival strategies and tactics that all should be aware of. The Vancouver Police Department has produced an eight-minute video portraying a workplace mass killing, which depicts the steps to survival and provides invaluable tips for safely escaping an active deadly threat. The video can be accessed through VPD's website at: https://vpd.ca/crime-prevention-safety/active-deadly-threat/

COMPLAINTS AGAINST ME:
REAL AND IMAGINED

A MEMOIR DRAWN FROM THIRTY-THREE YEARS OF POLICING couldn't be considered complete without a chapter dedicated to conduct-related complaints. Specifically, those made against me. By its very nature, police work often generates friction and animosity with citizens, resulting in complaints against officers. No one calls the cops to report that they're having a good day, or calls asking for a traffic ticket. Complaints about cops are inevitable, but when looked at in relation to the huge number of daily interactions between the police and the public, they are remarkably rare. Nonetheless, every complaint deserves investigation, or at minimum, a review to determine validity. In British Columbia, conduct-related complaints against the police, which do not allege serious injury to a citizen, are generally investigated by the Professional Standards Unit of the respective police agency (formerly known in the VPD as the Internal Investigation Section). All such, investigations are subject to the principles of civilian oversight, as applied in BC by the Office of the Police Complaint Commissioner. (See www.opcc.bc.ca for further insight.) Complaints alleging serious injury or death at the hands of the police in British Columbia are investigated by the Independent Office of Investigation. (See www.iio.bc.ca for further insight.)

I'm going to cover two complaints that were filed against me, one of which arose out of an off-duty interaction I had with a hostile male who had accidently rammed his truck into my personal vehicle in a parking lot and didn't wish to take responsibility. The other complaint was a wild accusation from a mentally ill subject that was taken a little too seriously, in my humble opinion, by the Office of the Police Complaint Commissioner. You'll see what I mean when you read the substance of the complaint.

The first incident occurred in the parking lot of a Home Depot store in the Vancouver suburb of Richmond, BC, the same parking lot in which I tried to shake the Russians a few years later during a botched surveillance. Anyone who knows me knows my penchant for cars. Mine are always well cared for and maintained in good condition. I habitually choose parking spots that I feel are the least likely to garner door dings due to the carelessness of others.

On this fateful occasion, my wife and I were in line at the Home Depot checkout. I was gazing out into the parking lot watching a beater pickup truck quickly reverse into a stall that I knew was in the proximity of where I had parked. I saw the truck lurch sharply to a stop, which indicated to me that it had struck the vehicle behind it. I kept my eye on the truck and told my wife that I was going into the lot to check if it was my car that had been hit. And yes, to my horror, it was.

I could see that the entire grille of my car was punched in. I could also see the offending driver, a large man in filthy coveralls, quickly walking away. I said, "I think you hit my car." His immediate response wasn't to apologize but to claim that he didn't cause all the damage. It was obvious that the height of his rear bumper far exceeded the height of my front bumper, which placed the point of impact at the most vulnerable part of most vehicles: the front grille. I said that he certainly did cause the damage, but rather than argue, I suggested we let the insurance company sort it out.

"I need to see your driver's licence," I told him. He refused, saying that all I needed was the plate number of the truck, and he kept walking away from me. I clutched him by the arm and told him that I was a police officer, and that I would arrest him if he didn't identify himself. He shrugged away my arm and tried to walk past me. I placed him into an arm-lock and told him that he was under arrest. At this point, he relented and said he would show me his driver's licence. I released his arm, and he adeptly pulled his licence from his wallet, choosing to hold his stubby thumb over top of all the pertinent data. After I finally convinced him of his legal requirement to produce his driver's licence so it could be viewed, he allowed me to capture his identity.

I sensed that this guy was going to be a problem for me one way or the other. I drove directly to the RCMP station in Richmond, filed an accident report, and provided details of the difficult encounter with the offending driver. All seemed fine for a few days; then came a call from the RCMP asking me to attend the station in response to the investigation of an assault allegation reported by the offending driver. *You can't be serious,* I thought, but I attended as arranged. I was escorted into an interview room and read my rights. As a cop that has read suspects their rights hundreds of times over the years, this felt completely foreign and a little intimidating.

"Do you want a lawyer?"

I didn't. What I wanted was a thorough investigation by the RCMP, believing that the truth would deliver justice. I read the statement submitted against me. It was partially correct but largely deceptive and rife with fabrication. It was correct in that he finally admitted causing the damage, but untrue in his description of our encounter.

He claimed that I had lifted him off the ground with an arm lock and thrown him over the hood of my car, which frankly was impossible given his weight of two hundred pounds or more. This feat of super-human strength could not be accomplished with the use of an arm lock. Our friend had sustained no arm injury or any other physical maladies from the encounter. Furthermore, there's no way that I would throw a person over the hood of my car! I'm the guy that's paranoid about door dings. I laid out to the RCMP all of the inconsistencies in the subject's story and invited them to examine the hood of my car for marks related to throwing a full-size male in coveralls onto it. But that didn't end the emotional and professional difficulties this creep would go on to cause me. Knowing that I was a Vancouver Police Officer, he filed a formal complaint with our Internal Investigation Section, alleging violent off-duty conduct. More Canadian Charter of Rights warnings and more statements were formally demanded of me. The subject also claimed to have initiated a civil action against me, seeking financial compensation.

I wrote to the RCMP, demanding that they conduct a full and thorough investigation of the allegations against me, and that they also investigate my complaint that the other driver was committing the criminal offence of public mischief. A public mischief occurs when someone intentionally engages the police in an investigation that they know to be false, which is exactly what the offending driver was doing. To their credit, the investigators went back to the subject, laid that concern out to him, and warned him that if evidence were to support a charge of public mischief, it would be proceeded upon. At this point, the offender's true motive became clear. In a tone described to me as glib and victorious, he said to the RCMP investigators that he had caused me enough trouble and now wanted to rescind his complaint. The investigators asked him if he was also intending to rescind the complaint that he had laid with the Vancouver Police and the civil action he had commenced. He said that he was. He agreed to sign a document the RCMP put before him that validated the quality of the RCMP investigation and recognized that the complainant (offending driver) no longer wished to pursue the investigation or any further action related to his spurious allegations. This signed document was faxed to the Vancouver Police internal investigators, in order to conclude their investigation as well. I was never served with papers initiating a civil action, so I'm not sure what transpired there, or if that was just another one of his lies.

It was a huge to relief to have justice prevail, though I was disappointed that the RCMP chose not to pursue a charge of public mischief. They had a point though; there were no independent witnesses to rely upon. I have to say that the whole series of events left me a little bitter, but a whole lot wiser. I considered initiating a civil suit against the offending driver but figured that would just prolong the misery. Interestingly though, I could now more closely relate to how innocent people feel when questionable allegations are waged against them. I can tell you, it's a very helpless and lonely feeling. And as a cop, in addition to all of the foreboding and anxiety inherent in such circumstances, your career is on the line.

This firsthand insight into the emotions surrounding false accusations served to make me more careful about taking complainants at face value. A little more digging can pay off exponentially for an innocent "suspect" during an investigation in which guilt may initially appear certain. While this complaint arose out of a real event—damage to my vehicle followed by actions intended to make my life and that of my wife miserable (she was affected by it even more-so than me)—this next complaint was triggered by a letter the complainant had received with my name at the bottom.

After becoming a senior-ranking officer in the Vancouver Police Department, I was assigned as the inspector in-charge of the Internal Investigation Section, where I had just spent several years as an investigator. (Note: The Internal Investigation Section was renamed shortly after as the Professional Standards Section.) I headed a team of high-flying investigators that thoroughly investigated every conduct complaint against a Vancouver Police officer that came into our office or the office of the BC Police Complaint Commissioner.

When those investigations were completed, pursuant to timelines imposed by the BC Police Act, a letter summarizing the investigation and its findings would be sent to the complainant with a copy to the Police Complaint Commissioner. The letter would also outline additional steps that could be undertaken if the complainant was not satisfied with the outcome. As I was the inspector in-charge of the Internal Investigation Section, the letters went out under my signature after I reviewed each investigation and concurred with the findings. That meant a lot of people received a letter from Inspector Rob Rothwell, concluding an investigation into a conduct complaint they had lodged against the Vancouver Police Department or its members.

It stands to reason that many of the recipients were not happy with the findings articulated. One such individual was a person well known to my investigators for complaints that were conjured up by a mind that was not well. Mental illness triggered the submission of fantastical complaints from him, usually with strong sexual content that had no basis in reality. Had the newscaster really removed himself from the TV screen during the six-p.m. newscast and sexually assaulted our complainant? You get the picture. Sorry for the pun.

After receiving several letters from me indicating that his complaints were being dismissed because they lacked "an air of reality" (in concurrence with the BC Police Act), I became this complainant's next target. Our complainant, who was prone to submitting long, aimless, meandering complaints, knocked one out-of-the-park when he wrote to the Police Complaint Commissioner accusing me of anally raping him. Yes, you read that correctly. He claimed in his disjointed allegation that I had secretly filled his home with acetylene gas, to render him unconscious, then had my way with him in a most egregious manner. To bolster the credibility of his complaint, he included a vial containing clippings of fingernails, toenails, and pubic hair.

Just how, in his unconscious state, our complainant would have known it was me that had violated him, I'm not sure. Or why I wouldn't also have been overcome by the gas, if that was even possible. As I understand it, acetylene gas is highly explosive and unstable if not properly contained under pressure. Not sure how a house could be filled with it without something more catastrophic occurring than that which was outlined in the written complaint. Of course, the Police Complaint Commissioner wasn't as eager to dismiss the complaint as I was. In misplaced wisdom, the commissioner forwarded the complaint and the forensic evidence to me, asking that I assign an investigator immediately and have the biological samples analyzed—for what I'm not sure. Naturally, I was slightly disappointed in his decision-making.

I had no intention of processing clippings for a case of fantasy and made it clear to the commissioner that doing that so would bring the credibility of his office into question. Dedicating precious lab time to such pointless folly would only serve to further delay legitimate cases in which public safety was of concern. With that, I said I would happily return the biological contents to him for reconsideration. After further discussion, the commissioner agreed to dismiss the complaint and instructed me to discard the clippings. Not sure what had affected his thinking, but glad that logic returned.

In relation to the biological evidence, I assume that our complainant had read, or knew, that poisoning by arsenic will interrupt the growth of hair and nails. Under microscopic examination, small ridges can be detected in hair and nails that correspond with the phases of poisoning. I imagine this investigative technique underpinned his decision to submit the biological evidence for forensic examination. The fascinating book *Murder by Milkshake* by Eve Lazarus (Arsenal Pulp Press 2019) outlines this investigative technique, which was the linchpin to convicting Rene Castellani of murdering his wife, Esther, by poisoning her with arsenic. The arsenic was delivered through a series of milkshakes he served her over a period of illness.

Sadly, what our complainant really needed was a health-care system that could provide meaningful intervention and treatment, but he wasn't the only subject suffering from a mental illness that wrote to us with some degree of regularity. Having read so many letters of complaint while I managed the Internal Investigation Section, I developed a sixth sense for the mental well-being of an author based on the length of a complaint, and if written by hand, by the messiness of the script. In general terms, the longer and messier, the less stable the writer. While complaints from those not well mentally were not uncommon, complaints that were either untrue or contained some degree of deception were encountered as well. Though such submissions cannot be prejudged, there are certain commonalities that can tip off an investigator and open doors to avenues of further investigation. I took a statement analysis course as a detective, which revealed some fairly reliable characteristics of deception in written and oral statements.

Statements that are needlessly and excessively long are early clues to deception. Untruthful individuals will provide great detail and truthfulness around superfluous elements of their day that don't directly pertain to the issue in question. You might read that they *got up as usual at eight a.m. and had half a bowl of Cheerios for breakfast, because they were out of eggs, which they usually eat for breakfast, but only two eggs because of the cholesterol.* And that their *coffee was weak because the new blend, which was on sale for $6.99, isn't as good as the old blend that they normally buy.* When they finally get to the part of the day in which they stabbed their roommate in the heart, it may go something like this: *'I slipped in the kitchen, and the knife accidentally hit my roommate, because he was standing too close to me.'*

It's as if they want the investigator to be impressed with the level of detail and honesty they are endeavouring to provide. And they want that notion to apply to the critical areas of the statement as well, despite being unable to provide the same level of truthfulness and detail without incriminating themselves. As a result, they gloss over the salient elements, hoping that the "awed" investigator won't twig to the weakness. It's a way of having their cake and trying to eat it too, but it doesn't work. Any reasonably competent investigator will see through the sham.

Ongoing training as a detective is essential to remaining abreast of the latest investigative techniques and governing jurisprudence. But training opportunities are also available to hone one's proficiency in dealing with deadly threats. I had the privilege of attending such a training course hosted by one of the world's top law-enforcement agencies: the US Secret Service.

US SECRET SERVICE'S DUAL MISSION

THE LAST MAJOR TRAINING COURSE OF MY CAREER WAS SET in 2008 in Washington D.C., during the same week that President Barack Obama was elected over Republican candidate John McCain. The course was an executive-level international program hosted by the US Secret Service. It was one-week in length and consisted of fascinating classroom discussion with key US Secret Service personnel in their D.C. Headquarters, along with on-site activities at the Service's premier tactical-training facility, the James J. Rowley Training Centre in Maryland.

Our class was comprised of thirty police officials from law-enforcement agencies around the world. I was the only Canadian candidate. Throughout the program, four of us gelled and chummed around together at lunch and after class. There was Jean-Phillipe from Versailles, France; Fernando from Madrid, Spain; and Paulo from Rio de Janeiro, Brazil. Getting to know these chaps and exchanging personal stories and police practices with them was truly enlightening. There is much crossover and similarity in police work that transcends all cultural and geographical boundaries. But as much as similarities may exist, a wide chasm exists in other areas of policing, tolerance for protest and civil disobedience being an example in which Canada shines in comparison.

The role of the US Secret Service is twofold. Firstly, it is responsible for protecting US currency from fraud, counterfeiting, and corruption. While many people associate the Secret Service with protecting the president, they may not realize that the integrity of the US greenback also rests squarely upon the shoulders of the Service. Historically, many completely separate currencies existed in the United States, which was certainly problematic as the union took shape. A single, consistent, and completely trustworthy currency was needed. The US dollar as we know it today was established nation-wide, with its integrity an unassailable founding principle. The Secret Service was formed as the agency tasked with protecting that integrity, which it has done since 1865. The protection of presidents, past and present, is its second *raison d'être*. It began protecting US presidents following the assassination of President William McKinley in 1901. In our discussions, the Service laid out concerns around its ability to protect Barack Obama if he became president-elect on Tuesday of the week we were there.

As everyone now knows, Obama was elected. Interestingly, I was more excited about his victory over the late Senator John McCain than many of the Americans I encountered. I felt it was transformative and highly progressive to elect a non-white president in the United States. Regrettably, many Americans failed to share that view. There had been so many credible threats against Obama's life during the run-up to the election that it generated unprecedented worry within the Service. Would they be able to protect Obama from every gun-toting white nationalist that vowed to never allow a black man into the Oval Office? Most of them apparently had no idea that Obama's mother was a white woman, that he was born in the state of Hawaii, and that he was not Muslim. Nonetheless, that didn't make the threats any less real. The Obama presidency was a game-changer for the Secret Service. They had to retool and rethink their strategies and tactics in order to deliver the most expansive protection any president, up to that point, had received.

The more dynamic components of our training program were delivered at the Rowley Training Centre, which is spread over 493 acres of rural Maryland forest and fields. The immensity of the facility includes thirty-six buildings comprising training rooms, gun ranges, gyms, and other assorted structures. More interesting to me was a faux village that resembled Main Street of Anytown, USA. It consisted of a central roadway lined with shops and services of such authenticity that I joked about popping into the barbershop to get a trim before asking the bank manager for a loan.

The roadway network used for driver training involved six miles of turns, intersections, and straightaways. There was even a highway overpass, which can be a lifesaving asset of presidential importance during a hurricane or aerial attack. Our next assignment, though, involved neutralizing a sniper in a tower, not on the road. The outdoor training facility included an area that resembled a typical laneway in an urban setting. A few abandoned cars, a mailbox, fencing, and other such items that could be used as either cover or concealment, and it's important to know the difference. Concealment will hide a responding officer from a threat but won't necessarily protect that officer from gunfire. A wooden fence is a good example of concealment; however, if bullets fly, the wood is unlikely to stop them. "Cover" is generally considered concealment that's solid enough to also prevent ballistic penetration. Concrete is a good example, and so is the engine block of a vehicle when nothing better is within access.

At the head of the urban laneway was an elevated shelter fabricated from a form of Lexan, which is a remarkably durable Plexi-glass-like product. The shelter simulated a tower and was fitted with a slot for use of a long-barrel weapon. Inside the shelter, armed with a long gun, was a sharpshooter. The shooter, played by a highly-proficient firearms instructor, used "simunition" ammo. Simunition ammunition is a non-lethal cartridge that shoots a bullet composed of hardened wax or a similar substance. Simunition will leave a coloured mark on any surface it strikes, enabling post-gunfight analysis. Heavy protective clothing along with a helmet and goggles had to be worn by participants for protection. Though they may be fabricated from wax, simunitions can be quite painful against unprotected flesh and could cause serious injuries if a subject is struck in a vulnerable location, such as the eye, ear, or . . . well, you get it.

In this exercise, students had to work in pairs. I chose Fernando, whose English was a bit dodgy at best. I couldn't complain though, as my Spanish was far worse. When I had been in the Drug Squad, our team was taught some basic Spanish in order to converse with an influx of Central American drug dealers who were violently dominating the Downtown Eastside drug trade. While the intent was commendable, the initiative showed its weakness when a Spanish-speaking dealer would respond to basic questions I had asked in Spanish with complex, rapid-fire answers. I simply couldn't match the pace of the exchange or sustain the conversation in his native tongue, which only served to undermine my credibility. I quickly reassumed the role of monolinguist.

Back to the sniper scenario. Fernando and I had to work as a team and were tasked with making our way through the lane and into a position close enough to accurately shoot the sniper. The only times the sniper would not fire at us was when he couldn't see us or when one of us was shooting at the tower. Otherwise, it was open-season on the trainees. Due to the language barrier between us, Fernando and I used hand signs to communicate our moves, which had to be perfectly timed and coordinated if we were to survive the sniper's attacks. While one of us quickly relocated to a position closer to the threat, the other had to lay down a steady stream of cover fire at the tower. We were armed with semi-automatic pistols, which fired simunitions.

An instructor on the ground assessed our performance in real time and carried a large supply of fully-loaded magazines (often incorrectly referred to as "clips"). We were not limited in how many magazines we were allowed. They would be dispensed to us by the assessing instructor whenever he saw us drop an empty or partially empty magazine from our firearm. This tidbit of information was key to a successful outcome.

Before taking our places, Fernando and I had agreed that neither of us would move to a new location until the other inserted a full magazine of ammunition, rather than relying upon an unknown number of rounds available in an existing mag. The other element on our side was time. We wouldn't rush this. Each of us had to be certain of what actions the other intended to take before putting wheels into motion.

We took to the course, each of us behind different sources of cover but close enough to retain visual contact. I'd point to where I intended to move to next. Fernando would acknowledge with thumbs up. He'd commence cover fire, at which point, I'd quickly reposition myself closer to the tower. The process would then be repeated to facilitate Fernando's advance. I'd continually fire at the tower while keeping an eye on Fernando's movement. When he was safely behind cover, I'd drop the used magazine and load a fresh one. Then I'd take a moment or two to plan my next move and communicate with Fernando.

Fernando and I repeated the cover-fire and move cycle a number of times. As we did, the tower would randomly fire at us between our moves, or if we presented a target, such as sticking our head out to have a quick look or leaving a limb exposed. And the sniper was deadly accurate (figuratively). Eventually, Fernando and I were both within range to take out the sniper. At this point, we both emptied a magazine of thirteen shots at the tower and ended the scenario. On post examination of our outer clothing and protective gear, some hits from the tower were noted. Seems the sniper put a round into the top of my helmet, judging by the smear of orange wax. This shooting exercise had been so adrenalin-inducing that I hadn't heard or felt a round striking the top of my helmet. The sniper said that I never raised my head to look, but that I had briefly misjudged how high I was holding my head when taking cover behind a low concrete barrier, and that's all it took. Good to know.

The week spent with the US Secret Service was truly a career highlight, and one that I'll always be grateful for. I'd like to thank the professionals at the Service for the exceptional care they took of us and for the invaluable training we participated in. Their work may reside in the shadows, but take notice: They are actively protecting the American currency and the American president 24/7 anywhere in the world.

Further, I'd like to recognize a friend and colleague, Mr. Greg Almaraz, who was then the resident agent in-charge, United States Secret Service, Vancouver Resident Office, for inviting me on the journey with the Secret Service.

THE ROAD TO RETIREMENT

WITH THE EXPIRATION OF MY EXECUTIVE CONTRACT, I RETIRED from being a cop in April of 2012 after thirty-three years with the Vancouver Police Department. The day I handed over my .40 calibre Barretta semi-auto pistol, my handcuffs, uniform, and police notebooks was a day of mixed emotion. On one hand, it was liberating to free myself of the jeopardy and accountability that goes with the badge; on the other hand, it felt isolating, leaving me with a streak of melancholy. I'd no longer be among my colleagues—individuals I knew would risk their own safety for mine and would be first to step up if ever tragedy were to befall me or my family. There's a deep-seated reassurance that comes from this level of commitment, which I'll always be grateful for.

Prior to retiring, I had been the superintendent in command of the Investigation Division of the Vancouver Police Department. This meant that all investigative units, be it Homicide, Robbery/Assault/Arson, Financial Crime, Special Investigations, and more reported through a chain of command to me. I reported to a deputy chief. As an executive member of the department, my role wasn't to actively pursue investigations, but rather to lead those highly capable individuals that did and to balance the public purse with the need to provide exceptional public safety. There is no endless pot of money to fund every investigation the police should ideally embark upon, nor are there the human resources needed. Nonetheless, crimes occur and they must be investigated to the furthest extent possible under the circumstances. Organized crime groups must also be focused on, and publication of the Annual Provincial and National

Threat Assessments assist the police in identifying the groups posing the greatest risk to the public and most urgently in need of police attention.

I'm not embellishing when I say that the Vancouver Police investigative units are highly skilled, competent, clever, and remarkably capable. They truly are. As their superintendent, I saw my role as that of facilitator in addition to that of executive oversight. Whatever investigators needed, to get the job done, I made it my job to get for them. I then stepped aside and let them exercise their inherent talents. It was a management style that was effective and greatly appreciated by the men and women in the trenches. A further management tactic I applied, which I learned from a rather eccentric supervisor when I was a detective many years before, was the art of managing by "walking around."

Managing by walking around is rooted in the practice of taking daily or semi-weekly informal walks through each investigative bullpen and connecting with frontline investigators and their supervisors. It's not about demanding stats and file updates, but rather about asking, "How are you doing? How can I help?" It's also about knowing a little something important to each person.

"Make sure you leave here today in time to get to your kid's (fill in the blank: ballgame, teacher conference, ballet, etc.)" was a typical directive of mine. I often cycled to work back then, so for added fun and superior time-management, I took to cycling around each of the investigative floors in the building to meet and greet the teams as they were embracing their morning coffees. The occasional Nerf ambush was a great stress reliever. We did our best to hide our massive nerf-gun battles from the deputy chief. Most of my investigative units had a supply of nerf weapons and foam projectiles. I was often ambushed during my "management by walking about" moments (or more clandestinely, in my office) by Nerf-armed Ninja warriors. Of course, I'd strategically retaliate. Maybe the same day, maybe not, but "I'll be baaack." My target would always be the team supervisor or manager. It's surprising how the investigators wouldn't "give me up," so to speak, as I used what I had learned with the US Secret Service to make my way unnoticed to the boss's office for a rapid-fire strike.

On the serious side, plenty of stress and negativity is experienced by detectives dealing with the worst forms of depravity that humans can expend upon each other. A little light-hearted fun in the office went a long way to boosting morale, and I'd argue, productivity. I was proud of the investigators and wanted them to know it. Despite the fun I chose to inject into the role of superintendent, the frequent one a.m. or later emergency phone calls and the continuous engagement became a burden that, after four years I was ready to excise from my life. Retirement was on the horizon, but not the rocking chair.

My planned departure happened to coincide with the VPD's need to hire a civilian manager to renew its aging fleet of patrol vehicles and manage its list of 525 fleet assets, which includes cars, motorcycles, trucks, trailers, boats, and more. This seemed like an interesting opportunity, which would allow me to remain a member of the department's senior management team while enjoying a post-retirement civilian management job. It was a win/win, which also dovetailed with a part-time career in automotive journalism I had been developing as a post-retirement gig.

I began my career in automotive journalism in 2002 and remained active in the field until 2018, during which I test drove new vehicles and wrote reviews for various online and print publications. I travelled throughout North America and Europe on lavish junkets, learning a tremendous amount about the automotive industry. I also learned that the life of a freelance journalist is not an easy or stable existence. As one seasoned journalist described it to me, it was like living the lifestyle of the rich and famous without being either. Nonetheless, I'm grateful for my foray into this glamorous but precarious profession; it provided me with a solid foundation to springboard into fleet management for the police.

On the Friday of my last week as a superintendent, I departed my executive office on the seventh floor of the building housing our investigative teams, leaving behind the view, the oak, and leather furniture, and the support of a wonderful executive assistant. On Monday morning, I entered the fleet building, which was, and remains, a temporary facility located within the parking compound with all of the patrol vehicles. My office there required a make-over. After paint, carpet, pictures, and furniture, it became habitable. From these meagre-but-welcoming surroundings, I worked closely with City of Vancouver engineers, technicians, and procurement personnel, along with many service providers in private industry.

The over-arching goal was that of advancing the quality, safety, and functionality of the police department's heavily-used fleet of patrol vehicles, specialty vehicles, motorcycles, boats, trucks, trailers, and pretty well anything with a gas tank and engine. A lot has changed since. The fleet now includes twenty-two full-electric vehicles, and sixty or more hybrid-powered vehicles. This year, another thirty-five hybrid SUVs will join the fleet along with forty-five more electric vehicles. Given that the annualized aggregate distance driven by the VPD's fleet is equal to driving to the moon and back roughly six times, the movement away from fossil fuel is critical for the health of the city and planet.

I've now been the VPD's fleet manager for nine years, far longer than I had ever planned. By year three, after achieving a number of goals around renewing the fleet and advancing it technologically, I submitted a proposal to Chief Chu for a reduced work week. I felt that I could fulfill one-hundred percent of my role in seventy percent of the time, and in doing so, allow thirty percent of my salary to be reallocated to the budget funding part-time personnel. The chief accepted. The extra three days off every two weeks has allowed me to pursue other passions, such as writing this book and co-producing a police drama series for TV, the latter remaining a "work in progress." I've also been enjoying semi-retirement with more time for recreation and relaxation, though it's the second "R" word I tend to fail at. Cycling is my new nirvana. I recently purchased a gravel bike, which I ride incessantly on-trail and on the road, leaving my mountain bike and road bike to gather dust in the garage. I eagerly refer to my gravel bike as my fountain of youth, medicine cabinet, and therapist distilled into two-wheels.

Despite handing in my pistol and badge nine years ago, the identity of being a cop never entirely leaves. I still look at sketchy people with suspicion and retain an unhealthy dose of skepticism for those driven by self-serving agendas. I continue to have vivid dreams of being in uniform, working with my patrol colleagues, feeling the close kinship and camaraderie that develops in police work. The frequency of these dreams is diminishing though, and so are the occasional fatalistic nightmares that would haunt me. I no longer find myself falling in front of a bullet that I can see but cannot stop.

Policing is one of those professions in which you never stop learning—a feature which one can embrace or resist. I always did my best to embrace, but over the course of thirty-three years, there are things that I'd do differently, given the chance for a do-over. I imagine that sentiment would apply to most who have pursued a single line of employment for three or more decades. Of course, all of us would've bought Microsoft stock when Gates was a tweed-wearing dweeb.

I recall my field trainer saying to me on our first day together, "Rob, policing will never make you rich, but you'll never be poor." Those words are true, but only as they apply to financial wellbeing. The real riches in policing are gained through the everyday calls and the daily opportunities to help others in their darkest hours. The totality of this may only be fully appreciated after vacating the front seat of society's rollercoaster. I hope the snippets of *Thirty-Three Years* have provided entertainment, but more importantly, a sliver of insight into a policing career well-lived and thoroughly enjoyed. While there wasn't a day in which I resented heading to work, my lengthy policing career wasn't rich in bravado and heroics. It was, however, rich in the little things that meant so much to so many on the worst day of their lives. For that, I'm proud.

In closing, I would like to acknowledge the men and women of law enforcement for their selfless dedication to helping others. I really believe that our unrelenting police officers and their tireless civilian support staff really are the last line of defence between good and evil. As I watched the news this evening, there was a feature story on the success of an anti-gang policing project named Taskforce Tourniquet, which resulted in convictions against twenty-seven major organized-crime gangsters for charges as serious as murder. The project also resulted in the seizure of more than 170 firearms, including automatic weapons, more than ten kilograms of deadly fentanyl, forty kilograms of heroin, methamphetamine, and cocaine, and more than $2 million worth of cash, jewelry, and high-end vehicles. All of the gangsters pleaded guilty and are now behind bars.

Without the hard work and determination of our police agencies, violent organized-crime gangs would become more deeply entrenched in our liberal society, eroding our safety and threatening the very fabric of our peaceful existence. Tourniquet is but one example of many similar policing projects undertaken regularly by Canadian law-enforcement agencies that conclude with similar success but seldom receive media fanfare. This level of crimefighting is expensive, time-consuming, and incredibly onerous given the litigious nature of Canadian criminal prosecutions. They are, nevertheless, of immeasurable importance in maintaining the stable, free, and democratic society we cherish in the welcoming and diverse country we love and call Canada.

Thank you all.

Rob Rothwell

Postscript: As of July 31st, 2021 I have retired from the Vancouver Police Department for a second time. I'm hoping it sticks!

About the Author

In his thirty-three-year career with the Vancouver Police Department, Rob Rothwell worked uniform patrol, bicycle patrol, and plainclothes crime task force. He was a school liaison officer, a Drug Squad detective, a member of the Vancouver Integrated Intelligence Unit and the Internal Investigation Unit and he was inspector in-charge of the Criminal Intelligence Section and the Patrol Support Section. He ended his career as the superintendent commanding the Criminal Investigation Division for Homicide, Robbery/Assault, Arson, Financial Crimes, and Special Investigations.

After retirement, he returned to the VPD as civilian manager of Fleet Operations, assessing fleet needs from patrol cars and trucks to motorcycles and boats. Rob lives in Vancouver, where he was born and raised, enjoying its outdoor activities, including cycling, skiing, and sailing his Laser in English Bay. He's now fully retired from VPD but remains active in TV development and production.

CPSIA information can be obtained
at www.ICGtesting.com
Printed in the USA
BVHW041006150222
629066BV00011B/753

9 781039 123427